COMPETING
FOR KIDS

**21 Customer Service Concepts that Public Schools
Can Use to Retain and Attract Students**

KELLY E. MIDDLETON

Edited by Mike Mavilia

Competing for Kids: 21 Customer Service Concepts that Public Schools Can Use to Retain and Attract Students

Published by Wheatmark®
2030 East Speedway Boulevard, Suite 106
Tucson, Arizona 85719 USA
www.wheatmark.com

ISBN: 978-1-62787-594-3
LCCN: 2017964047

Table of Contents

Customer Service Concepts for Public Schools

How to Use This Book

1. For school board members and superintendents who want to model service and develop a district-wide customer service plan for all students, parents, community members, staff, vendors, etc.

2. For school principals who wants to make customer service great to students, parents, staff, the superintendent and school board.

3. For transportation directors who want to make customer service a focus throughout the department, with the hope of bus drivers and monitors giving great service to students and parents.

4. For food service directors who want to make customer service a focus with managers and cooks in order to improve service to students and parents.

5. For teachers who want to give great service to students, parents, the principal, etc.

6. For school administrators who want to train their employees in customer service and improve the image of their school, a particular program, or the entire district.

7. For anyone who notices good and not-so-good customer service in their profession or their personal life.

8. For colleges of education who educate teachers, administrators, department directors, etc.

9. For training particular individuals who need professional growth in customer service.

10. For any leader in any organization who wants to improve customer service.

11. For anyone who wants to grow professionally regardless of occupation.

12. For any business who wants to model what the best companies do in the area of customer service.

Foreword

I remember the July day thirty years ago when I received a call that would determine my destiny for the rest of my life. I was offered my first job in education, teaching at a new alternative program in Rowan County, Kentucky. This job would give me the opportunity to be an assistant basketball coach, a tennis coach, and a school bus driver. The yearly salary at the time was an all inclusive $16,500. I was so excited that to this day I have kept that very first pay stub. It is a symbol to me that I finally reached my long-term goal. I was going to be an educator.

Being the first of my family to graduate from college, I called everyone to tell them the news. I was very proud of this job, my new salary, and my future. Landing a teaching job in 1987 meant that I could now begin thinking about marriage, having children, and home ownership. But most importantly, I was now a member of one of the best retirement systems in the world. I was truly excited and proud to be called "teacher."

Fast forward three decades and now public education is in a tailspin. Those of us who work in public schools have heard about it, and many of us have seen it firsthand. Across the country public schools are suffering from loss of funding, low student and parent satisfaction, poor perception in the national media, loss of quality teachers and administrators, downsizing of scholastic, athletic, and extracurricular offerings, and deteriorating infrastructures. As further proof of this tailspin, new forms of competition we never even dreamed of thirty years ago are popping up all over the county and accelerating at a feverish pace. Retirement systems for some teachers have already changed in many states, forcing teachers to work more years with lower-quality health insurance and fewer benefits. Public education can no longer offer the safety and security that I was afforded in 1987. Is it any wonder that now many of the best and brightest teachers are leaving public education or moving on to greener pastures in other sectors?

Even though I'm an administrator now, my mind is never far from what it was like as a public school student growing up. One of the reasons I wrote this book is that I've seen firsthand some of the mistakes that our public schools make, even with the best of intentions. I remember as a child one rule that literally made me sick.

As a kid, growing up in Kentucky, my family moved and I had to change schools in third grade. Anyone who has started a new school, especially at a young age, can testify to just how scary and lonesome it can be. One of the rules at this school was that, in the cafeteria, a student was not allowed to leave until he or she had finished everything on the plate. I can recall on one of my first days at this new school, sitting in the lunch room, struggling to finish a parmesan cheese sandwich that I could barely palate. I ended up vomiting after I finished it and got in trouble. Humiliated, I had to sit in the principal's office and miss recess that day. I could not believe how a school could be so mean.

Ironically, twenty years later, I would become assistant superintendent in that very district and I used this story during my interview. Thankfully, that particular policy no longer existed, but I am sad to say, in my thirty years of education, I have witnessed atrocities far worse than my cafeteria experience.

I think we all can agree that the goal of public education is to create a safe, caring environment in which our students can learn and grow. Most schools have a problem implementing a customer service mission. The purpose of this book is to get your school to the point where you and your employees think about the customer service ramifications of all school operations.

INTRODUCTION

The Competition Is Here

Wake up to the new enemy. Embrace it, for it will transform our lives and the way we work more profoundly than we can imagine, and nothing is going to stop it." – John Huey [1]

In my thirty years as an educator, I have watched public education ignore the competition, resulting in an enormous growth of educational alternatives. I am not placing the blame on teacher unions, legislators, school administration, or testing. Being a former teacher and current school administrator, I am as guilty as the next person and, earlier in my career, either made some of the mistakes mentioned in this book or was a part of a school or system where these mistakes occurred and stood by and did nothing to fix the issues.

As a superintendent and a former teacher and principal, I have witnessed some great accomplishments that public schools have achieved and I have also witnessed some poor decisions that have left me scratching my head. The decisions schools make—what to focus on, what to change, what to fix—all contribute to the successes or struggles of the school. These internal problems may be obvious to the school or they may not be. We often cannot see the forest for the trees when it comes to the places we spend the most time, be it work, family, or home.

Just some of the issues that plague public schools include food service mismanagement, signage issues, family day snafus, neglect for infrastructure maintenance, negative media coverage, and infighting. No wonder students and parents are seeking other forms of education.

A 2016 Gallup Survey found that due to the above issues, only 30 percent of Americans have a great deal or quite a lot of confidence in public education.[2] Is this an institution where you want your child to spend twelve-plus years?

Since the first public school, Boston Latin School, opened in 1635[3] there has been very little competition other than private school education for the past 350 years. Public schools served their segment of the population and private schools served theirs. The two types of schools coexisted (somewhat) harmoniously over the years. In nature, this is called niche differentiation. Think about how robins fly around eating their insects and berries, while squirrels hop from tree to tree eating nuts and seeds. The two species live side by side in relative harmony eating their separate foods. But education no longer has this niche differentiation that robins and squirrels enjoy. It's become a fight for students and survival.

Buyer's Market

As an author and a consultant, I have been afforded the opportunity to present to and interact with diverse audiences of educators, parents, and students across the country. Regardless of the setting (rural, suburban, or urban), student demographics (socioeconomic and racial backgrounds), or school size, they all say the same thing: we didn't see this coming. They saw the national news about charter schools coming in and pushing out public schools, and they heard about kids being homeschooled, while still using public school resources, but they all thought it would never impact them and their school or district. When the competition finally came, no one was prepared. Have I got your attention now?

Good. Because this increase in options has created a buyer's market for education. We are now seeing what buyers prefer when they have options and, across the country, in districts from San Diego to New York, it's not public school.

In the past, the types of schooling could coexist and feed off their own segment of the population, like squirrels and robins. But as our nation has changed, so too has the ecosystem of education. Kids who, in 1987, would have no doubt ended up in our public schools are finding alternatives that better serve them. Kids who are bullied at school and thus cannot focus and meet their scholastic potential can now be homeschooled. Kids who are great at sports get recruited to play at private schools, who in turn pay their tuition or offer scholarships so families can afford the school. Charter schools offer public school kids—often the best and brightest—a chance to enter their lottery. Just look at the following charts[4,5] that show the drastic increase in home school and charter school enrollment in the past fifteen years. It's not a good sign when a chart of your competition's enrollment looks like service bars on a cell phone.

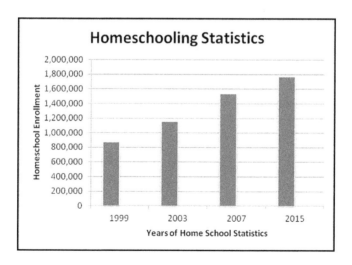

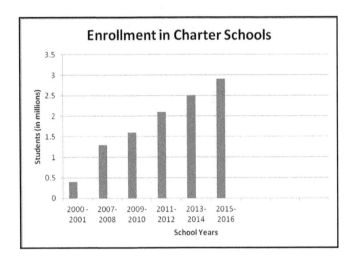

What is the impact on public education of more parents choosing these options? One of the consequences is a practice known as "creaming" in professional literature. This is where the best and most talented students are recruited away from public schools. Creaming creates public school populations that are less economically, academically, ethnically, and socially diverse. The weaning away of students and their parents who contribute to positive school cultures and positive school outcomes for diverse student populations creates a void within public schools.

> Only slightly more than half of public school parents (54%) say they'd stick with a public school if they were offered public funds to send their child to a private or religious school. (Assuming full tuition coverage.)
> – PDK Poll[6]

Furthermore, the students with complex and special needs who are not recruited to other schooling options leave public schools with not only a greater proportion of high cost-to-educate students than all other schooling options, but also less funds with which to educate them.

Given these trends, the future of public schools looks like pervasive programming for special needs, fewer gifted students, a less diverse student population, and an overall decrease in enrollment—hardly a recipe for success. What are public schools going to do about this? Can they really survive in a highly competitive educational market?

Add to this the governmental restrictions (like testing, tenure, and unions) that apply to public schools but not other forms of education, voucher programs, scholarship tax credits, sports recruiting restrictions, loss of funding for the arts, and the various state laws that draw students away from public schools and you can see just how much of an uphill battle it is for public education today.

> More Americans continue to oppose rather than favor using public funds to send students to private school (52% to 39%). And opposition rises (to 61%) when the issue is described in more detail.
> – PDK Poll[8]

You may remember the phrase "No stars upon thars" in the tale of the *Sneetches* from the godfather of children's books, Dr. Seuss.[7] In the story, the star-bellied Sneetches enjoy the best parties and exclude the non-star-bellied Sneetches from them. That is, until Sylvester McMonkey McBean rolls into town with a contraption that allows the non-star-bellied Sneetches to join the elite star-bellied Sneetches. What follows is a farce of adding and removing stars until Sylvester rolls out of town with everyone's money. Does this system of segregation remind you of anything? Perhaps this children's classic is a great metaphor for the battle between public education and private, charter, and homeschooling. Exclusivity, whether it's on the basis of intelligence, religion, athleticism, socioeconomic status, or parental legacy, is detrimental to the social fabric of our country and the values upon which the United States was founded.

Consequences of Declining Public School Enrollment

Given all these challenges to public education, should we be surprised that our competition is growing at such an alarming pace? How much longer can public schools last? As legislators continue to funnel resources to other educational options, consider one possible future.

In the city of New Orleans' main school district, Recovery School District, there is not a single public school anymore.[9] Following Hurricane Katrina, reorganization and redistribution of students caused the public school system to shut down indefinitely. The result was a publicly funded, privately managed school system. In other words, the school uses taxpayer money to fund a system that hires its own school board, effectively taking the voice away from the people who fund it.

The school choice movement may end up segregating and devaluing the diversity many champion as necessary for a democratic society. Certain school populations may become marginalized or more stigmatized, creating more cultural animosity and elitism within our communities. But perhaps most disappointingly, we may be perpetuating less tolerance among our students and stakeholders. After all, school choice advocates and programs get to choose who becomes a student and more importantly, who *doesn't* become a student in their schools. In the words of Dr. Seuss, they get to determine who their star-bellied Sneetches will be.

Do you see a theme here? The more competitors skim off the top of the best and brightest students from public education, the worse our public schools will get and the more criticism (warranted or not) they will incur until finally our school districts across the country mirror New Orleans, as public schools are run out of town.

Final Thoughts

As I accepted my first teaching job in rural Morehead, Kentucky in 1987, I never thought that public education could fail or even cease to exist. As I took undergraduate education classes at Georgetown, Kentucky, no one ever talked to me about how to handle our peers fighting from within, negative media coverage, and hate sites like Topix. I never thought for a moment we could lose our sense of purpose, and that parents could, or would, look elsewhere for ways to educate their children. I never thought for a minute that senior teachers could lose their jobs to declining enrollment, that new teachers—our brightest hopes for the future— would be the first ones to get fired when unheard-of budget cuts forced school boards' and administrators' hands. I thought my retirement age was safe and no one could add additional mandatory years for me to reach my retirement goal. When I started in education it was unthinkable that public school systems would have to merge or shut down altogether like in New Orleans. As a veteran administrator, I go to bed every night and thank my lucky stars that I am not a brand new public school teacher. To paraphrase Dorothy in *The Wizard of Oz*, "I've a feeling we're not in 1987 anymore."[10]

What Is Customer Service?

"Customer service is just a day-in, day-out, ongoing, never-ending, unremitting, persevering, compassionate type of activity."
—Leon Gorman, CEO L.L. Bean[11]

What do you think of when you hear the phrase "customer service"? Do you think of those smiling, handshaking Walmart greeters? What about that one checkout line at the store that's always the shortest, but only serves people who have returns or complaints? For many consumers, these are typical definitions of customer service.

However, in today's competitive market, the best companies view customer service very differently. Their definition includes:

- product quality
- building design and interior appearance (including cleanliness)
- how well employees are treated
- quality of leadership
- walking in the shoes of the customer
- quality of employees
- anything that would affect customer satisfaction

For the very best companies, customer service is an umbrella term for how well the company meets the needs of its customers. It is a guiding principle, a mindset, or, as J.D. Power and Associates say in their book *Satisfaction: How Every Great Company Listens to the Voice of the Customer*, a mantra that "flows like a waterfall from the top" down through every employee of the company right to the customer.[12] Shep Hyken of *Forbes* magazine says, "Customer service is not a department. It's a philosophy to be embraced by every member of an organization, from the CEO to the most recently hired employee.[13]

In Fran Tarkenton's book, *The Power of Failure: Succeeding in the Age of Innovation,* he describes how his business succeeded in spite of ruthless competition by having a relentless, fanatical commitment to doing their absolute best for their customers.[14] Every time a customer interacts with your brand, that exchange must be of the highest quality and offer the customer the utmost satisfaction. No company does this better than Disney.

Walt Disney was truly committed to customer satisfaction and personally checked that rides, tours, and games were run exactly right. Bruce Jones, senior programming director at Disney Institute, remembers one such "fanatical" moment with Walt Disney when Walt paid a visit to the Jungle Cruise ride in Adventureland.[15] After taking the Jungle Cruise, Walt pointed out that the ride lasted only four minutes, instead of the seven minutes it was supposed to be and that it went through the most important part, the hippo pool, too quickly. The manager of operations said he would fix it, and when Walt came back and rode all seven boats, he was satisfied, giving the manager a thumbs up and a nod. Jones says, "We still tell that story today to explain why whatever we do has to be the best possible experience for our guests."

Companies like Disney and Amazon are constantly innovating in order to improve the customer experience and thrive on the vision of their leaders (we will get into leadership later). Whether it's branching out into new industries like Amazon's Echo with Alexa or the attention to detail at Disney theme parks, the best companies know that they are not the only game in town. In fact, that knowledge drives their every move.

The Other Side of the Coin

Excuse the punny title, but customer service really can make or break any company. I've shown you some examples of sparkling service, but what about bad customer service? We've all experienced it.

Have you ever had any of these customer service headaches?

- Can't return items without receipt
- Nickel and dimed for napkins, condiments, extra cups, etc.
- Unable to get a real person on the phone no matter how many menus you go through
- Not getting the sale price, even though the sign is still up
- Waiting on hold far too long and being transferred to different departments with no one actually servicing you
- Staff refuse to acknowledge mistakes they make
- Cashiers that are unfriendly, careless, or who carry on conversations with other employees as they ring you up
- Going home or hanging up without your issue resolved

> "Business has never been tougher than it is today . . . the only businesses that are surviving with long-term sustainability are fanatical about differentiating themselves through the customer service they deliver."
> – DiJulius III, John R.
> *What's the Secret?: To Providing World Class Customer Service*[16]

I once had a cashier say straight to my face it was her last day and she didn't care about my complaint. With problems like these, I sometimes wonder why I even go to the store anymore!

It's fun to joke about these issues, but for executives, stories like these drive them nuts. They know just how important customer service is—not just to vault the company from mediocre to exceptional, but to survive at all.

Remember these companies that didn't make it because of their inability to change, poor leadership, and lackluster customer service?

- Toys "R" Us

- Blockbuster
- Borders Bookstore
- Circuit City
- General Motors' car companies Hummer, Pontiac, Saturn and Oldsmobile
- Polaroid
- Zenith TV
- Nokia
- The Sharper Image
- Tower Records
- Filene's
- Gawker.com
- Osco Drug
- KB Toys
- The Sports Authority

For the past eight years, *24/7 Wall St.* has published a customer service "Hall of Shame" list.[17] This list, based on a survey they conduct each year, asks those polled to rate each company based on the service they received. Here are the worst-rated companies for 2016. The percentage represents the number of respondents who rated the service they received as "poor."

15. Walmart—14.7%
14. Allstate—15%
13. Progressive—15.3%
12. Kmart—15.5%
11. Verizon—15.5%
10. Facebook—15.6%
9. Wells-Fargo—16.9%
8. T-Mobile—18.3%
7. AT&T—20.9%
6. DirecTV—22.3%
5. Dish Network—23.2%

4. Bank of America—22.9%
3. Time Warner Cable—24.3%
2. Sprint/Nextel—25.1%
1. Comcast—27.8%—their eighth year in a row in the Hall of Shame!

Are you surprised? If you've ever had to wait for one of these companies—either on the phone, in a line, or for a service person—you'll surely understand their presence on this list. Luckily for the eight telecommunications companies here, people put up with poor service because they have no better options and need television, internet, and phone service. But imagine what will happen when a better alternative comes around.

This list always reminds me of a *Flintstones* episode from my childhood. In the episode, Fred makes arrangements for two parties with "Cobblestone Caterers," one for his daughter Pebbles' first birthday party and the other for his adult pals from the Water Buffalo Lodge. Trouble ensues when Cobblestone Caterers, the self-proclaimed "only caterer in town," messes up by sending a children's clown to the Water Buffalo Lodge and dancing girls popping out of a cake to Pebbles' birthday party. The caterer could care less about the mix-up and flippantly explains to Fred that he's such a wise guy because he's "the only caterer in town."[18] No one has to worry about customer service mistakes when there is no competition.

Such a monopoly is an exception, however. In the wake of the 2007 financial crisis and the "too big to fail" controversy, companies are realizing more than ever that customer service is paramount to their success and survival. No matter how big or successful a company is, it is not immune to the economics of a highly competitive market. Perhaps we will be seeing some of the above "Hall of Shame" companies on lists next to the likes of Blockbuster and Circuit City some day.

Blockbuster didn't satisfy its customers. Didn't it drive you nuts when you got charged for not rewinding a tape? What about getting to the store *just* after it closed and having to pay a late fee? Blockbuster survived because it was the best option. Netflix and Redbox came along and suddenly the customers disappeared from Blockbuster. The other companies did things better, sure, but also, Blockbuster had no customer loyalty. People didn't *like* them; they *put up with* them. When another option came along, they went somewhere else. Does this sound like what's going on in public education?

These examples are here to give you a sense of just how vital the concept of customer service is in today's world, where the market for just about everything is highly competitive: where squirrels and robins aren't peacefully coexisting anymore.

This book is based on how the best companies do business. I've outlined the 21 practices that successful companies have in common. They can be applied to education just as easily as to business. Each concept works as a standalone practice, but they all work in unison, like a symphony, to produce a wonderful melody.

If you find yourself asking, "So how *do* these principles apply to me as a school administrator?" you're about to find out.

But Schools Are NOT Companies

Public schools have certain complexities that a company does not. For example, they cannot choose which students to teach; they must teach anyone who is legally allowed to attend the school. If a company doesn't want to go after a customer or even a whole demographic, it can choose not to. They don't need to sell football pads to people with mobility limitations, or picture books to the blind, but public schools must educate these populations.

> Frankly, if public schools were a business, we'd be out of business.

Treating a school just like a business would be a mistake. They are very different entities: one focuses on creating educated, well-rounded young people and the other focuses on selling a product or service. Right now, you may have some objections to the idea of incorporating customer service principles into your school, and that's understandable. Historically, for-profit business and public education have not played well together. Since charter schools have entered the picture, a categorical rift has even developed between schools run by "the public" and schools run by companies. I am not suggesting that a public school hire a CEO to run it, nor would I suggest that there be a constant focus on "the bottom line," (whatever that is) in education. I would, however, say that we need to see the writing on the wall. The *industry* of education has changed. We can see it in the way the competitors of public schools are focusing more on attracting and retaining students. In today's world, there is a correlation between the long-term viability of ANY entity, whether it's for-profit or nonprofit, and its ability to satisfy its customers, whoever those customers may be. Education is no different. The answer is customer service.

CONCEPT 1

Customer Service Must Be the Top Priority of Leadership

"Everything rises and falls on leadership."
– John Maxwell[19]

Great leaders must occasionally make tough, unpopular decisions. Tylenol is the most well-known name in pain relief and a product that built its reputation on being a very safe drug, even for children. But in the early 1980s, the country was shocked by the news that Tylenol was killing people.

In a matter of two days, seven people in the Chicago area died from taking Tylenol laced with potassium cyanide, including a 27-year-old postal worker named Adam Janus. When his family converged at Adam's home after his death, even more tragedy struck. Stanley, Adam's brother, and his wife, Theresa, both took capsules from the poisoned bottle and quickly collapsed and died. Instead of one funeral, the family would now have three at one time.[20]

James E. Burke, chairman of Johnson & Johnson (the maker of Tylenol), set out to determine what was causing the deaths from taking Tylenol. But more importantly, he wondered how he should handle this crisis. News had broken about the deaths and the country was in shock. Would Johnson & Johnson recall all Tylenol bottles in the Chicago area? Would they discontinue the Tylenol brand? After all, who would buy a Tylenol product again?

Chairman Burke decided to meet with the Federal Bureau of Investigation and the Food and Drug Administration in Washington D.C. Burke had begun to advocate a recall of all Tylenol capsules, but both the FBI and the FDA counseled him against recalling the drug precipitously. The FBI said doing so would say to whomever did this, "Hey, I'm winning, I can bring a major corporation to its knees." The FDA said a recall would cause massive public anxiety.[21]

After hearing the arguments from both the FBI and the FDA, on October 5th, 1982, six days after the first death, Chairman Burke decided to issue a nationwide recall on Tylenol products and ordered the destruction of all thirty-two million bottles in circulation. This controversial decision had an approximate retail value of $100 million dollars, but may have saved the lives of many of Burke's customers.

Chairman Burke stuck to his guns and followed the Johnson & Johnson credo written in 1943. This credo is chiseled into the wall of its New Jersey headquarters:

> We believe our first responsibility is to the doctors, nurses and patients, to mothers and fathers and all others who use our products and services. In meeting their needs everything we do must be of high quality . . . [22]

After investigations found that the bottles had been tampered with, Tylenol responded with an unprecedented triple-seal package that we still see today: glued outer flaps on boxes, plastic shrink rap around the neck of the bottle, and a foil seal over the mouth of the bottle.

Within just a few months of the largest recall the FDA had ever seen, Johnson & Johnson had returned Tylenol to the market, and it took just one more year before the company recovered its position as the top-selling over-the-counter pain reliever.

How did Tylenol go from a deadly killer to top painkiller within a year? Both the public and investors had confidence in the leadership of the company. In 1982, large-scale recalls were unheard of. Yet, when his customers' lives were on the line, Chairman Burke responded quickly in a manner that ensured their safety, while having no regard for "the bottom line." He was aware that if people could not trust Tylenol, the brand would fold. However, a short term loss that admits a wrong and fixes it completely will ultimately bring its customers back. We will talk more about recovering in a crisis later on.

If you look closely enough at the business world you'll find that behind every successful company is a great leader. Disney had Walt, Southwest Airlines had Herb Kelleher (whom we will discuss later), Amazon has Jeff Bezos, Apple had Steve Jobs, Johnson &

> Customer service must "flow like a waterfall" from the top of the organization, according to J. D. Powers and Associates.

Johnson had Burke. But more than being exceptional leaders, they had their fingers on the pulse of what people wanted and they delivered it to them at the highest possible quality.

A Born Leader

Southwest Airlines is one of the leading names in air travel today. From 1972 to 2002, Southwest (or LUV, it's stock symbol) had the highest returns on investment of any company.[23] Furthermore, in 2014, Southwest was the number one stock on the S&P 500 with a 110 percent growth rate that year.[24] So how has an airline—in an era when all the major airlines have shown decreases in revenue or even declared bankruptcy like Delta, United Airlines, American Airlines, and US Airways[25]—been able to not only increase its revenue, but become one of the top companies in the entire country?

When you visit Southwest's About page on their website, you see the following mission statement: "The mission of Southwest Airlines is dedication to the highest quality of customer service delivered with a sense of warmth, friendliness, individual pride and company spirit."[26] For Herb Kelleher, cofounder and former CEO of Southwest, his company's commitment to customer service is the top priority and the reason he repeatedly cites for their success over the years.

Consider this description of Kelleher from Terry Maxon, airlines beat reporter:

He's found himself in many different places over the years — regularly loading luggage onto airplanes every Thanksgiving Day and cooking Christmas dinner at Ronald McDonald Houses in the cities where Southwest flies. He'll show up anywhere a Southwest employee is stationed, even if it means climbing over a locked fence to make a surprise reservations center visit.

He's dressed up as Elvis Presley, a woman, the Easter bunny, a leprechaun and as a flight attendant to promote Southwest. He performs in rap songs for training tapes — or any other occasion. He seems unable to walk through Southwest offices, airport ramps or along the terminal gates without schmoozing. He works the crowds at Southwest's frequent parties and hosts meetings in Southwest's 32 cities.[27]

As you can see, Herb Kelleher's actions are influenced by his customer service mindset. He understands what it means to be a servant leader, not only for the employees but for the various communities where Southwest Airlines flies. Herb Kelleher's understanding of the customer experience and his interactions with the passengers reflect his commitment to excellence and the importance of training employees to create a culture of making the customer feel valued. That's what it means to have leadership "flow like a waterfall" from the top. Mr. Kelleher was a walking mission statement for Southwest Airlines. With such a dynamic and committed leader, it's no surprise that Southwest has gone from a small twenty-three plane operation, servicing only the state of Texas,[28] to a major airline competing with the likes of Delta and Jet Blue — and often winning.

What Is a Student?

When we consider what customer service–based leadership looks like in public education, we have to start with identifying the customer. Who are we serving? Here's one definition:

What Is a Student?

A Student is the most important person ever in this school . . . in person, on the telephone, or by mail. A Student is not dependent on us . . . we are dependent on the Student. A Student is not an interruption of our work . . . the Student is the purpose of it. We are not doing a favor by serving the Student . . . the Student is doing us a favor by giving us the opportunity to do so. A Student is a person who brings us his or her desire to learn. It is our job to handle each Student in a manner which is beneficial to the Student and ourselves.[29]

This poster hangs in my school in an area prominent to both teachers and students. It was created by William W. Purkey, a writer, inspirer, and lifelong educator. When I came across this ideology, I was instantly hooked on its message to put the student first. But what I didn't know was that while William W. Purkey created this poster, he borrowed it from elsewhere.

It turns out, this poster came from the outdoor and clothing chain, L.L. Bean.[30] Purkey simply changed the word "customer" to "student." In the process he found himself a great concept for schools. It fits nicely into any school's rule system and not only that, it shows how customer service and the mentality behind working in a school are quite compatible ideas.

Leadership in Public Schools

In a crisis, where tough decisions had to be made, Chairman Burke went back to the Johnson & Johnson credo, which stated that the health and safety of its customers trumped profit. In the world of public education, we can learn a valuable lesson from Chairman Burke's response to this crisis. Many difficult decisions have to be made in our schools—from everyday

> "When you're dealing with parents, you have to remember the other name for them . . . the customer."
> —Steven Harper on the TV series *Boston Public*[31]

problems to major crises. It takes customer service–driven leadership, like that displayed by Chairman Burke, to make students' needs and well-being a leader's top priority.

If we remember to use customer service as the guiding principle behind our decisions and actions, we can feel confident in those choices, whatever the outcome may be. Customer service must be imbedded in mission and vision statements like the Johnson & Johnson credo. Everyone must be able to quote these missions and visions and be able to refer back to these company values each day, especially in critical times.

But it is not enough to merely remember mission statements. John Maxwell says that, "Personal and organizational effectiveness is proportionate to the strength of leadership."[32] In other words, organizations cannot rise above the level of leadership. Taking his statement a step further, leaders who don't value and practice great customer service cannot realistically expect their employees to value and practice it either. Leaders need to both preach *and* practice giving great service.

Examples of Leadership in Public Schools

Principals are the leaders of the school. Teachers are the leaders of the classroom. Those of you who are or have been a principal understand the difficult decisions that have to be made on a daily basis as the leader of your school. On the TV show *Boston Public,* principal Steven Harper faces the problems of terrorism, racism, sex scandals, bullying, student protests, and cheating in his school. Despite having tough choices to make as a leader, he never loses sight of the main objective: to serve the best interests of his students, whatever that looks like.

In an episode from *Boston Public,* remedial education teacher Harry Senate talks with a student who is depressed and suicidal. During class, Mr. Senate brings up the idea of suicide and decides to start a club where students can talk about these thoughts and feelings. When word gets out about the club, parents speak out in outrage about it, fearing that it will tempt kids to consider killing themselves.[33]

But Mr. Senate persists with the club because he sees that the students need a safe place to talk about these issues. He sees the need from the students and acts with their best interest in mind, even though it was met with criticism and anger. The students are thankful for the club and for their teacher's genuine interest in helping them navigate this scary path. Furthermore, participating in the club also creates a desire to do well in the class, and some of the underperforming students start to take an interest in their schoolwork.

The story behind this story is the support that Mr. Senate received from his principal, Mr. Harper. If the principal didn't put his students first, like Chairman Burke did with his customers, then he would have caved to the parents' pressures and told Mr. Senate to disband the club. It's this commitment to service that allows teachers (real or fictional) like Mr. Senate to follow their instincts and do what's best for their students. This is what John Maxwell meant by, "Organizations cannot rise above the level of leadership."[16]

Teachers and principals are not the only leaders in schools. We find leaders in all sectors of public education. Take the transportation director for example. A transportation director is responsible for handling accidents and complaints, calculating costs and budgeting, and ensuring buses are in working order and up to code. That's the job description, but what would a transportation director who was also a great leader do? Let's look at a scene from the movie *Forrest Gump* to find out.

"I remember the bus ride on the first day of school very well," the adult voiceover of Forrest says as he waits at the bus stop in his leg braces. When the bus pulls up and the door opens, we see a woman smoking a cigarette and scowling, waiting for Forrest to get on. When she says, "Are you coming along?" Forrest insists on formally meeting each other before he steps on the bus. After they do so, he gets in and looks for a seat. All the kids on the bus tell him "seat's taken," and don't let him sit with them. Finally, one little girl offers him a seat and he lights up at her acceptance of him. Had she not invited him to sit down, Forrest would have had nowhere to sit.[34]

There are several opportunities here for a customer service–driven transportation director to change this bus experience for the better. First, she can instruct bus drivers to be friendly and inviting to students, especially on the first day of school, when nerves are running high for most students. Next, she can make a school bus policy that prohibits saving seats, enforced by the bus driver, so students like Forrest will not feel rejected. Lastly, the fact that Forrest refuses to get on the bus until he and his bus driver have introduced each other speaks to a fundamental desire in human nature. We are much more likely to be kind and interested in the well-being of a person we know than a stranger. Something as simple as knowing a student's name creates a relationship between the bus driver and the student. A customer service–driven transportation director could make it school policy that each bus driver take five seconds on the first day of school to meet and greet each student. She could even go a step further and tell bus drivers to learn each student's name and have a conversation with each student by the end of the first week of school. Starting off a school day with a positive interaction with an adult can go a long way.

> "I am not afraid of an army of lions led by a sheep; I am afraid of an army of sheep led by a lion."
> —Alexander the Great[35]

Final Thoughts on Leadership

Every school employee's behavior and attitude matters. Customer service must "flow like a waterfall" from the top of the organization and must seep out the pores of all employees. As a school leader, it starts at the top with you: your priorities and your actions. Communicating your vision, your values respective to that mission, and the reason customer service is a priority to you as a leader are all vital to get employees on board. If customer service is the top priority of the school board, and thus the top priority of the superintendent, it will then be the top priority of the transportation director, who will ensure it is the top priority of every school bus driver. One thing is for sure, if Walt Disney, Chairman Burke, or Herb Kelleher were in charge of Forrest's school, there's no way that scene would have unfolded as it did! Without customer service–driven leadership, student experiences like Forrest's are bound to occur. Remember what John Maxwell says, "Everything rises and falls on leadership."

CONCEPT 2

Every Touch Point Matters

"The devil and the magic are both in the details"
– Kelly E. Middleton

Thirty years ago, a top executive at an airline company changed the way his industry and other industries across the globe viewed customer service. Jan Carlzon of Scandinavian Airlines had a hunch that if a passenger's first experience after boarding a plane was a negative one, that person was more likely to assume other aspects of their experience would be negative.[36] He conducted a massive survey of 60,000 passengers. The survey was looking for feedback on the cleanliness of the plane, the cleanliness of the bathrooms, the competency of the pilots, and the mechanics of the engine. The surveys were filled out and collected before the plane took off.

What they found was just as Carlzon had predicted. The survey answers came back overwhelmingly saying: the airplane was meticulously clean, bathrooms were very clean, pilots were overly competent, and the mechanics of the engine were above average. There was one caveat. The surveys from the third row of the plane came back saying: the airplane is dirty, the bathrooms are dirty, the pilots are incompetent, and the mechanics of the engine are substandard.

Why such a drastic difference for just this row of passengers? It turns out the airline staff had placed a coffee stain on the tray tables in this row. When passengers got on, sat down, and flipped down their tray tables to fill out the survey, they saw this stain and assumed all of these negative qualities about the airplane. Remember, the surveys were collected before the plane even took off, so these passengers hadn't seen the bathrooms, hadn't seen the pilots flying nor the engines in use. All of these negative assumptions came from that one row's tray tables. Something so small can totally change a customer's experience. That's why it is so important that every detail be of the highest quality. Otherwise, you end up with undeserved bad reviews. This is the basis for understanding touch points in customer service.

What Are Touch Points?

Touch points are moments in time when the customer interacts with your brand — whether you're a public school, airline, fast food restaurant, or mass transit company. A touch point, also called a "moment of truth" by Jan Carlzon,[37] is any chance a customer has to make a judgment of the entire company, much like how passengers judged different facets of the plane after seeing the coffee stains. When an employee answers a phone, that is a touch point. When a customer pulls into your parking lot, that is a touch point. When the air conditioning turns on (or doesn't turn on), that is a touch point. Customers believe that an employee will take care of their needs when that employee answers the phone with a cheerful, friendly voice. Such an attitude makes the customer feel welcomed. But what happens when the employee does not follow this protocol?

During my first year as principal, I was having a conversation with a parent who told me she hated my middle school. When I asked her to explain, I thought she was going to tell me some big, horrific story about a teacher or another student doing something unspeakable to her child. Sensing her anger, I braced myself for her response. She told me that she was treated rudely on the phone by my school administrative assistant, stating, "That lady is just as mean as they come!" It was an "a-ha" moment for me early on in my career: a person will possibly base their entire perception of a school based on one interaction with one employee. I had no idea how prevalent this concept was at the time, but as the years went on, I would see conversations like this one play out year after year with parents and students.

Touch Points Are the Responsibility of Leadership

In the Leadership concept I explained the importance of leadership setting an example to employees by acting and making decisions based on the best interest of the customer. Being mindful of all your touch points is a major part of such decision making and, just like leadership, will flow from the top like a waterfall. What if a school leader has never thought about or been trained how to manage the various touch points of a school, and thus has no idea how to ensure his employees give great customer service at each touch point? Perhaps, at his school, administration doesn't even know who is responsible for certain touch points. I have a saying about that: "If everyone is responsible, then no one is really responsible." Let's look at a hypothetical situation to better understand why giving great customer service at all touch points must come from the very top.

Steve is the Superintendent of East Nowhere School District. His transportation director, Karen, is truly amazing with customer service. Karen passes her customer service philosophy and practices down to district bus drivers. She trains, monitors, and evaluates all her direct reports with a customer service mindset. When Steve speaks with parents in the community, rarely do they ever mention issues with bussing. In fact, they don't mention buses at all—a true sign she's doing things right.

On the other hand, we have Mark, the food service director of East Nowhere School District. Mark is very knowledgeable about food-related issues, but doesn't think that giving great customer service is important. In fact, he doesn't know much about the concept of service. Since customer service is not important to Mark, it's not going to be important to his direct reports, including the cafeteria managers, cooks, servers, and cashiers. Needless to say, Steve regularly hears complaints from parents about their kids' lunchtime experience.

Steve begins to reflect upon his own leadership and his focus on customer service:

> *If some of my top leaders are giving great customer service and some leaders are not giving great customer service, the problem might be me. I might need to be more clear on my customer service expectations and the impact on our district of not practicing great customer service. Am I monitoring and evaluating my leaders on customer service by personally checking on their various touch points?*

If customer service was really a major focus for Steve and flowed like a waterfall from him, the heads of each department would demonstrate it. By leaving the responsibility of giving great customer service to his department heads, he leaves it to chance. The result is that Steve's employees give sporadic service and his desire to lead each department down a road of great customer service doesn't come to fruition. As Branch Rickey stated, "luck is the residue of design,"[38] and I believe when it comes to customer service practices, the less you leave to chance, the more luck will come your way.

Just like Chairman Burke at Johnson & Johnson and Walt Disney at Disney Corporation, only Steve has the power to influence the entire school organization and all its various touch points. After all, the transportation director isn't going to teach the food service director how to give great service. Given this type of perfunctory leadership, there might be pockets of good or great service within the school district, but until Steve puts customer service as a top priority himself, East Nowhere School's performance in these various touch points cannot and will not rise above the level of Steve's mediocre customer service leadership.

The Very Best in Customer Service Touch Points

When a school leader ensures that everyone in every department knows the importance of giving great customer service and trains them to do so, only then can a school truly feel confident about all its touch points. The Disney Corporation continues to serve as an excellent model to illustrate and inspire organizations to address customer service from various touch points.

The goal of the leadership at Disney World is absolute perfection. When trash flies across a walkway, it is swiftly snatched up by the nearest employee—regardless of whether or not it's her job to clean the park.[39] When customers step out of their cars in the massive Disney World parking lot, they are picked up by a train, which brings them into the park. It's the sum of the great parts plus the *absence* of any negative parts that break the spell of being in the Wonderful World of Disney, that makes their park so magical. It is because of this gold standard quality of customer service that Disney is the world leader in family entertainment, taking in over $52 billion dollars in 2015[40] and experiencing a 59 percent increase in annual sales over the last ten years.[41] No wonder CNN called Disney "the most magical company on earth."[42]

> A touch point, also called a "moment of truth" by Jan Carlzon, is any chance a customer has to make a judgment of the entire company.

One example that I love is a story shared by my colleague, Amy, from when she went to Disney World. While walking past the Cinderella Castle, she had noticed a dead bird off the beaten path. Amy had heard me go on and on about how perfect the experience is there and decided to test it out. She found a phone nearby and called to report the dead bird to the staff. For a few minutes, she looked around in anticipation of a worker coming along to take care of the problem. Suddenly, she thought she saw something out of the corner of her eye. She looked down and saw a small square of grass sliding to the side and a person popped out of the hole. He swept up the dead bird, disappeared back down the hole, and replaced the ground piece. She couldn't believe it; there was an underground tunnel where workers could secretly travel around the park and come up wherever a problem occurred! The vision here was to avoid cluttering the park with workers and keeping those things that ought to be out of sight really out of sight (we'll talk more about this idea of keeping backstage issues backstage a little later). Who really wants to see a guy walking around with a broom and a trash bag, picking up dead animals? Disney World truly understands what it means to minimize customer exposure to unpleasantries that are bound to happen anywhere. This is just one example of how Disney has a plan that is carried out by all employees for every single touch point in order to make the customer experience as great as it can be.

Giving great customer service at every touch point is only possible with total buy-in from all employees, and it starts at the top, with leadership. Disney World doesn't just have great workers who are committed to giving the best service. Walt Disney had the vision, translated vision into expectations and practices, and then communicated it to his leaders, who in turn model it, monitor it, and provide feedback on it with the employees.

Touch Points in Public Schools

Let's consider what giving great service at all your touch points looks like in public schools. In the Leadership concept, I gave the example of Forrest Gump feeling unwelcome on the bus ride on his first day of school. How stressful that must have been for him! That bus ride was a touch point for the school. What if Forrest's story unfolded with a student at your school? As a leader you must begin looking at all of the practices within your school with an eye for customer service. When we spend so much time in a place, we become blind to the problem touch points. It happens to even the best customer service–driven leaders. The best way to overcome this blindness is to take some time to break down the touch points at your school. There's no way to list every touch point in a school, but the goal is to start thinking about them. Below is a list of touch points, broken down by departments, to get you started. Remember, a touch point is any time a customer (student, parent, community member) interacts with your school. This interaction can be with a person (such as a bus driver) or a thing (such as a confusing sign).

TRANSPORTATION:
Do drivers give great service to students?
How clean are buses when they pick up students?
Does the driver greet or speak to students entering or exiting the bus?
FOOD SERVICE:
How is the food presentation?
Is the food nutritious?
Do kids like the food? How do you know?
Do workers give great service to students?
Are the tables cleaned before every lunch period?
FACILITIES:
Are restrooms cleaned and checked regularly throughout the day?
Is signage clear and free of spelling errors?
Are things dusty?
Are classrooms themed for what the teacher teaches?
Are there decorations, or is the room bland? You should be able to walk into a classroom and know what class you're in.
Are air ducts and vents working properly?
Are fences rusty?
For events, can you understand what the person is saying into the P.A.? If not, do you need a new microphone or speaker?

These are the questions that you as a school leader should be asking for each area of your school. Again, this list is nowhere near exhaustive, nor could it be, as each school is different. Knowing your school's touch points and thinking about how you can improve service at each one will get your school on the track to giving *consistently* great service.

When it comes to touch points in schools, it's good to look at how the best do it. I would argue it's not Space Mountain, Cinderella's Castle, the food or shows that truly makes Disney

World great. In my opinion it's the combination of all the little-things: From the time you look up how to purchase tickets to the park on the website to the train ride to and from the park and everything in between, that makes it a total magical experience. As a school leader, using Disney as a model to think about touch points will put you well on your way to creating your own magical experience for your students, staff, and community.

> **Where are your coffee stains? At which touch points in your school or district could you give better service?**

Final Thoughts on Touch Points

It's all in the details. Rest assured, schools will be judged on the basis of a single interaction, like the vignette about Scandinavian Airlines earlier. We need to make those interactions count. Since we never know when someone interacting with our school will be judging us critically, identifying and training at all of our touch points ensures that whenever, wherever that interaction occurs, it will be a positive one for that person.

As a school administrator, there is one truly indispensable step when thinking about touch points. Henry Ford said, the best leaders are able to walk in the shoes of their custom-

> "Experienced teachers know that what you do and what you say in the first few seconds of the first day of school can make or break you." —Harry Wong[43]

ers.[44] As stories abound how Walt Disney would walk the theme park incognito and test rides, leaders must walk in the shoes of their students and parents observing all the touch points (I'll talk about walking in the shoes of the customer more later on). Have you ever rode the school buses, stood in the lunch lines, or went through the enrollment process of your schools? I wouldn't have run into the parent who hated our school because the administrative assistant was rude to her had I just been holed up in my office. Walking the grounds of your school as much as possible not only allows you to survey all the touch points—new graffiti, overflowing trash barrels, gum on a carpet, vents blowing cold air onto lunch tables—but it also gives you the opportunity to see your students and employees interacting with your school. As you are able to implement practices at each touch point, you'll start to see more employees taking pride in improving their touch points until eventually high-level customer service becomes routine!

Think about one student's day at a school. Let's say that student has four interactions with a school staff person in the first hour of that day: a bus driver, an administrative assistant, a homeroom teacher, and a first period teacher. Multiply the number of interactions by the number of hours in a school day (seven, for example). Now multiply that by the number of school days in a year (175, for example). Then multiply that by the number of students in your school (Four hundred, for example). That's nearly two million "Moment of Truth" experiences in your school in just one school year! If just one of those four people that the students interacts with routinely gives poor service, that's 500,000 poor reviews over one "coffee stain" of a touch point.

Most companies wouldn't survive such an employee and, in today's competitive educational environment, neither will a school. I believe we can change the entire perception of public education and our schools if we decide to have an intentional focus on customer service. This focus requires leaders and their employees paying Disney-like attention to detail at every touch point.

CONCEPT 3

Hire the Best

"Hire attitude, train skills."
– Southwest Airlines[45]

The TV show *The Apprentice* bills itself as "The Ultimate Job Interview." Contestants, or interviewees, are put through a series of elaborate business-related tasks to determine who gets the job as "the apprentice" in Donald Trump's company. The stakes, as well as the drama, are enormous on the show, as the contestants pursue their dream job of working at an international conglomerate. They endure a series of interviews where Trump utters his famous catchphrase "You're fired!" thus signaling the end of one person's dream. After weeks of hands-on tasks and debriefing sessions in the boardroom, one contestant stands out as the best of the best and is finally crowned the apprentice. Now, if only we could devote so much time to finding the right employees in public education. Wouldn't that be great?

Since public schools are not quite in the position to go to such lengths as a reality show, we have to work a little smarter and harder at hiring. What do you think of when you hear the term "hiring process"? Do you think of it as a necessary evil? Something that you'd rather not be doing, as you have so many more important tasks to accomplish? Have you ever kept an employee simply because it was too much work to find a replacement? Have you ever hired a teacher just because they have the certification required? If you answered yes to any of these questions, I'd like to shine a different light on the dreaded hiring process.

For many public schools, the hiring process is organized chaos, consisting of posting available positions, groaning through interview after interview and finally hiring based more on desperation than whether the candidate is a great fit for the school. In addition, candidates who are not hired leave with a negative opinion of your school. You make one person happy, but a handful of others leave the process with a bad taste in their mouths.

Sound familiar? What if there was a way to hire customer service–driven candidates and make the hiring process more customer friendly? No, this is not a sales pitch from *The Apprentice*, it's an attainable goal. You can tweak your hiring process to get more qualified applicants and put the right people in the right jobs. All it takes is a team commitment to customer service and some out-of-the-box thinking. It's really that simple.

Hiring in Public Schools

The best companies know that in order to hire the most desirable customer service–driven candidates, they need to attract the best. Certainly, *The Apprentice* gets the best and most promising candidates, but do public schools get equally high-caliber applicants? They can by following a few simple principles.

In many public school hiring situations, we end up with a small pool of applicants and hire quickly in order to check this off our summer to-do lists, or possibly out of desperation because there is only one candidate with the proper certification. Sometimes we hire a person because one of the teachers or school leaders knows the applicant personally or needs to do someone a favor. After the candidate is hired, we are all just happy that the entire process is over so we can go back to our daily routines. If any of this sounds familiar, you probably don't need me to tell you it's not working.

Over my years as a public school leader and consultant, I've seen leaders use the same lackluster interview questions year after year, interviews that only proved a person's competency at doing a job, interviewees who got hired merely because they knew someone on the inside, and an overall apathy of hiring committees.

These are just some of the shortcomings of the hiring process I've seen. Fortunately, we don't have to reinvent the wheel in order to improve our hiring. We just need to borrow ideas from our high-flying customer service friends in the business world.

Hiring for Customer Service in the Business World

The best companies know just how vital hiring well is to their overall success. There are two focal points during the hiring process in the business world that stand out. They include:

1. Identifying the right candidates for the company
2. Treating the hiring process like a courtship

What does "the right candidate" look like? At the beginning of this concept, I shared one of my favorite hiring quotes: "Hire attitude, train skills." This philosophy, championed by Herb Kelleher of Southwest Airlines, embodies how some of the most successful companies view the hiring process. At Southwest, the most important factor is *who* they hire. Herb Kelleher has found that while skills are important, they can be learned, but an employee's attitude—especially as it pertains to agreeableness, desire to be part of a team, and going above and beyond the call of duty—are the hardest qualities to try to instill in an employee.

If we follow Herb Kelleher and Southwest's lead, we can emphasize looking for customer service skills in people. This includes having a friendly, positive attitude, understanding they are there to serve the customers, and showing a commitment to giving the very best service to those customers. In order to ensure that these people even apply to a company, some legwork needs to be done. It all starts with recruiting candidates who have the right attitude.

Before a position even becomes available, the best leaders already have a list of potential hiring sources or specific people they want on their team. This is the essence of recruiting. So how do you find people who give great service? The best leaders notice who has the right attitude and who gives great customer service in their daily lives—certain companies and employees—and they keep a list for when they need to fill positions. When those vacancies occur, they can refer back to that list to reach out to these candidates to apply. This practice is particularly helpful at conferences or any other professional gathering.

Recognizing who has the right attitude doesn't just help with recruiting. It also helps hiring committees define who to hire during the interview process. For example, when Google interviews a candidate, they are looking for "Googliness"—a term Google coined that encompasses their main qualities like going above and beyond the call of duty, being friendly, being playful, and being creative.[46] Those on the hiring committee know the essence of Googliness (even though its exact meaning defies definition) and can spot it when they see it. While a lack of hard skills (like years of programming experience) may count against a candidate, one simply cannot be hired without fitting into the mission and culture of Google: without Googliness.

Hiring Is a Courtship

The second main component of hiring is treating the process like a courtship. The best companies never forget that even though they are asking the questions, they are not the only ones being interviewed. In fact, the best candidates *always* have other options. Therefore, it is important for the interviewers to wow their candidates. At Zappos, potential hires who are coming from out of town get picked up in a Zappos van at the airport and taken to the interview. Now *that's* service![47] But there is another reason for this shuttle service. The driver takes note of how the applicant interacts with him or her. Zappos wants to ensure that every employee (even the shuttle driver) is treated with respect, and this practice helps ensure candidates are the right fit.

Some companies spare no expense in order to court the best and brightest—flying them out, putting them up in fancy hotels, taking them out to meals, sporting events, casinos, or concerts. While those are great if a company can afford it, some less expensive ways to entice applicants can be just as effective. Here are a few touch points where the best companies give great service to candidates:

- Courteous, enthusiastic staff returning calls and setting up interview times
- Friendly employees greeting interviewees as they walk through the building, showing that the company has satisfied employees and a culture that is welcoming
- Having a clean waiting area with comfortable seating for interviewees
- Offering interviewees water while they wait or during the interview
- Offering to take interviewees' coats
- Thanking interviewees for their time and for expressing interest in the company
- A clear, specific interview process with timelines for decisions, especially with regard to a call back about a job offer/decline

Making an applicant feel special and welcomed is very important to the best companies. They want *all* their potential hires to leave the interview thinking, "Man, I wish I could work here!" Companies should not overlook the importance of such an exclamation. Recently, hiring resources from *Forbes* to *USA Today* to *Fortune* have been saying what was unheard of before the turn of the century: people should look for good jobs that make them feel fulfilled over jobs with higher salaries.[48,49,50] The evidence is there too. People of all ages, especially millennials, are saying no to jobs that overwork their employees and underappreciate them. Making your school a desirable place to work doesn't have to mean offering the highest salaries. It can be as simple as giving great customer service during the interview process and making sure the applicant knows they will be *cared for* while employed at your school. I'll talk more about this idea in Giving Great Service to Employees later on.

Applying Customer Service Hiring to Public Education

Now that you have a good idea of what works in the business world, I'd like to share a story about what customer service–based hiring looks like in a public school.

As a new principal of a school in a small town, I had an administrative assistant opening one summer. While I knew how important this position was for me and the school, on the surface it just seemed like a routine hire. I could not have been more wrong!

In just a couple of weeks I had over sixty applications and fifteen different people who wanted to meet for "just a few minutes" to pitch their friend, spouse, neighbor, or babysitter to me. Even the superintendent asked me to hire his administrative assistant!

I spent all summer on this one hire; I didn't want to rush this important decision and I had to stay focused on finding the best customer service–oriented person. I role-played customer service scenarios and various school situations with each candidate. In the end, I decided to hire someone on my recruitment list: a bank teller from my town. Besides her great answers, she had the very best attitude throughout the entire process, and I felt very confident with my hire, even though she would require more training than the school administrative assistants I interviewed.

I am proud to say that the woman I hired over twenty years ago continues to be a great customer service employee at that same school. Even though I had to put several important aspects of my job on hold, the simple fact that the school didn't have to worry about hiring for that position for *two decades* was payoff enough. The icing on the cake is the immeasurable positive customer service impact she's had on this school over her thousands of interactions with the community.

Twenty Years of Lessons Learned

1. Pretty resumes are not an indication of a good candidate. Ivy League applicants can be just as good or bad as candidates from a community college.

2. Always check with a candidate's immediate supervisor before hiring. If a past immediate supervisor is not listed, it is a red flag. Check with those not on the reference list.

3. Experience does not mean quality. They may have hurriedly thrown together lesson plans one year and simply reused them 19 more times.

4. Use the interview to let the applicant know that customer service is important to you. Constantly check for how the applicant fits into the mission of customer service.

5. Ask the teacher applicants about doing home visits before the school year begins, and then ask them how they plan on working with students after the teaching day is over.

6. Keep the position open until you find the right applicant.

7. If you find a great candidate that doesn't exactly fit the job description, think about where the applicant might fit within the organization. Whenever possible, never let someone walk away that would be a great fit for your school.

8. The school and district must be a team during the hiring process. Give great customer service throughout the process; you want every interviewee to be impressed with your school.

9. Be willing to take a chance to make a great hire.

10. Recruit candidates – don't just wait for candidates to come to you.

11. The entire process of hiring, from the initial call to the interview to the call regarding the hiring decision, is a customer service touch point. Be strategic from beginning to end.

12. Set up the interview questions to get future commitments from the candidate, if hired. For example, asking the candidate, "if you are struggling with a student, would you be willing to go to his or her home to talk with a parent or guardian?" will allow you to hold the employee to that standard if such a situation arises.

This example shows how much is riding on hiring the best customer service–oriented people, not just in the short term by not needing to hire another replacement in the next few years, but also in the long term with regard to student happiness and overall success of our schools. We all know how rarely school personnel get fired, so each hire, especially if they qualify for tenure, can impact the school—for better or worse—for decades. In that sense, hiring in public education is immensely important. I would argue it's *more* important than hiring customer service–minded employees at Google or Southwest. At least at those companies, if a bad hire is made, they swiftly show the individual the door! Can we confidently say that we do the same in our public schools?

> **Hiring the best matters!** In a study conducted in the Dallas Independent School District, when students had a highly effective teacher three years in a row, their test scores rose from the 59th percentile in fourth grade to the 76th percentile in sixth grade. If students had an ineffective teacher, their test scores dropped from the 60th percentile in fourth grade to the 42nd percentile in sixth grade.[51]

In the course of public school interviews throughout history, how many times would you say interviewees were asked customer service–related questions? There is a correlation between the school's customer service philosophy and the quality of its employees. Every single person must fit into the school's philosophy or else those who don't fit will undermine the school's mission, washing away what is good about it like the tide washing away the beach. Remember what John Maxwell said, "Organizations cannot rise above the level of leadership." If a board does not hire a customer service–minded superintendent, he or she will not pass that value down to the entire district. Therefore, we must ask ourselves:

1. What are the qualities or characteristics important to the position?
2. Do we have customer service standards for this position? If so, what are they?
3. What are the customer service needs of the school?

A Few Sample Customer Service–Based Interview Questions:
1. "Give some examples of times you've really connected with students."
2. "How will you communicate with parents and guardians?"
3. "How will you make contact with your students before the first day of school?"
4. "How are you going to let parents and students learn a little about you?"
5. "If a child is struggling in your class, when would you contact the parents? How would you contact them? What might you say to them? If the parent blames you, how might you respond?"
6. Role-play for an elementary school: A child gets to school but school is called off. As a guidance counselor, how would you ensure that this child gets home safely?

Asking a few customer service questions will enable the hiring committee to determine whether the candidate has the right attitude for your school and will be a good team member. These questions will also show the interviewee the importance of customer service at your school and potentially weed out candidates who do not want to work in such a culture.

Once you know what to look for in candidates, you'll spot a customer service–oriented employee working everywhere you go and even on the telephone or computer. You'll also be able to see what your intuition has been telling you all along about people who have the wrong attitude and just aren't clicking with your school. Honing this sense will improve the culture

What are the consequences of not giving great service during an interview? In a study by American Express, researchers found that a person will tell twenty-four others about a bad service experience. If thirty people apply for a job at your school, that's 720 people who hear about this bad experience over just one open position. Let's say over the course of a year your district has twenty-five open positions. That brings the total to 18,000 people![52]

and productivity of your school as well as the happiness of your students and staff.

Keep in mind that providing great customer service to interviewees is important for the *reputation* of your school. Do you want to be known as the school that doesn't treat potential hires well? If a candidate walks into a school and doesn't feel welcomed, what do you think they will assume about how welcomed they'd feel as an employee? Word of mouth spreads quickly, especially because for every position you only hire one person; the rest have to be told they didn't get the job. A school should aim to make a great impression on candidates so that even a "no" answer doesn't sound like a rejection or leave a bad taste in all those mouths. The goal is to create great connections with these applicants with the hope that they will want to apply again in the future. If you've ever had to reluctantly pick one of several great, qualified candidates, you know the value of encouraging those people you didn't hire to apply for a future position at your school.

> When hiring, ask yourself: Is this person best for our students, our customers? Who is benefitting most from hiring this person, students or someone else?

The Customer Service–Based Hiring Process

Imagine we are working at a school that gives great customer service; let's call it ACME Customer Service School. We will have a system for the hiring process. It will be a structured step-by-step method that includes training the hiring committee to ensure everyone knows what to look for in candidates and understands each person's role.

> "You're terminated. Hasta la vista, baby!"
> —Arnold Schwarzenegger on *The New Celebrity Apprentice*[53]

Recruiting: We begin with recruiting to ensure that we have a qualified pool of applicants. Leaving it up to chance is not good enough. So just as college coaches recruit athletes to ensure they have a winning team and businesses recruit candidates, so too must schools recruit the best employees to enhance the quality of their staff and school culture. We can borrow the idea from the business world, mentioned earlier, of keeping a list of people who would be fitting team members so that when vacancies occur, there are already leads on who could fill the position, cutting down on time and energy spent blindly interviewing candidates who end up not fitting into the school's mission.

When seeking the best candidates, every avenue must be pursued, from formal networks like job-seeking sites to informal networks like people you meet in your daily life and recommendations from current customer service–minded employees. Earlier in this chapter, I mentioned a bank teller who I hired as an administrative assistant. That's the kind of outside-the-box thinking that can take your school's hiring to the next level. While your rival school the next town over entertains applications for *only* people who have experience as public school administrative assistants, you can enjoy a wider applicant pool by considering applicants from the business world with years of experience in customer service.

> **Success does not happen by chance; a school can only be as successful as the individuals they employ. No amount of training will help a bad hire!**

Screening: What's the point in granting someone an hour of your time when after five minutes you can rule them out? This is the eyeball test. If you've ever gone through the process of hiring someone at a public school (or hiring someone anywhere, for that matter), you know just how many applicants throw their hats in the ring but are simply not a good fit for your school's mission. Screening ensures they take up only a few minutes of your time.

Interviewing: Before starting the interview process, schools should craft a set of questions that are congruent with the school's mission and values. Does your district have a set of customer service values that can be given to the potential candidate to ensure the position is a good fit for both the interviewer and the interviewee? For example, in the ACME School District we want every student to receive a home visit by a teacher before the student's first day of school. We also want every teacher to give his or her personal cell phone number to parents in case of emergency. If the teacher does not want to do either, it might not be a good fit.

The interview questions should be tailored to the position and include questions specific to customer service. For example, "Who would you identify as your customer, and how do you develop a positive relationship with this individual?" They may be taken aback by such a question, but they need to know that giving great customer service is expected from all employees. A grumpy cafeteria worker versus a friendly, polite cafeteria worker can make a huge difference in the outcome of a kid's day—every day for the duration of that worker's employment.

The other side of the interview coin is the interviewee's response. Just like in the business world, those involved in the interview should have a clear idea of what a good response sounds like. This will ensure your hiring team are all on the same page when it comes time to evaluate each candidate. If you were a teacher, would you grade students' essays on a rubric or by how much you liked each one? Having a clearly defined system for assessment eliminates biases (we all have them!) and allows the best to be recognized as the best.

According to a study of 108 nationally representative school districts by the Center for American Progress, only 13 percent of schools required teacher applicants to perform a demonstration lesson during the interview process at any time before being hired. Furthermore, only 33 percent of schools required an interview with the school principal as part of the hiring process. In my opinion, both of these numbers should be closer to 100 percent.[54]

Sometimes a second interview is necessary when

it is hard to determine which candidate should get a position. This interview puts the candidate in his/her role, performing the duties that will be asked of him or her. Many hiring experts recommend this type of simulated experience. I suggest recruiting students for a teaching simulation with the applicants. Additionally, having a student or group of students walk around the school with the applicant gives insight into how well that applicant will interact with students. In my meetings with student ambassadors after their tours, I get a sense of their impression of the candidate. Generally, when the students are excited about the candidate and that candidate gets hired, it ends up being a great hire. Students truly have a sixth sense for who will be a good fit in the school and who won't!

The last step is to make the critical decision of who to hire. In our busy world it's easy to rush to a decision and get on with our work. My

> Secretaries that call candidates to set up interviews always have stories about candidates acting rudely to them on the phone. Hearing about school staff's interactions with the candidate is important because it shows you the side of a candidate that you will not see during a formal interview.

advice is that if you're not thrilled with the best candidate, keep looking. Success does not happen by chance; a school can only be as successful as the individuals they employ. Still, some schools view hiring as simply one more thing they need to check off their to-do lists. We owe our students, our customers, and ourselves much more. The concept of hiring well is one of the most important functions of any school or district. *Ask yourself questions like these:* "Would I want this candidate interacting with my child?" and "Do I want this secretary to be the face of our school?"

Final Thoughts on Hiring

As school choice continues to grow, parents will choose schools based on the quality of people interacting with their children. Thus the very survival of public education depends on hiring employees that give great service. The business world knows this all too well. There's an old saying from the business world:

> *A corporation may spread itself over the whole world and it may employ a hundred thousand [people], but the average person will usually form his judgment of it through his contact with one individual. . . . If this person is rude or inefficient, it will take a lot of kindness and efficiency to overcome the bad impression.*[55]

This is why every employee is critical to achieving the customer service vision of the district.

Hiring is a tough, time-consuming task. As school leaders, we are already short on time doing our regular duties, so when an employee gets fired, it can be hard to find the time to devote to finding a replacement employee. But when we take hiring as seriously as *The Apprentice* does, keeping in mind the potential long-term costs or benefits to each hire, we can see just how much it pays off to look for customer service skills and get the person with the right attitude on our team.

> Sixty-eight percent of customers stop patronizing a company because of "an attitude of indifference and rudeness toward the customer by owner, manager or employee."
> – Dr. Michael LeBoeuf, *How to Win Customers and Keep Them for Life*[56]

I've included sample customer service questions for several different positions, interview checklists, and employee guidelines in the Appendix of this book.

Concept 4

Forge Relationships with the Customers

"Sometimes you want to go
Where everybody knows your name
And they're always glad you came . . . "
—Theme song from *Cheers*[57]

We all need a little place like Cheers in our lives, don't we? Whether it's our home, work, social club, or something else, it just feels good to be among people who understand us and care about us. Building trust with another person opens so many doors for that relationship, allowing each person to share his or her feelings, take chances, and eventually to strive for the other's approval. When applied to the business world, the idea of building relationships is essential to providing great customer service. In fact, it may be the most important concept of them all.

Whenever I present to schools on the subject of forging relationships, I always share one amazing and unexpected customer service experience from my life. I enjoy playing blackjack as a way to unwind, so when I decided to take a Christmas vacation with the woman I was seeing, Janet, I was excited to make a quick stop at a casino on the way. This is where I met Dave, the blackjack dealer.

Dave was a towering individual with a booming voice like a giant, but I could instantly tell that Dave loved what he did each day and his fellow employees and customers loved him, too! He would question card choices in a comical way, make beverage suggestions, yell to guests walking past, and banter and joke with anyone who made eye contact with him as he got to know every person at his table. Dave was able to do all of this and still keep total control of his table, remain focused, and ensure that all people followed the rules.

From the very beginning, Dave and Janet would tease and banter back and forth. I would chime in that I was glad that he was there to listen to her so I could focus on the cards! Early on in the game, we were joined by another couple and gentleman and, with Dave's help, we laughed and played blackjack for six hours! Dave would even pass up his break time to stay with us at the table. There was one empty seat at the table so Dave placed a marker to indicate the seat was taken to keep others from joining our group. It was like we had all been friends forever, and I know that it was a direct result of Dave making connections with his customers. I now realize that Dave's enthusiasm had an impact on many of the other dealers and thus the entire culture of this casino. I'll talk more about that infectious attitude in the Give Great Service to Employees concept.

The other couple at the table asked if we would return the next day. Janet and I hadn't really planned on staying, but Dave, being "in the moment" and listening with one ear, yelled to his pit boss, "Kelly and Janet need to stay so they will all come back tomorrow." The pit boss made a call, and we were given a free room and two complimentary meals.

We ended up staying overnight and returning to Dave's black-jack table the next day to find the couple there again. The lady turned to Janet and in a small whisper thanked her for the enter-tainment and fun that we had all shared. You see, she said this would be her last Christmas due to her cancer, and she had chosen to run away for the holidays and not think about her illness or be a burden to her family. The time that we all had shared, with Dave leading the way, made her laugh and forget for a few short hours! What started out to be an hour at a blackjack table turned into a two-day experience.

On the one year anniversary of our unplanned weekend at his casino, I received a text from Dave wanting to know why we were not at his blackjack table. For the past three years Dave has occasionally texted or emailed me asking when Janet and I will be returning. To date I have made five more trips to Tunica to stay at the Roadhouse Casino to play five-dollar blackjack with Dave.

I later found out that Dave makes less than six dollars an hour and has to share any tips with the other dealers. From Dave's attitude, one would think he made $100 an hour as he kept a smile in his voice and on his face and he made an intentional effort to connect with all his customers. I was so impressed, I even contacted his manager to make sure they understood what a valued asset that man was to their establishment. It wasn't the fancy rooms, free dinners, or money we won that mattered; we were repeat customers because of Dave. He continues to be my gold standard for forging relationships in the business world.

How the Best Companies Forge Relationships

The leaders at Zappos, the shoe retail giant, know the importance of forging relationships with their customers. As a web-based company, they don't have the opportunity that stores like Walmart have to interact and make great connections with their customers. So Zappos has to make an *intentional effort* to create personal relationships with customers. They target a young, tech-savvy demographic that doesn't mind buying shoes online as opposed to trying them on at a shoe store. One of the ways they build relationships with this market is by interacting on social media. They start with clever Twitter posts like "Dunn nun . . . Dunn nun . . . Duunn nun Duunn . . . Dun nun Dun nun Dun nun Dun nun," then show a picture of shoes with designs from the movie *Jaws* on them.[58] Zappos has amassed a huge following on social media because of its clever marketing and interactions with customers.

Zappos broadcasts live videos from launch events such as a Nintendo partnership with the shoe company Vans, creating classic Nintendo game–inspired shoes.[59] They have giveaways for people who watch their broadcasts on Periscope and for those who follow them on Snapchat. One such contest gives winners a very special delivery: instead of the usual Fed-Ex delivery person, their package is delivered to their door by record producer and radio personality, DJ Khaled.[60]

All this is just the tip of the iceberg of what Zappos is doing to connect with customers and show the human side to their web-based business, and it's paying off.

> **Poor or weak relationships generate a host of negative effects, including chronic elevated levels of cortisol, which can destroy new brain cells, impair social judgment, reduce memory, and diminish cognition (Sapolsky, 2005).[61]**

When I think about companies that make an intentional effort to forge relationships with me, I see a lot of it happening on a local level. I regularly visit a particular Waffle House in my town. I've had so many conversations with one waitress that, when she brought over my coffee one day, I was greeted with a pleasant surprise. You see, this restaurant had sugar packets, Sweet 'N Low packets and Equal packets, but not Splenda. Unfortunately for me, Splenda is my sweetener of choice, and I always have to go with one of the others instead. So what did I see when she brought over my coffee? You guessed it, a pile of Splenda packets. "When did Waffle House start carrying Splenda?" I asked her. She leaned in close and said, "Don't tell anyone, but I felt bad you keep coming here and we never have your Splenda, so I went across the street to McDonald's and swiped some for you." She then proceeded to flip the *M* on the McDonald's packet upside down to form a *W* for Waffle House. While I am not advocating stealing, this waitress found a way to do a little extra, make me smile, and thus strengthen our relationship.

Think of a business that you go to on a regular basis. It could be a bar for a particular bartender or restaurant for a particular waitstaff, a barber, an auto mechanic, a hotel chain, or a coffee shop. Why do you keep going back? For many people, it's because they've established some kind of relationship with the business or an employee at the business. Whether that relationship is with a person, a product, or an experience, the familiarity, consistency, and comfort people get from knowing and being known by a company creates brand loyalty, which keeps them coming back. To quote *Cheers* again, "You wanna be where everybody knows your name." From millennials to baby boomers, customers love it when a company or product speaks to them as an individual. The best companies know this, and that's why they try to succeed at making each customer feel special. Shouldn't every student in our public schools feel special too?

From My Experience

Dave, the blackjack dealer, reinforced the idea—formed in my early days of teaching—that establishing connections is at the foundation of any job that requires interactions with others. However,

> "No significant learning occurs without a significant relationship."
> – Dr. James Comer[62]

something else clicked when I got home from that trip. The casino knows more about *me* than most public school staffs know about their *students*! This realization, to me, is inexcusable. The cornerstone of any successful school should be building relationships with students.

I was in my third year of teaching when I walked down the hall of a high school in Eastern Kentucky and overheard one of my more disruptive students, Stephen, talking about working on a tobacco farm. Though I was a novice at the craft, as a teenager I worked with my stepfather on his father's farm as a way to earn extra money. I interrupted Stephen to ask him how many tobacco sticks he could cut in a day. While I do not remember his number, I exaggerated (which is a teacher term for telling a white lie) that on a good day I could cut 1,000 sticks. He eyed me suspiciously, as a boy who had farmed all his life would to a young, inexperienced teacher dressed in a three-piece suit. However, I had used enough of the proper tobacco lingo that he knew I had some experience in the craft. After a long consideration, he smiled and we both had a good laugh. The next day he asked me if I had ever "dropped sticks." (Harvested tobacco plants are skewered with these sticks and hung to dry.) I then told him I could carry about a hundred sticks on my shoulder, but that I prefer to drop them from a "high boy." Stephen continued to ask me tobacco questions and I held my own mostly, though sometimes I pretended I had to run to a meeting when I had no idea what he was talking about!

About two weeks after that first conversation, I started to notice Stephen's work habits change in my classroom. This was a big deal as he had not only been a major disruption in my class but, as a leader among his peers, his attitude had rubbed off on the other students. In high school, every classroom has its own personality and at the time this was my least favorite class. As Stephen's behavior improved, the entire class environment began to change. I began taking a few minutes each class to get to know each of them and allow them to get to know me.

"Unless someone like you cares a whole awful lot, Nothing is going to get better, it's not."
– Dr. Seuss, *The Lorax*[63]

The moment that changed my entire teaching career occurred just two weeks later when I received a new student. I could tell from this student's body language and the fact that he did not bring paper or a pencil to class that he had the potential to be a class disrupter. If that wasn't enough, he immediately headed to the back row of my classroom.

Sure enough, during the lesson, the new student yelled across the room to another student. Then, amazingly, Stephen (whose behavior three months earlier mirrored that of the new student) turned around and told the new student that he was not going to act this way in this class. He went on to say, "Mr. Middleton is teaching us and you need to settle down."

The next day, the new student was sitting right by Stephen and began contributing to the class. I not only began talking more with this class, I began making it a point to speak with them in the hallway and during lunch. I noticed myself being able to make my lessons more relevant to them as I began to know them, and I ended up enjoying this once-dreaded period more than any other class I taught that year.

> "Relationships will make or break your school."
> – Eric Jensen[64]

The symbiotic relationship between teachers caring about students and students responding by seeking teachers' approval by doing their best in class made it one of the more successful classes I had that year. It truly opened my eyes to the importance of forging relationships with students.

The Importance of Forging Relationships in Public Education

The 1995 film *Dangerous Minds* stars Michelle Pfeiffer as a young teacher who has been given the task of teaching English to a high school class of "problem students."[65] Within the first minute of standing in front of her classroom, she is unable to handle it and races out to get help from another teacher. But she is determined to get them to learn, so she scraps the usual lesson plans and curricula for songs and poetry about issues that will speak to these inner-city teenagers. She then teaches by using dialogue—challenging her students to say what they think.

At first they are reluctant to speak, especially the class leader and tough guy. But after she breaks up a fight, then follows up by visiting the suspended students and bragging on them to their parents, the class starts to trust that she truly cares about them as individuals and doesn't just see this as a job. When the end of the year comes, she surprises herself by deciding to stay to teach again next year. It turns out they forged relationships with her as well!

One year, when I was an assistant superintendent, a new teacher stopped me during the first week of school to thank me for

> What would happen if I ever received bad customer service from Dave or another employee? Because of our established relationship it would take numerous bad experiences before I would change my opinion of this casino. We need this type of relationship insulation in our public schools.

the home visit program. The teacher had placed a student on the wrong school bus, and for about thirty minutes the parents and everyone else were panicked. After the student was found, the teacher was dreading telling the parent it was her fault. The teacher, who had been trained on how to recover well (a concept I'll discuss later), took the student home and apologized to the parent face-to-face. Surprisingly the mother was not upset at all. She just smiled and said, "I know you did not mean to do it and I know you care about my child." The teacher went on to tell me that she knew it would not have gone quite so smoothly if she had not done the summer home visit, which began a dialogue and relationship with this parent. Thinking about relationships this way, we can see that they are actually a form of job security. They allow us, as school personnel, to be given the all-important *benefit of the doubt*. Everyone makes mistakes—even the best companies—so it is imperative that we prioritize building relationships with the customers so that we will be forgiven when those slipups occur.

> In a study of public school students, more than 80 percent of student athletes said they believed their coach cared about their grades, and three-fourths of the students rated their coach as one of the top three most influential people in their lives (Newman, 2005).[66]

When I researched for my book *Simply the Best: 29 Things Students Say the Best Teachers Do Around Relationships*, I surveyed thousands of students about what makes the best teachers.[67] Twenty of the twenty-nine answers given were relationship-based. In fact, we found that the number one concept that the best teachers practice was "getting to know their students." They know their students' names, interests, life goals, and families. It turns out, *students just want to know the adults around them care about them.*

What Forging Relationships Looks Like in Public Education

So what exactly does making an intentional effort to forge relationships look like in a public school? There are endless ways to get to know students, but here are some of my favorite examples of how school personnel can build a solid relationship with a student.

- Home Visits: During the summer, have teachers visit the homes of their students to check in on how they are doing, meet their family (if they haven't already), and most importantly, spend some one-on-one time with the student and family to establish a connection that can lead to greater trust.

- Move-Up Day: During the last week of school, having a full, step-up day dramatically reduces the amount of anxiety students have on the first day of school the following year. Spending a day in their future class-room with their future teacher takes away the fear of the unknown. "What if my teacher is mean?" "How do I work the combination lock on my locker?" These are common thoughts that run through a student's mind all summer. By taking the mystery out, students can know what to expect and not be so anxious. Furthermore, if the teacher is welcoming by smiling, being friendly, and engaging students, the students might actually *look forward* to being in this class all summer long instead of dreading the start of school. The school also benefits from Move-Up Day because students' enthusiasm for the start of next year means that they are less likely to decide to switch to a competing form of education.

- Graduation Day: Have a student's favorite district employee hand him or her the diploma. This is an emotional day for students; they are saying good-bye to their home away from home. Allowing students to have a favorite teacher, coach, or school employee hand them their diploma can be a great way to celebrate the formal end of their relationship. But be warned, if you try this in your school, be prepared for some misty-eyed staff and students. And don't be surprised if you well up yourself! It's a great way to thank your students for their hard work over the years. (An observant leader will take note of which employees end up on the stage year after year.)

- Assign an adult advocate (staff member) to every student in school. This advocate will reach out to his or her assigned parents and guardians to get to know them personally. Where do they live? When and where do they work? When is the student's birthday? Does the student have a pet and what is its name? This staff member should exchange cell phone numbers and be the first point of contact on any school issues. Just like how every teacher has a union rep who has their back, each student should have such an advocate.

These are just a few examples of how school personnel can connect with their students. It doesn't really matter *how* you do it though, as long as you do it. Make relationships part of your school identity by incorporating questions and follow-ups on weekly staff agendas. The goal is to move toward a day when you, as a school leader, can put the names of every student on a wall and have staff write something about that student next to his or her name, so that every name has several personal details next to it. Would activities such as this help change the perception of public schools?

Final Thoughts on Forging Relationships

Implementing the strategies outlined in this concept can create a brand loyalty (think: your favorite coffee shop). Research has shown that if students feel connected with the school, they're less likely to leave. In a 2014 study by the High School Survey of Student Engagement (HSSSE), 29 percent of high school students who had thought about dropping out cited not liking their teachers as the reason, while 62 percent of them cited not liking the school as a whole.[12] Because students and families have more schooling choices than ever before, each year they have to decide whether they will stay in the public school system or go with one of the other options available to them. Many choose to stay in public schools because they don't want to lose their connections. A great teacher, coach, extracurricular leader, or any other staff person with whom the student has a great connection can make

> According to Lee and Burkam (2003), students were less likely to drop out and more likely to graduate when they felt a positive bond with teachers and others at school.[68]

the student decide to stay in the school. Conversely, a student who feels that the school doesn't know her or care about her is easier to sway toward another schooling option.

All it takes is one or two school employees to care about a student to make that student work hard in the classroom, behave well, and buy into the school's mission. I see students like Stephen turn the trajectory of their futures around all the time. It truly is a magical sight to see when these challenging students begin to believe that school is not their enemy.

When administration understands the importance of forging relationships and passes that idea down through each employee at the school, amazing things can happen. As Dr. Seuss wrote in *The Lorax*, "Unless someone like you cares a whole awful lot, Nothing is going to get better, it's not."

The Importance of Building Relationships in Order to Decrease or Prevent School Violence

"[E]ducators can play a part in prevention by creating an environment where students feel comfortable telling an adult whenever they hear about someone who is considering doing harm to another person, or even whether the person is considering harming themselves. Once such an environment is created, it will remain important that the adults in that environment listen to students and handle the information they receive in a fair and responsible manner."

— US Secret Service and US Department of Education,
"Implications for the Prevention of School Attacks
in the United States"[247]

"Promoting healthy relationships and environments is more effective for reducing school misconduct and crime than instituting punitive penalties. . . . Students who are committed to school, feel that they belong, and trust the administration are less likely to commit violent acts than those who are uninvolved, alienated, or distrustful."
... "Peers and teachers who talk with problem students can often provide the most useful information about when such students are in trouble. Establishing school environments where students feel connected and trusted will build the critical link between those who often know when trouble is brewing and those who can act to prevent it."

— Edward Mulvey and Elizabeth Cauffman,
"The Inherent Limits of Predicting School Violence"[248]

CONCEPT 5

Train for Customer Service

"The expense of training isn't what it costs to train employees.
It's what it costs not to train them."
– Phillip Wilber, President, Drug Emporium, Inc.[69]

I was with my friend Sarah after a long day outside in the hot weather. We decided to quench our thirsts at a restaurant that she and I both knew did not give good service, so we did not have high expectations. With no other dining options, we decided to give it a shot.

We stood waiting to be seated for over twenty minutes in a mostly empty restaurant with plenty of employees working—several of whom walked right by us. After finally being seated, we waited again for a waiter to come and take our drink orders. Exasperated, I asked Sarah if she wanted to leave. I was not prepared for her response. She jumped out of her seat and yelled across the restaurant, "We're thirsty over here!" I sat, mouth agape, watching her fume at the waitstaff. In fact, it seemed everyone in the restaurant stopped mid-bite, forks clanking to their plates.

Well wouldn't you know a waiter came on a dead run and actually slid up to our table like Tom Cruise's sock slide in *Risky Business*.[70] Then he got down on one knee and said, "You're not my table, but I will be your server anyway. I'm Adam." Even though his run and slide were impressive, I could tell Sarah was not pacified. She reported how long we had been waiting and how thirsty we were. After we told Adam our drink orders, he jumped up and ran to get us our drinks and came back with an extra of each, then again got down on one knee to take Sarah's order. Everyone seemed to be watching our table, so Sarah took the opportunity to exclaim to the whole restaurant, "I love to bring men to their knees!"

We received our meals promptly after placing our orders. From time to time, Adam would playfully yell across the restaurant to see if Sarah was still happy. The entire mood of the restaurant seemed to change, and it was all because of Adam's great service. When we finished our meals, Adam brought us two warm chocolate chip cookies on the house. By that time, Sarah's (and my) experience had turned around completely. She even had me take a picture of her giving Adam a hug at our table. I have to admit, I wanted to offer this gentleman a job.

As we were saying good-bye to our impeccable waiter, I asked Adam what customer service training he'd had. He looked around then leaned in, and said in a low voice that at this restaurant they don't really train for customer service, but at his previous job he'd been trained very well. Now it finally made sense.

This story is a great example of how much of a difference customer service training can make (and an instance of recovering well, which I'll discuss later). The disparity between Adam and the rest of the staff just shows how much a customer's experience can change when the staff has been properly trained in customer service.

The reality is, most employees—across all industries—have very little or no customer service training. I'm sure you can think of a few establishments where you routinely receive mediocre or poor service. For the best companies in the world, such an experience is simply unacceptable. Do you think Southwest would let their flight attendants work a flight without making sure they knew how to charm a crowd, handle miscues and take people's guff with a smile on their faces? Absolutely not!

Cue customer service training. It can turn a promising, well-intentioned employee from a sub-par performer into a superstar. But it doesn't happen overnight; it takes practice to master the skill of giving great customer service. In order to reach the point of customer service mastery, one must look at it the way one looks at athletic training. We can see such a connection in the following passage from *Exceptional Customer Service: Going Beyond Your Good Service to Exceed the Customer's Expectation*, by Lisa Ford, David McNair, and William Perry.

> *You see, developing an exceptional customer service program is much like developing a fitness routine. It's a workout; it's aerobics. It's not a one-time grueling workout. It's a long-term program of constant activity. After all, you don't talk about running to become a marathon runner. You are not simply inspired to become an Olympic swimmer. If you truly understand the positive impacts of a distinguishing service program, then you must work at it constantly and consistently.[71]*

If we look at customer service in this way, we can understand the time and effort it takes to train employees to consistently give great service to customers.

Customer Service Training in the Business World

The best companies understand the importance of customer service training. One of the best customer service companies has a unique approach to training. Zappos, the largest online retailer of shoes, utilizes layers of training. It starts, believe it or not, during the interview process.[72] The company makes each hire based on several rounds of interviews, during which the company learns the applicant's skill sets, experience, and whether the applicant is a good fit for the culture of Zappos.[73] After this process, every hire—regardless of job title or department—goes through two weeks of training focusing on learning the company's history, culture, and philosophy on customer service. Then, for another two weeks all new hires, again regardless of job title or department, work as *actual* customer service representatives for Zappos. That means, they answer phones and emails from customers, interacting with them to find out what the issue is and how to resolve it quickly and painlessly.

After the first week of paid training, each new hire is offered a bonus of two thousand dollars to quit.[74] The rationale behind this practice is that the people who just want a paycheck can take the money and go, but the people who want to be a part of the team are the people they want. Zappos is so confident that they are an amazing place to work that they're essentially saying, "We dare you to take our money and leave." Less than 15 percent of new hires accept this cash-out offer. Zappos's enculturation process is critical to aligning employee behaviors with the core values and practices of the company, whose mission is to "Provide the best customer service possible!"[75]

Where Public Education Falls Short

We've talked about how the best companies train employees to give great customer service, but on the other end of the spectrum we have public schools. Historically, public schools are not known for providing customer service training to employees. In fact, during our school years, many of us can recall at least one employee of whom we were terrified. For me, it was the school administrative assistant. She was always barking orders at kids, demanding to see hall passes, questioning whether kids were

Why Is Customer Service Training So Overlooked in Public Education?

1. For the first 200 years, there has been very little competition for public school students.
2. Public schools tend to train based on how they are evaluated. Currently, public schools are evaluated based on test scores.
3. There are limited resources for training.
4. The argument that "a school is not a business" keeps such principles out of schools.
5. Customer service is not important to leadership.
6. Giving great customer service is hard to measure and evaluate.

telling the truth, or calling the teacher to make sure the kid was not lying about his or her purpose in coming to the office. My heart definitely beat faster every time I walked by her office.

Employees like this might be a familiar sight in our schools, even the norm in some cases, but they wouldn't be tolerated for very long at the best companies. Of course, you can't go around just firing everyone who's not giving great service. In fact, their failure to give great service may not even be their fault. While sometimes the problem is employees not following through with the school's protocol, it's often the case that they simply were not *trained in customer service.* When it comes to training, I've noticed that public schools do a decent job of covering the fundamentals of a position. For example, a front office administrative assistant's fundamental job is to staff the desk in the front office, answer phones, and deal with whoever comes into the office. Public schools do a good enough job of training employees in those areas. However, they fall short when training employees how to go from just doing a job to doing it in a way that creates a positive working and learning environment—that is, in a way that gives great customer service. Without such training, we leave *the way* the administrative assistants do their jobs open to interpretation, which we cannot be assured will be up to our standards and expectations. Only through a well-planned training program on which employees are monitored regularly can a school expect to consistently give great customer service.

> A question I like to pose in my district presentations is, "Have you ever had any customer service training?" Ninety-five percnt of school employees have responded, "No."

A colleague of mine called me one day, fuming about his administrative assistant. He said, "Kelly, I'm so fed up with her not screening my calls! You wouldn't believe the calls she puts through to me." On and on he went until finally I stopped him and said, "Greg did you ever sit down with her and tell her which

> Tip for front office personnel when someone enters the office: when you greet them, acknowledge that you've met the person before or point out that you haven't met them before. It either invites them to think back to those previous (hopefully good) interactions or gives them a window to explain their purpose without that impersonal, all business, "Why are you here?" question.

callers go through to you and which callers she should take a message from?" He responded meekly, "No." "Well then, how is she supposed to know?" I said. He fell silent for a few seconds, and I knew the light bulb had turned on in his head.

The administrative assistant ended up working out for him after he took some time to train her on how to screen calls. One major mistake I constantly witness administrators make is assuming the employee knows what to do. How does that famous phrase go? "Never assume, because when you assume you make an ass of you and me."

Customer Service Training in Public Schools

So what does such a training program look like? As stated in the Leadership concept, in order for any organization to be great at customer service, it must flow like a waterfall from the top of the organization down through every employee. That means the very top of public school administration needs to be trained in customer service principles so they can in turn train their employees in the customer service aspects specific to employees' positions. For this reason, an initial training in customer service and yearly refresher courses will ensure that employees stay focused on this goal. All school leaders and each department (maintenance, food service, teachers, substitute teachers, transportation, office personnel, volunteers, etc.) should have their own customer service training sessions each year—tailored to fit their job specifications. I also recommend that school leaders attend their staff's customer service training so they'll know what staff have been taught and can follow up to enforce expectations, creating a culture of accountability.

I've found that modeling what the best companies do works well for customer service training. Just like at Zappos, a school should incorporate an induction program for all new workers. This induction program would be a two to three day session training with a major emphasis on giving great customer service. Public schools tend to throw their new hires right into the fray, without any customer service training. Frankly, should any new employee be in front of customers without being trained?

Induction programs should make sure staff learns both specific customer service directives (like teachers conducting home visits or custodial staff attending school functions like science fairs in order to further forge relationships with students and families) as well as tips on how to perform typical functions of their jobs with a customer service twist. Here are a few examples of induction program training:

- Training administrative assistants to answer phones and greet visitors
- Training cooks to speak to children
- Training teachers to conduct effective parent-teacher meetings and to involve parents
- Training facilities staff to see and fix problems with infrastructure before others see them
- Training coaches to relate to athletes and parents, especially in regard to cuts, playing time, or roster changes
- Training school board members to give great service to each other or making sure service flows through the whole school system
- Training everyone to recover well after making a mistake

This is just a small list to get your mind thinking about customer service training. Some of these topics could even be their own training sessions. One stand-alone customer service training that I highly recommend is home visit training.

For those who haven't jumped on the home visit bandwagon, in my experience, these are invaluable customer service tools for our teachers. Not only do home visits get teachers thinking outside the box about the lives of their students, but they really push teachers to forge relationships—and you know how I feel about that concept!

Home visit *training* is important because a home visit is so far outside teachers' regular job description. This is important to keep in mind because as leaders, we sometimes tell employees to do something but don't tell them how. Giving teachers specific instructions and advice will help home visits go smoothly.

You can start with general tips like:

- dress down/wear casual clothes
- talk about something you have in common with parents to break the ice
- you don't have to stay in the house
- don't bring clipboards—it looks too investigative
- remember to just be yourself, not a teacher

I've found teachers even appreciate training on how to leave. It can get awkward cutting off a parent once they are on a roll talking about their child. Tips like getting on the edge of the seat or saying you've got another visit to go to can help. I also recommend having a discussion about cultural sensitivity. For example, some families ask to take shoes off or are offended if guests don't eat something.

At the end of the day, though, there are two magical sentences that drive a home visit: "Tell me something about your child," and "What are your child's talents?" This also gives the teacher insight into the student's interests in order to motivate and further build a relationship with that student throughout the school year.

However you choose to do it, the most important thing is that you have some form of customer service training—*even if it's thirty minutes* the first time. As I mentioned earlier in this chapter, incorporating the concept of customer service into an organization, whether it's a public school or a Fortune 500 company, takes time. Start however grandiose or small as is realistic and comfortable for your school, and just make a pledge to do better each time. After all, that is a customer service motto. Once you start thinking about what great customer service can look like for a particular position, the possibilities are endless!

Final Thoughts on Training

As school leaders, we know the importance of learning. We also know that working for a school is, at the core, an interpersonal experience. It only makes sense that we train our employees to reflect these two beliefs. If our mission is to mold intelligent, capable students, we must ensure that all staff reflect that mission in their service to students. It all starts with training. Most people who work in public education want to do right by their students. We just need to give them the tools to do so.

Concept 6

Walk in the Shoes of the Customers

*"If there is any one secret of success, it lies in the ability
to get the other person's point of view and see things
from that person's angle as well as from your own."*
—Henry Ford[76]

What Is Walking in the Shoes of the Customers?

I've been told that great chess players like to get up and go to their opponent's side to see what he or she sees. It helps them to get a better idea of what he or she may be thinking or planning. They find that each time they get up and go to their opponent's side, they see the game in a totally different light—one that gives them a more holistic view of what's going on—and it helps them plan their moves and countermoves.

Similar to the chess game, when we talk about walking in the shoes of the customer, the goal is to understand their perspective. Walking in the shoes of the customer is a philosophy as much as it is an actual physical activity. We ask, "What is it like to *be* one of your customers?" This is the heart of the motivation behind walking in the shoes of the customer. If you can see what they see, you'll be able to pick out the details of their experience that are not up to your standard of excellence.

In the 1930s American Airways (now called American Airlines) was receiving many complaints about lost luggage from passengers. General Manager LaMotte Cohn had tried to fix the problem but the improvements were minimal. Cohn then came up with an idea. He held a meeting at the company's headquarters and required all his station managers to attend. Cohn then made

68

sure that every manager's luggage never made it to the meeting. Needless to say, the managers were furious when they arrived and found out all their luggage was lost. After cooling off, they realized the reason behind their GM's actions and from then on the amount of lost luggage was significantly reduced.[77] Message received!

What does this tell you about the way customer service works? Cohn tried to implement changes several times to improve this problem, yet only after his employees felt firsthand what it was like to land somewhere without their personal items did the problem improve. People are generally empathic, but without the opportunity to connect with another person's struggles, the expression of empathy does not occur. Once the managers knew what it felt like, that is, once they walked in their customers' shoes, they realized just how important it was to make sure the bag follows the passenger to the destination. Just like all of our customer service concepts, the end result relies on leadership (in this case the general manager and then, in turn, the managers) prioritizing the need and passing that priority down to each of their employees. In one fell swoop, Cohn was able to get his managers on board with fixing this problem, and it paid off with lower lost baggage counts and more satisfied customers.

Undercover Boss

On the television series *Undercover Boss*, a top executive puts on a disguise and takes a front-line position at his or her very own company.[78] In each episode, the undercover boss discovers employees who are hidden jewels within the company, and every once in a while he or she finds an employee who must be retrained. Regardless of what happens while undercover, the bosses always discover information that not only helps the company, but also helps them become much better bosses.

Undercover Boss demonstrates a form of walking in the shoes of the customer, because the boss must step out of his or her management role and assume a wholly different job. Taking on the identity of another, just like going to the opponent's side of the chessboard, creates a shift in vision that cannot occur without first relinquishing one's typical viewpoint. When a leader can do this, the possibilities for changing procedures in order to give better service open up. Another way of saying this is that a leader must periodically *kick the tires* of her or his organization in order to ensure that the quality is up to the leader's standards.

In public education, we can't rely on students and families to report when they have a problem. Many public school families just assume that public schools can't or won't help them, so they don't bother asking. Relying solely on them to report is not a good model for a school. Public school administrators need to periodically *kick the tires* and walk the halls and grounds themselves in order to ensure they are providing the best service to their customers. I'll show what this looks like next.

Undercover Sup

I must admit, as a fan of *Undercover Boss*, I've taken to emulating the show over the course of my career in public education. Actually, one of my favorite things to do is to pop in unannounced (and usually unnoticed) to see what *really* goes on in the school. I'll never forget the day I discovered the multitude of issues in one department in my school. I call it "Spork Day."

During a meeting with my student feedback group, "Kelly's Kids," I came across an opportunity to truly walk in the shoes of my customers. They reported the good and bad experiences they have had at school, and the cafeteria seemed to be a common complaint. There were many problems they wanted to share, but the food was the most predominant. One young lady shared a complaint about something so simple it made me shake my head. She said, "I just wish there was another kind of salad dressing for the salads."

Yes, you guessed it. They only served ranch! Good, old, faithful ranch salad dressing. I remember asking her, "Don't we have any other choices?" In her cute little middle school voice, she replied, "Yeah . . . but you have to ask." There was just something in her tone that let me know that it was not as simple as asking. Something had to be done about the problems, and it was important that I see it myself, through the eyes of my students: the customers.

I decided the next day I would go through the lunch lines with the students. I did not tell anyone of my intention; I feared people would prepare for my visit just as they always did when they heard "suits are in the building." I stood in line with the students, and I noticed that the young lady who had told me about the salad dressing happened to be standing a couple of students ahead of me. I watched as students were handed their plates of food. The only alternative to the main dish was a salad. This is not your typical salad. This is the salad I have affectionately named "peek-a-boo" salad, as it is served in a white styrofoam container with a closed pop-up lid. The students are to take it for granted that there is a salad inside because they are not permitted to open it up . . . but that's a problem for another story. I watched as the young lady ahead of me chose one of the salads.

> Any time a school board, superintendent, principal, teacher, or other staff member implements a rule, it must be based on a philosophy in order to transmit a clear, consistent message. Using "Walk in the Shoes of the Customers" (or "How would *you* like it?") as a philosophy will help guide those rules and decisions toward a customer service model.

When she got to the last cafeteria worker, and let me add, not one of them seemed happy to see the students, the girl seemed to stand two inches taller (I think she knew I had her back on this one!) as she asked, "Can I have another kind of salad dressing?" This was not the million-dollar question, apparently, by the way the cafeteria worker dropped her eyebrows, slumped her shoulders, stomped to the refrigerator, retrieved the Italian dressing packet, and slapped it onto the plate next to the "peek-a-boo" salad. The girl glanced back toward me and raised her eyebrows as if to say, "I told you so!" It was at this time that the cafeteria ladies realized that I was in line. But by then, I'd already confirmed my student's story.

Next I made a trip over to the elementary school to investigate my students' lunchroom complaints. When I walked in, I was welcomed by the sounds of busy, little elementary schoolers being yelled at to "shut up" and "be quiet" by the cafeteria monitor, who apparently was under the impression that this was an effective type of behavior management. I made a note about training and continued on.

As I jumped in the serving line with the students, I noticed that I had to turn my back to the food in order to make my milk choice. The students were doing the same thing and, while I know that it was very quick for me to grab my chocolate milk carton, deciding on white or chocolate milk when you are six or seven years old can be a very long and serious decision! I could see the problem with this setup, as I heard the cafeteria servers yelling across the counter to the students things like, "Hey, do you want gravy? Hey, hey! Hurry up and turn around! Do you want gravy?" The students would get the milk, turn around and answer the question after being yelled at several times, and then proceed to the next cafeteria server and answer to her list of demands like they were in an interrogation room instead of a lunch line.

Next came the question: "Do you want peas or green beans?" which was quite perplexing to some youngsters because they only know they are green, and they struggle with really knowing the difference without seeing which one is which. The students hemmed and hawed and, as a result, the cafeteria lady kept asking, "green beans or peas?" while getting more frustrated with each repetition.

For dessert, cobbler was offered. The students were very confused because, again, they couldn't see the cobbler, and thus they couldn't identify it. Meanwhile, the server continued to yell, "Hello?! Do you want cobbler?" My head was spinning as I sat down with my food, afraid of what might happen next.

The entrée for the day was salisbury steak. As I settled in at the table with the students, I noticed that my only choice of eating utensil was a spork. What?! How was I going to cut and eat my salisbury steak with just a spork? One of the little students sitting next to me must have realized the futility of trying to eat steak with a spork, as he just grabbed the meat patty, dripping with gravy, and began chomping into it. The cafeteria monitor continued to scream at the students to "shut up" and "be quiet," but she appeared to have learned a new sound management tool while I was in line because she would flick the lights off and on to signal the students to get quiet. It was like trying to eat at a dance club! I am thankful that this kind of noise control does not go on at any restaurant that I visit or I would not be eating out anymore.

I had seen enough and I had a better understanding of what my customers experienced each day. My Kelly's Kids were spot on, and I knew that changes had to occur. I went to my next Kelly's Kids meeting and the first thing I told them was "You were all right. It was just as bad as you told me it was!" I could tell by the looks on their faces that they loved that an adult believed them.

Had I not gone down into the trenches and looked at things through the eyes of a student, I would have never known how bad it was in the lunchrooms in my schools. For example, even if I'd walked in and observed, I wouldn't have gotten all the important details, like why it was so loud in the serving line. I'd only know that it was too loud and the staff were impatiently trying and failing to communicate with kids. It wasn't until I went through the line myself that I saw the flaws in this operation. Afterward, it was a pretty easy fix, but that's a story for another concept!

The Folly of the "Tryouts Board"

Most of us remember the scene that unfolded when a teacher or coach posted the cut for sports teams or stage and music productions on the big board in the school hallway. Kids would crowd around, reading the list of names, begging, pleading, praying theirs would be up there. Others would show up just to see the drama of who made it and who didn't. It seemed the whole world was watching these students being judged, like it was their version of *American Idol*.

In my opinion, the tryouts board is a lazy relic of the old days of public education. Don't students deserve an explanation as to why they did not make the team? Teachers or coaches should bring students into a one on-one meeting, tell them they appreciate them trying out, offer them an auxiliary role on the team (like being a manager or keeping stats), and inform them about intramurals or other options. They could also give students feedback on what they did well and what they needed to improve to try out next year or later in the year if the team ends up needing another player.

Can you imagine if the tryout board was also used to announce which teachers and staff would and would not be coming back to work for the school next year. Instead of an in-person conversation or even a private letter, the school would post the list in the hallway on a corkboard. How do you think your employees would feel about this? When thinking of customer service principles, asking if the practice, rule, or behavior is good enough for you and your employees is a great barometer. This type of walking in the shoes of the customer really shows us just how differently we tend to see students compared to adults. In a customer service–driven public school, a student should get the same high-quality treatment as the adults. After all, they are the reason we all have jobs.

So I challenge you to try this little exercise as often as you can—and especially for rules and policies about which you've heard complaints. Just be sure to remember that there will always be problems when students do not have a voice. Those silently suffering are as important a customer as those vocally suffering. No experience taught me this lesson more than the day I paid a visit to the house of one of my second graders.

Sometimes You Have to Walk the Walk

I was settling into my first superintendent position in Newport, Kentucky when I received a call that would test my commitment to customer service. The call was from Ms. Franklin, a grandparent of one of our second graders. She had requested that the school bus come to her house to pick up her granddaughter Lisa. She explained that her request was denied because she didn't live far enough from school. In Kentucky, schools are only reimbursed for transportation when they transport students over a mile from school, and Lisa lived within a mile of the school. Ms. Franklin was very distraught, and I could tell she really feared for the safety of her granddaughter. Since I teach not to use policy as a way to say no, I decided to find a way to fix this problem. I told her I would be at her house in fifteen minutes to check out the path Lisa would have to walk to school.

Ms. Franklin gave me her address on Ann Street and I immediately knew I was heading to one of the more impoverished areas of town. As I pulled up, Ms. Franklin met me at the door and immediately she began to tell me about how her granddaughter's parents were in jail and how she was going to be taking care of Lisa indefinitely. I thanked her for taking on the parent role and also told her I had been raised by my great-grandparents for a few years in elementary school. I also shared that my stepfather was put in jail when I was in middle school, so I knew how hard it must be for Lisa to cope with losing her parents. I told her I would not make any promises, but I would be in touch later.

After talking with Ms. Franklin, I started on the walk to the school. It did not take many steps for me to realize that I would not let my own daughter walk more than a block in this neighborhood, but I continued my journey. I walked by a bar and a few other unsafe areas, making mental notes. As I got closer to the school, I reached the intersection of Eleventh Street, one of the busiest roads in Newport. As I watched cars zooming by on both sides of the street, knowing that this little girl was going to have to cross this street by herself, I realized this was going to be a defining moment.

I brought this issue to my next cabinet meeting—a meeting where my top leaders and I discuss issues and problem solve. I decided I would teach all our leaders about walking in the shoes of the customer. I had Bob, our transportation director, state our policy on transporting students less than a mile from school. Then I told them about Lisa.

"We've done it this way for years," Bob said, "and if we made an exception for this girl we would be heading down a slippery slope. We would have to do it for everyone." It sounded like the entire school district would implode if we transported this little girl. While I knew I could just override the decision, I felt this was a teachable moment. I stopped the meeting and had everyone drive or ride with someone to Lisa's house. We then walked Lisa's future path on the way to the elementary school. It was fun watching these full-grown adults struggling to get across Eleventh Street! We went back to the office and then I asked the question, "How many of you would be fine with letting your second grade daughter walk this path to the school?" Silence. I then explained that she lived with a grandmother who was physically unable to walk Lisa to school. Some leaders were visibly upset with themselves for not seeing the big picture. Bob was still defensive as he again went back to policy. It was then that our finance director, Jim, a good friend of Bob's, said "Damn it, Bob, Mr. Middleton wants us to be about kids!" Jim postured himself as if he was ready to fight. I then jumped in and thanked everyone for their impassioned discussion, then stated we would be transporting this student and that I would deal with future ramifications. It's been five years since that very intense cabinet meeting, and I've received zero complaints about making this one exception.

Final Thoughts on Walking in the Shoes of the Customers

When school leaders get in the lunch line and eat in the cafeteria with sporks, or walk the path a little kid has to travel just to get to school because of a ridiculous policy, they are able to empathize with the customer. It is only when we get out of our subjective school employee perspective and enter theirs that we can truly understand what the students experience on a daily basis. Whether we are talking about a school administrator, a teacher, a coach, or any other employee, walking in the shoes of the customer is essential to finding the faults and shortcomings of the school's customer service. By implementing rule and policy changes based on reflections on what would help solve these problems, school leaders will be well on their way to making the school a better place for students to live and learn.

CONCEPT 7

Collect Reliable Information

"What Gets Measured Gets Done."
– Unknown

The game "Telephone" is fun to play as a kid, but as a school leader, it is nothing but a headache.

One year my middle school principal was dealing with a rumor that a girl in the school, Shelly, was pregnant and had an STD. Shelly had been teased by other students during the school day, so when the principal's secretary rang his phone and said Shelly's mother was on line two, he didn't wait to hear any more and said to put the call through. When he picked up the phone, he immediately explained to the mother that the situation had been handled, and that the school nurse confirmed that, while her daughter was pregnant, she did not have an STD. The mom gasped and told the principal she and her husband would be over immediately and hung up the phone.

Befuddled by Shelly's mother's response, the principal asked the secretary what the nature of the call was, only to find out that he had been speaking to *Kelli's* mother, and her call was in regard to the spelling of her daughter's name on the honor roll.

The principal could not believe he misheard the student's name and had just told the wrong parent that her daughter was pregnant and a rumor was going around the school that she had an STD. By cutting off his secretary when she was about to explain the nature of the phone call, the principal caused massive panic in a parent and made her drop everything to rush down to the school. The principal eventually conveyed that he made a mistake to Kelli's parents, but not until the damage had been done. Had the principal just followed protocol and let his secretary tell him why the parent was on the phone, this terrible game of telephone would have been avoided.

Sometimes collecting reliable information takes a little extra time, but it takes a lot more time to correct issues on the backside when you have wrong information. Since trust is also built on correct information, ensuring that the information you have is correct and reliable is a must for any school administrator.

The best companies are constantly monitoring their customer service practices. Whether it's following up on training procedures, tracking employee behavior, or general service trends, they always have their fingers on the pulse of what's going on in every aspect of their company. It's not enough for leaders to rely on their own eyes and ears to make decisions and policy: kicking the tires themselves won't cut it. They need other voices.

It all starts with training. Training builds the groundwork for ensuring that your customer service practices are clear and carried out by employees. Once trained, employees have a standard, an expectation, to which they can be held accountable. But it is only after training that the real work begins.

The following three chapters build off each other. In this chapter, you'll learn methods to collect reliable information about your customer service practices by monitoring employees after

Drew Stevens, world-renowned consultant and customer service guru, explains how grossly companies overestimate the quality of their service. He says, "Ask any firm and the Pareto Principle prevails. Eighty percent of most organizations believe they deliver exemplary customer service. Ironically, less than 20 percent actually do."[79] Stevens goes on to say that a study by Bain & Company found that only 8 percent of companies actually deliver exemplary customer service. Whether we are talking about a Fortune 500 company or a small town public school, organizations tend to overreach when stating their successes, stunting their progress and preventing issues from being corrected.

training. Collecting reliable information gives leaders a good reason to take action when employees do something that needs correcting (the Confront concept) or when employees give exceptional service (the Praise and Reward concept).

How do the best companies ensure they deliver a high quality product to their customers? I will explain three common practices of some of the best companies.

Focus Groups

The first practice, and possibly the most important in my experience, is focus groups. A focus group is a sample of customers—either randomly picked or chosen specifically to represent all demographics within the customer base—that are brought together to report to the company and answer questions about service. These focus groups provide information that could not be obtained by the leaders as their perspectives are skewed by working for the company.

A school can use an outside group or person to bring parents, students, or staff together to have a meal and ask questions about the school in total anonymity.

In the Walk in the Shoes of the Customers concept, I mentioned my "Kelly's Kids" group, which is made up of a representative sample of students from each school level. I meet monthly with these students to discuss everything from transportation to cafeterias to the use of cell phones and technology to picking out paint colors for new school additions.

In addition to a student-based focus group, I also have an employee focus group. My classified employee advisory group and I meet monthly to discuss what is going on in our schools. I provide breakfast and use this time to form relationships and build trust with this important group of people. We have representation from administrative assistants, bus drivers, cooks, custodians, and maintenance and cafeteria managers. We have good, open, honest, and frank discussions that have helped me solve several district issues. Any principal or superintendent who is not having such meetings is truly missing out on a great way to communicate with classified staff.

Focus groups don't have to be in person. In today's digital world, companies are turning to the internet for a new spin on their tried-and-true models. Frito-Lay has been using social media since 2008 to get customers' opinions on new products. One of their first forays into digital focus groups was a contest called "Do Us A Flavor," which utilized Facebook to find out which flavors of Lay's chips customers wanted. On their Facebook page, the company allowed users to suggest flavors. Taking the place of the "Like" button on Facebook, users could click an "I'd Eat That" button to vote. "There's a big difference between liking something and wanting to eat it. We wanted something really visceral so people could get excited right away," said Ann Mukherjee, the chief marketing officer at Frito-Lay. The app proved so popular it crashed on the day it launched.[80] Talk about a successful focus group!

Mystery Guests

No, we are not talking about the old game show *This is Your Life*, where the contestant would hear the voice of a familiar person talking about her and have to guess that person's identity. In the business world, a mystery guest is someone who poses as a customer but is actually there to gather information about an issue or the experience of interacting with the brand and then report back to management. The mystery guest can be utilized for just about anything you believe could use a fresh pair of eyes.

One example of a mystery guest you may have heard of is the mystery shopper. Mystery shoppers are people who fit a brand's demographic and are hired as consultants. Let's use a department store as an example. Say Acme Department Store is wondering what customers think of the new layout of the women's apparel department. They hire a dozen mystery shoppers to give them feedback. The people chosen are similar to those who will shop at their store.

Next, the mystery shoppers are briefed on their purpose. This is a crucial step because it is where management primes the shoppers for what their role will be. The shoppers are given criteria—what to look for, where to go—and told they will report back after their shopping experience. The briefing can be done in person or online.

Then the shoppers go into the store with their agenda in mind. After shopping, they again report back to management. They may fill out questionnaires or surveys or give a verbal account of their experience. After this, their job is over and management collects all the information to make a determination on how effective the new women's apparel layout is or what needs to be changed about it. Mystery guests allow companies to get inside the customer's head and see what they really think.

Many restaurants hire companies to bring in mystery guests. As someone who utilizes them myself, I frequently volunteer to be a mystery guest at local restaurants. After the meal, I would have to fill out forms about every touch point. I am sure the restaurants received a lot of good information, and it also holds all the servers and leaders accountable.

As superintendent, one year I divided all my employees into various groups and held a districtwide customer service training. The result of the training was a new school district guideline pamphlet that was given to all administrative assistants and office staff. In the months that followed, I collected information on how well our employees were following through on the training by having a few mystery guests call our school offices pretending to be prospective parents.

The conversations were recorded and our mystery guests asked the administrative assistants everything from "What is the mission statement?" to "How are the school's latest test scores?" They asked about taking a school tour and even about the steps to enroll their children. One of the calls lasted over an hour and even sucked the unwitting principal into enrolling three of these fake students. (We later had a good laugh about it!) I then played these recordings back in leadership meetings to discuss how we could improve upon our customer service.

Five years later, we hired a new administrative assistant at one of our elementary schools. As I introduced myself to the new hire, she asked for me to give her a few weeks before I had a mystery guest call to test her. After all this time, administrative assistants were still worried about the mystery guest calls!

A word of caution about mystery guests: if people know a mystery guest is present, it defeats the purpose. That may sound like common sense, but you'd be surprised how easily this can happen. A restaurant I patron frequently had their mystery guest come in on the same day each month, and everyone working at the restaurant knew it. Of course, employees stepped up their game and that day the service was much better than on other days. Not only did management fail to gather reliable information from this practice, but they undermined their own purpose in the process.

Exit Surveys

An exit survey is simply a set of questions given to someone upon leaving, whether it is an employee or a patron. Exit surveys can be helpful tools to gather information about specific employees or practices. However, many people are afraid of telling the truth on surveys because, if they say anything negative, it might get back to someone who will then cause trouble for them. In my experience, their concerns are valid!

In my school district, we used to have substitute teachers fill out evaluations on teachers for whom they subbed. On several occasions, if the subs gave any constructive criticism and the teacher was asked about it, the teacher would then blackball the sub from ever subbing again in his or her classroom. Public schools have a hard time keeping information confidential, and sometimes it is just impossible to address a situation without someone being able to figure out the source. A student who is asked to take a survey by his teacher knows full well the teacher will be able to figure out who said what!

Here are a few ways public schools can use exit surveys:

1. Survey staff members who are retiring or leaving your school or district.

2. Survey students and parents as they leave each school— If students are leaving eighth grade to go to high school, survey them the last week of school. Survey graduating seniors about their high school and their entire experience in the district.

3. Call parents who took their students out of your school or decided to homeschool their students. Ask them about your school or district.

4. Ask substitute teachers about their experiences in other schools in order to gain some insight into what can be done differently.

The Importance of Anonymity

Anonymity is vital when collecting information. When people know they're being watched or are confronted about what they think of something, they tend to sugarcoat the negatives or simply tell the person what they want to hear. In scientific terms, this is called the acquiescence bias. Have you ever had a boss ask you what you thought of his tie? No matter how ugly it was, you said you liked it, right? That's acquiescence bias. In order to avoid this data-skewing nightmare, anonymity is a must. Now let's say that instead of directly asking employees, your boss gave each person in the office a piece of paper that said "yes" and a piece of paper that said "no," and had everyone drop one in a box inside a voting booth. You can bet his answers would be quite different!

In public schools, I've noticed a lack of anonymity when it comes to asking for feedback. When students are asked to fill out end-of-the-year surveys for teachers, my Kelly's Kids have reported that they tend to leave out any criticism out of fear that the teacher would recognize their handwriting and punish them in some way.

Years ago, I was a basketball player and senior captain of the Georgetown College men's basketball team. One ritual our team had was going out to eat for a pregame meal of country-fried steak. By that, I mean that we were all *required* to eat country-fried steak before *every* game! I was on full scholarship and my parents were unable to provide me with additional spending money, so eating out was a special treat. Still, eating country-fried steak before every game for four straight basketball seasons was torture . . . even for a poor boy like me!

Coach Reid was a "man's man," and was respected by his players. He took his basketball, his routines, and his rituals quite seriously and was not all that receptive to his players' opinions and suggestions. Behind his back, there had been much grumbling and frustration among his players about having to eat country-fried steak before each game and we all thought Coach needed to allow us the freedom to eat something different. The team collectively agreed that, as captain, it was my job to be that representative.

One day I courageously and reluctantly approached Coach Reid, explaining how passionately the whole team hated the country-fried steak and that the whole team wanted something different to eat for the next pregame meal. Coach's response was just as I had expected. His volume increased and his posture changed while he enlightened me on the reasoning behind rituals—specifically, country-fried steak. He then wanted to confirm that it was something the whole team wanted, and I assured him that was exactly what we all requested.

He was silent for an agonizing minute. As sweat rolled down my forehead, I started to wish I had never asked him. Miraculously, he agreed to allow us to eat a pasta dinner before the next game. I told the team and everyone was so thankful to have a break from the country-fried steak. I was now the hero to my teammates.

And then we lost.

Not only did we lose the game, but it was a major upset and we had not played to the best of our ability. I knew what was coming. We boarded our bus and waited with dread in our hearts as our coach stepped onto the bus and addressed us with his postgame speech. Before he could begin the play-by-play breakdown, he looked at the faces on the bus. Then his booming voice demanded, "Who told 'Worm' (my nickname) that they did not want to eat country-fried steak?" Sure enough, nobody said a word. No one wanted to speak against Coach, especially after the embarrassing loss. My teammates acquiesced to what Coach wanted to hear, fearing being blamed for the loss, even though that meant throwing me under the bus, figuratively speaking, of course.

As the team captain, I just went from being the hero for getting us pasta, to being the scapegoat who changed the pregame ritual meal that caused us to lose the game! "Think we'll go back to eating country-fried steak," Coach said and sat down. Just like that it was settled for good, even though my teammates all continued to complain behind his back about the pregame meal. After that, I told my teammates never to bring me another issue again.

Unfortunately, these situations happen all too often in public education. Students and parents don't feel like they can speak the truth for fear of repercussions. This results in giving very skewed information to those in charge. In fact, if you want true, reliable information, I suggest you use outside groups to gather information, and there must be no chance that anyone will ever know who said what during interviews or surveys.

As a side note, while I still love Coach Reid, I do not eat country-fried steak to this day.

Collecting Reliable Information in Public Schools

So how do schools measure up? Usually, not very well. Can

you guess the one thing that we monitor better than anything else aside from test scores? It's attendance. We track attendance like a bloodhound tracks a squirrel. Public schools keep immaculate records of not just attendance, but how long students are in classes and when they are dismissed or sent home. Now, when it comes to what they *do* when they are in the classroom, we don't seem to care much (if we are going by what we monitor). They could be fast asleep in the back of the class, but what gets reported is simply that they were a warm body in a seat.

Why? It's all about funding. I won't get into school politics, but what I'm getting at is this: as a public school administrator, you're probably not going around town boasting about how great you are at attendance. Wouldn't it be nice if public schools monitored employee customer service performance as well as they do attendance? Just think about how your school monitors the following:

- An administrative assistant who has a negative tone when answering the school phone
- A staff member who does not get back with people within 24-48 hours
- A cafeteria monitor who yells for students to be quiet in the cafeteria
- A staff member who bullies other staff members
- A teacher who has 3-5 years of bad test scores
- A custodian who doesn't help the group that rents the school at night
- Restrooms that are always dirty
- A teacher who does not use the new technology he or she was given for the classroom
- Vents that are always dirty in the classrooms
- The administrative assistant who does not do a good job screening calls before they are forwarded to the leader

While you probably have your own spin on these examples, the fact is that at most schools, problems such as these go unchecked

> One of the strategies the best companies use is P.I.M.E., which stands for Plan, Implement, Monitor, and Evaluate. Try going through these steps with your next new customer service practice.

and employees get away with cutting corners. By monitoring employee customer service after training, you can ensure your training is effective. As a leader, it is your job to really scrub the cracks between the tiles of your school with the toothbrush of monitoring. So roll up your sleeves and get to that dirty work!

Final Thoughts on Collecting Reliable Information

Focus groups, mystery guests, and exit surveys are just a few methods you can use as a school leader to gather information about your customer service. You can also refer to the concept of Walking in the Shoes of the Customer to learn how to really see all the nooks and crannies of your service. However you do it, keeping tabs on what's going on in your school is vital in order to follow up on employee training. I think about the many administrators who hire me to speak to their entire district or train a segment such as their entire secretarial staff, yet many times leaders do not attend these trainings. In my opinion, leaders must know what their employees are being taught in order to monitor them afterward. Sure, training ideas and concepts might stick with some employees, but without monitoring employees to see if they are doing what they've been taught, the effectiveness of training will not last.

Of course, monitoring is not an end in itself. In the next chapter, I will talk about what to do when employees implement their training by giving great service (Praising and Rewarding). This is a vital next step after monitoring that will keep employees following through with training goals. But what do you do when your monitoring uncovers service that is not meeting the expectations laid out in training? I'll cover confronting, retraining, and firing later in the Confront Poor Customer Service concept.

CONCEPT 8

Praise and Reward Employees
for Giving Great Service

"There are two things people want more than sex and money . . .
recognition and praise."
—Mary Kay of Mary Kay Cosmetics[81]

One of my colleagues was visiting a friend who had twin three-year-old girls. The family was getting ready to go to the beach and part of their ritual was potty time so that they could go without a diaper. The mom took the first girl into the bathroom. A few minutes later the girl ran out proclaiming, "I went poop in the potty!" and the family proceeded to shower her with praise, high fives, and even a few M&Ms. Then the second girl went in with the mom and a few minutes later came out, chest puffed, and yelled "I went poop and pee in the potty!" Again she made the rounds getting praise and rewards from the family like she'd just gotten into Harvard. This is the college acceptance letter of child development.

My colleague told me that it was an interesting sight to behold as an onlooker, with no stock in whether the girls went potty or not, but it was fun to see how thoroughly the girls responded to this system. As soon as they came out of the bathroom, they knew they had done a good thing and welcomed, even expected, their recognition for doing a basic human function that most of us take for granted.

A quick search on Amazon shows over 2,500 books on potty training.[82] It's a rite of passage that humans have gone through for centuries, yet

> How much longer would it take to train these toddlers if, instead of celebrating positive behavior, we chose to scold them when they soiled their pants?

there is no one way to do it. There are dozens of potty training methods, but one thing they all have in common is the component of praising and rewarding the child for going in the potty instead of in their pants. If only we could use the philosophy of "potty training" on our employees to help promote positive customer service within our schools!

Luckily, in the context of a work environment, people really are no different than toddlers. I'm sure you have great stories about the childish behavior you've seen at work, but that's not what I mean. People of any age are "potty trainable" if you find the right words and motivations.

I'm not talking about praising employees when they perform basic functions of work, like arriving on time each day. Instead, praising and rewarding should be done at times when an employee makes a choice to perform some aspect of his or her job in a way that shows he or she is practicing customer service principles. Think of this as a cause-and-effect phenomenon. The employee does something you want them to do, which causes you to reward them. The value in doing this is that the reward makes the employee more likely to repeat that behavior in order to get the reward again, which creates a cycle of reinforcing behavior. When done in the proper scenarios with the right motives, praising and rewarding is a wonderful way to get what you want out of your employees while also thanking them for their good work.

Below are just a few examples of ways to praise and reward an employee. I'll talk more about what to do (and not do) when praising employees a little later on.

- Telling a teacher she did a great job introducing the new student to the classroom, in particular the name game they played at the start of class.
- Praising the physical education teacher for going out to get more balls for kids on his lunch hour because the previous class had lost several of them. Then thanking

him by getting him a can of golf balls (his favorite sport) and delivering them in person, while saying that he'd gone above and beyond the call of duty and that you're very grateful for his commitment to the students and the school.

- Finding out a bus driver was so well-liked by all of her riders, and then one day getting on the bus while she drove the students home from school and treating her to an ice cream after she'd dropped off the last student, making sure to verbally express how thankful you are that she's there each day to brighten the students' morning and afternoon.

John Maxwell had this to say about the concept of praising and rewarding: "How do we know if people need encouragement? If they have a pulse, they need encouragement."[83] We know that employees like being praised and rewarded. But what are the benefits for you? After all, they also like getting paid more, but paying employees more won't necessarily make them do their job better or make the organization more successful. There has to be an incentive for the employer for praising and rewarding to be a mutually beneficial action.

Whale Done Customer Service

One of my favorite attractions at Sea World in Orlando, Florida is the Orca show. I am always blown away at how well the whales are trained, and I imagine just how much fun it would be to swim with killer whales! They dance on the water and soar through the air with such grace that I forget these are 8,000-pound creatures at the top of the ocean's food chain. The trainers apparently work with these whales for years before the whales ever get "called up" to be in the show. During these years, the trainers not only gain the trust of the whales, but also use the same praise and reward system that we are talking about here.

In his book, *Whale Done: The Power of Positive Relationships,* Ken Blanchard highlights the methods used by orca trainers at Sea World and explains the ramifications for managers and employees.[84] What he found was

> **Lessons from Sea World: Who wants to yell at a killer whale and then get in the water with it? Now consider how the same behavior affects your employees.**

that, "the more attention you pay a behavior, the more it will be repeated," and "if you don't want to encourage poor behavior, don't spend a lot of time on it." He says that managers tend to focus on a "gotcha" mentality; that is, managers are constantly on the lookout for employees doing something wrong in order to chastise them for their mistakes. Blanchard says that instead, managers should focus on looking for the "whale done" (a play on the phrase "well done") behaviors—catching employees doing something *right* and *rewarding* them.

Here's what the "Whale Done" response looks like:
1. Praise employees *immediately*
2. Be *specific* about what they did right or almost right
3. Share your positive feelings about what they did
4. Encourage them to keep up the good work[85]

A Delicious Example

While visiting the leadership at the Yum! Corporation, I got to see Yum!'s Walk of Champions. The Walk of Champions is a a beautifully decorated hallway with photos of Yum!'s leaders presenting unique and clever rewards to their employees. The leaders at individual companies under the Yum! umbrella, which includes Taco Bell, KFC, and Pizza Hut, give personalized awards to employees who perform well. They call it "catching people doing things right."[86] Just like in the "Whale Done" example from Sea World, the focus here is on rewarding employees who are giving great service. Yum! gives employees awards with fun names like "The Game Ball Award," "The Helping Hand Award," "The Bull Dog Award," and the "Whatever It Takes Award."

If you spend time at the Yum! Center you will likely hear cheers breaking out at unexpected times. Shirlie Kunimoto, vice president of operations excellence, says, "It's okay to disturb everyone with a Yum! Cheer. Another thing that will get your attention is the Recognition Band." This is a corps of employee volunteers who play instruments and are periodically called together to honor a fellow coworker with a song.[87] Yum! itself deserves an award for praising and rewarding their employees so well!

Former CEO of Yum!, David C. Novak, has shared some of his best practices, which I think stand out as both innovative and reliable methods to praise and reward his customers properly. He says:

> People are starved for direct feedback. . . . The best way to give feedback is to start out with, "This is what I appreciate about you." They might have great strategy, good vision, they're good at execution, or whatever you think they're really doing well. When you start out by talking to people about what they're doing well, that makes them very receptive for feedback because at least you're giving them credit for what they've done.[88]

So not only does recognition improve employer-employee relations, but it also takes away employees' dread when the boss walks over to talk with them about their work. He goes on to say:

> [While at KFC] I gave away these rubber chickens. They were called floppy chickens. I'd go into a restaurant and I would see a cook who'd been there for 25 years and the product was great, so I'd give him a floppy chicken. I'd write on it and tell him his "Original Recipe" was fantastic, and take a picture of him with me.[89]

> David C. Novak of Yum! on praise: "One, it needs to be deserved. And, two, it needs to come from the heart. . . . People leave companies for two reasons. One, they don't feel appreciated. And, two, they don't get along with their boss. . . . To me, with recognition, if you've got to err on the side of anything, recognize more than you should."[90]

He has a lot more to say on these topics, as he has been an executive at Yum! for over fifteen years and has written two books about employee recognition.

From employees at Yum! to potty training toddlers to orcas at Sea World, we see the benefits of praise and reward on just about anything with a brain! It's hard to understand why this practice is so often underused, misused, or simply ignored in the business world.

The Importance of Sincerity and Personalization

Sincerity is a huge part of praising and rewarding. A personal touch goes a long way when reinforcing an employee's behavior. Going back to the Sea World example, Ken Blanchard emphasizes this idea:

> The killer whale knows if you are insincere, you cannot fool killer whales. They feel the insincerity in your hands when you give them a rubdown. When the animal knows you're not interested, he won't want to work with you. He'll swim away.[91]

People are no different than whales. If you give them a reward but your attitude, tone, and demeanor don't say thank you, then the reward could very well mean nothing to the employee, thus not reinforcing the behavior. Showing your sincerity when giving a reward goes back to a previous concept (surprise, surprise!): Forging Relationships. Leaders who are good at establishing warm, personalized relationships with people (staff and customers alike), will be given the benefit of the doubt more often when it comes to interpreting the meaning of receiving a reward. In other words, if you're a sincere person all the time, people can see that. So when it comes time to praise and reward, your employees will be less likely to question your motives. However, regardless of your track record, if you fail to be sincere in your rewarding, not only can it result in failure to reinforce the good behavior, but it can also damage the relationship that you spent so much time forging. If an employee notices that a reward is not heartfelt, he or she may feel manipulated or controlled through gifts. What a huge backfire that would be!

In addition to sincerity, *personalization* of the praise or reward is essential. Giving someone a Santa pen when they don't celebrate Christmas would be a pretty costly mistake. Not only does it instantly fail to reinforce a desired employee's behavior, but it also shows the employee that you do not know her and perhaps don't even care about her. Of course, this was not your intention, but execution is all that matters when it comes to employee relations and, in this case, it was a total crash and burn.

I interviewed companies that were giving great customer service, and found a common theme: the leaders seem to really know their staff and have personal connections with many staff members. In public schools, the ratio of employee to administrator is much greater and makes this task a little more difficult. However, school culture is vital to the success of a school and district, and we must do our best to connect with our staff. How can we do that?

One way is to ask each member of your staff to fill out a "Getting To Know You" form. Information that might be included is listed below. Keep in mind, these rewards do not have to be expensive. In fact, you'll find that people enjoy a simple, personal, heartfelt reward as much as one of higher monetary value!

Getting To Know You:
  1. Favorite music
  2. Favorite restaurant

3. Favorite scent or candle
4. My favorite way of being recognized for doing a great job
5. Spouse and/or children's names and ages
6. Hobbies
7. Favorite movie
8. Books or magazines that I enjoy reading
9. Interesting fact about me that most people are unaware of
10. My proudest moment
11. High school or college attended
12. Favorite snack or junk food
13. Favorite beverage
14. Knickknacks or collectibles
15. Favorite breakfast or lunch food

The simple fact that you care enough to give this survey to employees will encourage them to view you as a caring administrator. This is the first step in forging those relationships! But following through by using this information is the *crucial* next step. By keeping these forms on file for all of your employees, you'll have quick and easy access to some ideas for personalized rewards for each employee, ensuring that you don't have a "Santa pen" moment!

Larry the Custodian

It doesn't take much to make an employee feel great about the job he's done. With a little practice it becomes second nature. Whenever I think about praising and rewarding, I think of how I recognized one of my former employees, Larry, after my inspirational visit to the Yum! corporate office.

Larry, the custodian, knew his job and performed it well. But Larry was not one who was willing to work after hours or go beyond his job requirements. One cold, rainy night after a high school basketball game, Larry approached me to explain a situation that he just encountered. One thing that I have discovered as a leader is when your employees know your expectations and you model them, then they will perform those expectations without being told to do so because they know they are important to you. Larry's exact words were, "Mr. Middleton, I know that you do that 'customer service stuff.' There is a lady from the other team in the parking lot that has a flat tire. Am I supposed to change it for her?" Now, I know Larry is going to help her out because it is the right thing to do, but he just wanted me to know that he was working beyond his time!

Despite the rain and dropping temperatures, Larry changed the tire and sent the lady on her way. The next day, I received an email from the same lady, bragging on Larry's kindness and recognizing that he went "above and beyond" his job expectations. She even referred to him as "superman"!

I approached Larry to express my appreciation to him for buying into our customer service initiatives. I knew that telling Larry that I appreciated him was not enough; he needed more tangible recognition.

Most people assume that recognition has to be a grand ceremony with much pomp and circumstance, but simplistic recognition can be just as effective to promote and encourage good customer service.

I was once told that I know how to put "the moose on the table" — an expression for giving totally honest feedback regardless of how uncomfortable the feedback might make an individual feel. After visiting Yum!, I chose to make a stuffed moose my signature reward for employees being caught giving great customer service. My staff understood that even though it was a very small token of appreciation, it was heartfelt and personal. In order to get as much mileage as possible, I would then look for just the right time to bestow this moose award. Larry was going to be my next well-deserved recipient.

Our opening day, back-to-school breakfast was held each year and included all employees from our district. It was my turn to speak, and I was going to tell Larry's story. I displayed the email I received from the lady with the flat tire on our big screen. Then, I bragged on Larry and told how she called him "superman." I said how thankful I was Larry had performed "that customer service stuff" that I encouraged! I asked Larry to come up on the stage to receive his stuffed moose. He came up to the podium and accepted his award as the crowd gave him a standing ovation.

I wasn't certain that Larry thought it was a very big deal until a while later when Larry got up from his table to get a drink. I glanced toward his seat and watched him walk away, then turn back around only to retrieve his little moose! I guess the little stuffed moose even means something to "superman" when given in the right situation.

It's stories like these that demonstrate just how big a deal such rewards can be for an employee. It makes me want to have these recognition events more often. A boss coming over to you to check in and say hi can pick up your whole day. You've got to spend time with your people; take time to do this on a regular basis. It creates happy workers, which makes them work harder and may prevent future problems. What does good recognition really look like? "You did a great job today," doesn't cut it. Praise and rewards must be genuine and personal. It could be something like covering a teacher's class for thirty minutes so she can have a longer lunch. I've found that spending your own time is the highest level of showing appreciation. If you haven't yet, give it a try!

Good vs. Bad Recognition

Sometimes it helps to know what *not to do* in order to see the clear distinction, especially when it comes to the nuanced difference between impersonal recognition and personal recognition. I've found that this distinction eludes many school administrators, but it is essential in order for your reward system to work.

If done incorrectly, there may be no benefit or even a negative effect! Have you ever had someone compliment you in such a vague way that you were left wanting to know what exactly you did right? What about someone saying: "I like your shirt—

Possible Ideas for Personalizing Your Reward System

- Do you collect something?—I know of one leader who gave away mounted baseball cards to employees. Another leader gave out decks of playing cards.
- Do you have a nickname?—One principal was called "Sheriff Steve," and he would give out badges to employees who performed well or went above and beyond.
- Be creative—One principal's last name was "Campbell," and she gave out a decorated can of Campbell's Soup to staff members caught giving great service.
- Praise—Some people don't like public recognition or get embarrassed when singled out, so for them, maybe a handwritten note would be better.
- Involve staff—involve everyone in the process of creating awards to promote ownership of recognition.

---

green is my favorite color"? That's not exactly a complement to the person, it's just sharing information about yourself. However, saying, "I like your shirt—green looks good on you," is a much better way of giving a compliment to a person about his or her shirt. Remember, little details such as word choice are important when giving praise.

I was in the car talking with a superintendent one day and he was bragging about how good he was with customer service. This gentleman called his main administrative assistant and reminded her to purchase flowers for herself and for all the other administrative assistants in the office to show his support of Administrative Assistants' Day. How much of a reward do you think it was for his administrative assistant to have to buy her own gift? Making a person get it themselves, especially when it's lumped in with all the other to-do items of her job, takes away the "specialness" of receiving a gift. I didn't have the heart to tell this superintendent what I really thought.

On another occasion, I talked with a superintendent who had purchased a jogging suit for his wife, but she didn't want it. He then brought the suit to school and told his administrative assistant that his wife didn't want the suit and she could have it as her Christmas gift. How impersonal can you get?

I know a principal who allows her staff to take an extended lunch on Administrative Assistants' Day each year. However, she neither pays for nor attends the lunch. I think this is a big misstep on her part. She's missing out on a great chance to connect with her employees on a very personal level and to really show how much she appreciates their hard work on the one day that is dedicated to their recognition.

Final Thoughts on Praising and Rewarding

When it comes down to it, as David C. Novak of Yum! says, if you have to err, err on the side of over-recognition. Thinking about it that way and then looking at what your current practices are helps you see just how much room you have for improvement. And when it comes to personalization, when in doubt, face-to-face eye contact and even physical contact, will trump any tangible prize dropped on an employee's desk.

CONCEPT 9

Confront Poor Customer Service

*"The culture of any organization is shaped by
the worst behavior the leader is willing to tolerate."*
– Gruenert & Whitaker[92]

In the 1999 movie *Office Space*, Jennifer Aniston's character, Joanna, is working as a waitress at a chain restaurant when she is confronted by her manager about the amount of "flair," or decorative buttons, she has on her uniform.[93] A stunned Joanna points to her buttons and says she has the required fifteen pieces of flair on. Her disappointed manager retorts that fifteen is the *minimum* number of flair required, pointing out that her coworker Brian has thirty-seven pieces, and encourages her to wear more flair. He says, "Look, we want you to express yourself, okay? Now if you feel that the bare minimum is enough then okay, but some people choose to wear more and we encourage that."

Later in the movie, he confronts her again about wearing only fifteen pieces of flair, asking her what she thinks of a person who "only does the bare minimum." Infuriated, she says if he wants her to wear thirty-seven pieces of flair, he should just say that. Then she "expresses herself," by extending a certain finger toward him and quits.

Now, no boss wants an employee who only does the bare minimum, but as we can see from the exasperated Joanna, confronting employees is a skill and not all managers have it. Leaders need both the will and the skill to confront bad service. In this example, I would say the manager had the will, but lacked the skill. In school administration I find that many leaders have neither the will nor the skill. In this chapter, I'll explain the importance of confronting employees who are not giving great service and offer a few tips.

Walt Disney and Confrontation

LifeLock, an identity theft protection company, has a commercial where a gentleman in uniform is observing a couple's staircase. He looks up and tells them they have termites. The couple tells him to get rid of them. To their dismay, the gentleman says he is not a pest exterminator, he's a pest monitor, and he only lets people know when there's a problem. At that moment the couple's daughter comes down the steps and falls through the staircase. As half the girl is looking at them through the staircase, the pest monitor says flatly, "There's a problem." He then leaves the house, pulling the door completely off the hinges in the process. A graphic pops up on the screen, reading, "Why monitor a problem if you don't fix it?"[94]

Going back to a previous chapter, I talked about collecting reliable information about your customer service practices. Once you've collected that information, what you do with it is critical. It's not enough to simply gather information; you need to act on those findings. What do you do when an employee is not giving the great service that he or she was trained to provide? The first step is confronting employees and implementing changes— whether it's retraining or something as simple as redirecting them from one behavior to another. Here's one example of confrontation in action that is also a great example of walking in the shoes of the customer.

In his ongoing effort to collect reliable information about his park's service, Walt Disney would test rides and games to make sure they were up to par. In one such instance, he found that the boat captains (the "skippers") of one of the rides were simply not performing as well as they were supposed to.

Ron Dominguez, former executive vice president of Walt Disney Attractions, retold this story of the days when he was a supervisor at Disney World. He said Walt approached the ride supervisor, Dick Nunis, and told him that the skippers operated the ride correctly and recited their lines accurately enough, but it was the performance, the *acting*, that was so severely lacking. Walt felt as though the skippers lacked enthusiasm, energy and showmanship. The skippers needed to convince the passengers on their boat that they were as surprised to see a hippo pop out of the water as the passengers were. Walt said, "I want the skippers to act as if every trip on the Jungle Cruise is their first trip."[95]

Afterward, Dick met with his skippers and told them what Walt had said. Dick rode with each one and critiqued their performances afterward until they performed with the energy and excitement that Walt desired.

As a leader, Walt was able to confront his employees about how to do their jobs correctly and hold them accountable by monitoring and observing them in action. By running a tight ship, Walt was able to build his empire on giving great customer service. This should be the model for all leaders.

Confronting Our District Cafeteria Customer Service

Remember the cafeteria story from the Walk in the Shoes of the Customers concept? After I went through all the breakfast lines and lunch lines throughout the school district, I called a group meeting with the food service director, school principals, and all the cafeteria managers. Here is a list of the findings I presented to them:

- We do not offer our students enough meal choices
- We do not ask the students their ideas and opinions about the food
- We do not have enough side items like chips and drinks for students to purchase to supplement the serving line meals
- The restrooms off the cafeteria were not monitored, so students would go there to smoke cigarettes
- Cafeteria monitors were negative with students during

lunch. They flicked lights on and off for sound control. Children were yelled at by cafeteria monitors
- Table setup was not conducive to good student interaction
- Students had to eat with sporks, which were useless for many foods they were served
- Students needed to be able to see the salads, but they were hidden in Styrofoam containers
- Students needed more choices for salad dressing
- Students preferred milk in bottles instead of cartons
- Food presentation could be greatly improved
- We do not offer ways for students to sample new cafeteria offerings
- Cafeteria employees do not wear uniforms with school logos
- Tables were not effectively cleaned between lunch shifts

I gave the food service director, managers, and their staff a few months to create and implement solutions to these problems. During this period, I brought food service managers on visits to other school districts that were doing a much better job with customer service. After each trip, I sat down with staff for a reflection meeting on what we could do better in our own school system.

Within three months, our entire food service had changed into something very special. Even the media caught wind, as they published several newspaper articles about our new food service program. The food service managers were asked to speak at a few major conferences on the subject as well. All school principals began to see a major drop in cafeteria discipline issues, and soon districts from all over the Midwest were setting up appointments to visit our cafeterias!

All this success wasn't without its downside. When I started to implement changes and confront employees about their service, many of them left our meeting with hurt feelings. Nobody wants to hear that they're not doing their job well, especially those who work in the thankless field of education. As a result, several employees decided to retire at the end of the year. However, we hired great replacements and became better than ever. Being unpopular when necessary is truly the price of leadership. If you are not willing to confront, do not apply to be a school leader. You will not be happy, and you will end up cheating your primary customers, the students.

Being Unpopular When Necessary Is the Price of Leadership

Mr. Collins is late to school every day and all staff members know about it. The students in his class are unsupervised for so long each day that he has them take attendance themselves. Everyone knows that Mr. Collins is going to retire this year. A few teachers told the principal earlier in the year about Mr. Collins's tardiness, but administration has done nothing about it.

Assuming that being on time must not be important to the administration, several other teachers have started showing up late each day. The principal, Mr. Stein, sees this happening, decides he has had enough, and sends a stern email to all teachers and staff about the importance of arriving to school on time. If this continues, the email states, he will have to begin giving written reprimands to those who are late.

All the teachers laugh at Mr. Stein's email, as they know he will never follow through on his warning, and that the only reason he sent out this blanket email is because he is afraid to confront Mr. Collins or the other late teachers one-on-one. Though Mr. Stein is well-liked amongst the school staff, they do not respect him and they believe Mr. Collins and other teachers who are taking advantage of Mr. Stein's nonconfrontational style are making a mockery of him. To make matters worse, a few teachers who are always on time and very supportive of Mr. Stein are now very upset that they received this email. Another group has decided that they do not need to worry about being on time as well. The entire issue could have been resolved if Mr. Collins would have been confronted in the first place. Yes, Mr. Collins may have had his feelings hurt and may eventually have been suspended. Yes, Mr. Collins may look the other way when he passes Mr. Stein in the hallway. However, this one issue could define Mr. Stein as a leader, and failing to confront staff for not adhering to their customer service commitments tears at the very fabric of a customer service–driven school.

I recall another situation where a few elementary school teachers were taking additional recess time, and their students were monopolizing the playground equipment. By failing to confront a few teachers early in the year, the principal caused a playground war between the entire staff.

Among the top ten biggest mistakes a leader can make, according to *Entrepreneur* magazine, is trying to please everyone.[96] This idea makes sense in the business world, but it also applies to public school administrators. We need to understand that we are certainly going to make people upset along the way; it's just a part of the job.

Customer Service Training Makes Confronting Easier

Back in Concept 5, I talked about training. Well, that concept goes hand in hand with confronting. Training lays the groundwork for confronting employees because you've already given *clear expectations*, and there is no excuse on the employees' part for not following through. If he or she had a problem or a legitimate reason for not following through with training, it's their job to come to you and say so. If they don't, you can safely and rightly assume they are holding up their end of their agreement. When you find out—through monitoring—that one of your employees is not implementing the training, you can now begin the confrontation and evaluation process. If the issue persists, begin the process to remove the employee.

I have a saying: "If you have the power to stop an injustice with a student, parent, or community member and you do nothing, you have sided with the person doing the injustice." This is an important mantra for me when I have to confront someone, whether it's an employee, administrator, coach, or parent. Repeating this line while deciding what to do helps remind me of my ultimate mission: to serve the students' well-being. Most of the time, the right choice is confrontation, and this line is my "backup," my patrol partner, when I go into confrontation mode.

Below are a few examples of situations I've had to confront during my career. Some have been easier than others, but I've found that each confrontation was essential.

- A staff member who sold drugs to students
- A teacher who had an inappropriate relationship with a student
- A staff member who came to school drunk
- An employee who stole school supplies in order to start her own school
- Custodians who clocked in and then went to nightclubs
- DUIs by staff members
- Teachers who were late for work or left early
- Staff who let their children run wild after hours throughout the school
- Unprofessional administrative assistants who should have never been placed in a school office
- Teachers who could not manage their classrooms
- Parents who behaved poorly at athletic events
- Coaches who had terrible conduct during sporting events
- Bus drivers who had no control of their buses
- Principals who did not show up for major events at their schools
- Board members who did not know their roles and responsibilities
- Custodians who could not keep restrooms clean or stocked

- Custodians who fought with one another
- A cook who cussed at students going through the lunch line
- Major events that did not go well. Graduation/football game/Move-Up Day/Home Visit Day/ First Day of School
- Teachers dressing inappropriately or provocatively
- Teachers using of group punishment because of the actions of a single student

My Tips on Confronting

Confronting staff can be tricky. On one hand, you know you have to do it. But on the other, you may face backlash when you do, like insubordination, staff spreading word to other staff that you are unfair, or even staff giving you a bad review. Still, you've got a job to do. Here are a few tips I've found to help make the process easier.

1. The quicker you confront an issue the better. You have the opportunity to stop a small problem before it grows into a larger problem.
2. There is nothing people hate more than a face-to-face confrontation. As much as you may dread it, the other person dreads it even more.
3. Never leave a school day feeling more frustrated than the person who is causing the frustration. Especially on a Friday. I do not want to think about it all weekend.
4. If there might be political ramifications, let your immediate supervisor know about the issue.
5. Always confront in private, but remember the employee will talk and the message will spread throughout the school.
6. While people will publicly feel sorry for the employee that was confronted, secretly most will be glad you did it.
7. Many people might be able to do your job; however, a lot of people are afraid to confront others.

8. If you will not confront an adult mistreating a student, you are stealing from your school. You might as well embezzle money too.
9. Good training coupled with written expectations make it easier to confront.
10. The better hiring decisions you make, the less you will have to confront.
11. Confronting can be both quick and painless. The more you do it, the easier it gets.
12. The closer you are to someone, the harder it is to confront. Always keep a little distance between yourself and those you supervise.

As an administrator for the past twenty years, I have hired, fired, and transferred many employees, from custodians and administrative assistants to principals and district leaders. Because of such decisions, I have been the object of criticism from teachers, parents, unions, and press. I have been sued, investigated, targeted on social media, and had people picket in front of my schools because of my sometimes unpopular commitment to making personnel decisions consistent with the philosophy of putting students first and giving them the greatest customer service possible. If you are going to make customer service a focus at your school, you will need to confront employees when they are not complying with the district's customer service standards and not implementing the customer service training that has been provided.

If you are not willing to confront your employees for giving subpar customer service, you need to consider going back to the classroom or at least get out of public school administration. Just as there are employees who are simply not cut out to work at the likes of Disney, Chick-fil-A, or Southwest Airlines, there are also people who work in public education who are not cut out to work with children. How long would managers with no customer service skills last in great companies? Probably not long. The same should be true for our public school administrators.

Final Thoughts on Confronting

While it can be a lot of fun to praise and reward your employees for giving great customer service, you are simply not doing your job and cheating your students and parents if you do not confront bad customer service.

In the story about Mr. Collins, the situation demonstrates that if the administration doesn't prove it will act, nobody will fear consequences. Let's face it, nobody wants to reprimand or fire an employee. We, as public school administrators, are able to see the good and worth in all of our staff, so it can be difficult to confront them. Making matters more challenging is when you've established a relationship with them. Who wants to fire someone they've shaken hands with and said hello to everyday for many years?

Confronting subpar customer service is one of the many challenges of our jobs, but it's also a necessary part. We need to always keep in mind that the students are our primary customer. It's all about the students. So when we have to make these tough personnel calls as the leader, perhaps a little of the discomfort and sadness can be alleviated by knowing that we are not only staying true to what is expected of us as leaders, but also doing right by the students. If you make every decision in the best interest of students, then you're doing what all of your employees would say they want. I have found that, at the end of the day, you have to be able to look at yourself in the mirror and feel good about how you do your job.

CONCEPT 10

Facility Maintenance Is a Top Priority

"Design is how you make your first impression with your consumers.
Make sure it is a lasting one."
– Jay Samit[97]

Las Vegas is home to some of the best and most elaborate hotels, restaurants, and entertainment venues in the country. It boasts world class facilities, ambience, and sensory gratification. All of the senses are catered to, down to the calming sounds of the fountains and the subtle fragrances in the air all around. All of this as thousands come and go, twenty-four hours a day, 365 days a year.

Las Vegas is a model for the best businesses, showing just how important appearances are to guests and customers. One also gets the feeling that these amazing hotels are using their facilities to attract customers. Each business is trying to one-up the other, and it is a given that they will be both spectacular and immaculate.

From psychology science to *Forbes* magazine and *Business Insider*, research shows that people will judge a whole institution in the first seven seconds of interaction with it.[98,99] And in most cases, those first seven seconds are spent with facilities.

Facilities in this chapter are much more than physical buildings, however. Schools need to recognize this. For the transportation department, the goal should be the school buses being "Vegas clean" on the inside and out for our guests, the students. The outside of the bus must be constantly washed and everything must be working mechanically. The bus must be swept out each day and any graffiti removed immediately. Rips and tears in seats must be fixed, and each passenger window must be able to open in case the students need fresh air.

For food service directors and managers, the cafeteria is their facility. The cafeteria needs to be well-lit and the floors should be wet mopped each night. The tables must be washed with a clean cloth between lunch shifts and be at an age-appropriate height. Windows and serving areas should be clean at all times.

For teachers, their classrooms are their facilities. I have witnessed classrooms with graffiti on student desks, flickering lights, smelly carpets, electronics that did not work, and stained ceiling tiles. Some classrooms are not even decorated. I hate to see dirty vents in all of the pre-mentioned areas as that is the air that everyone is breathing. I have seen vents in school districts that have probably never been cleaned. During rain days, I have seen buckets in classrooms and schools because of leaks that have never been fixed. I can go on and on, but I will leave on this last note. My mother always told me that we might not have a lot of clothes, but there will be no excuse not to be clean. I believe school leaders should strive for "Vegas clean" facilities; our students deserve it.

Facilities Ground Zero

One major mistake schools make is not paying attention to a place in the school that everyone will visit. I'm talking about the restroom. Your students and staff will visit them several times each day. Parents and guests will use them when they patron your school for plays, parents' nights, concerts, or science fairs. What will they think when they walk into a restroom and they smell cigarette smoke or see cigarette butts in the toilets? What about broken mirrors or graffiti on the stalls? I know we've all experienced this one: no toilet paper. I have even known schools to remove the doors on the stalls because they cannot keep them from being damaged. Having to use the restroom with no doors? Is this a school or a prison?

The restrooms at my school used to be a never-ending source of complaints. Since restrooms are so important to me, I borrowed an idea from the business world. I found that some of the cleanest restrooms had a form mounted by the door on a clipboard that the custodian initialed each time he or she cleaned, usually 3 or more times a day. We started doing this for each restroom in my school several years back and now we have much fewer complaints. The restroom is the one spot all of your customers will visit, so it better be clean!

When I need a restroom, I always look for a Dunkin' Donuts, as they consistently have the cleanest, most well-kept restrooms. They don't mind if you go in and just use the restroom—there is no

> At Disney World, it is every employee's duty to pick up trash whenever they see it, regardless of if they are a ride operator or the Senior VP of Sales. This buy-in keeps the facilities pristine.[100]

sign that says it's for customers only, like many places. And by having good restrooms that are open to the public, surely some of those people buy something anyway, while they're there. I'm surprised I don't see more fast food establishments taking care of their restrooms like Dunkin' Donuts.

I know of gas stations with signage declaring the best restrooms in town in order to try to earn people's business. The best companies know that the restrooms are important to their customers. Since we implemented the checklist system in my district, I have started to notice them in other establishments. Leaders need to remember that facility maintenance is a reflection on your organization and leadership, so they'd better be well kept.

A Defining Moment

I had just accepted the assistant superintendent position in Mason County Schools. I remember my first drive onto the campus as second in command and the first thing that greeted me was this rusty, dark yellow sign that said, "No Trespassing Violators Will Be Prosecuted." I pulled the car over and took a picture of this sign. (I have used this picture in presentations ever since). At one of our first leadership meetings I sarcastically asked just how many people had been prosecuted for coming onto our campus. Everyone looked at me as if I had four heads. I then asked why we would have such an ugly, rusty sign threatening our customers as soon as they entered our campus. They all nodded their heads like it was a revelation. Taking down that sign was the first of many customer service changes that we would make in our school system.

> We should not have to ask what subject matter is taught in a particular classroom. History teachers should have images and relics from the past—get creative! Students love that. Teachers who show enthusiasm for their subject matter infect their students with it. Challenge your teachers to dig down and find the passion for their subject, and encourage them to express it and share it with students via their classroom décor.

Other blemishes that were picture-worthy included dead trees, unsightly dumpsters, and rusty fences. On another occasion there was a rotting tree right in front of the middle school. My grounds crew and I went up to the tree, which was at least twenty feet tall. I pushed on it and, to my surprise, the tree fell completely over. We all just had to laugh as there is no telling how long that dead tree had been there.

I have always had excellent maintenance and custodial staff, but none of them generally came to me looking for extra work. As I walk the grounds, I like to use my cell phone to take pictures of facility items that need to be fixed or replaced. I will then send these pictures to appropriate personnel. While they usually thank me for bringing this to their attention, I usually can feel some sarcasm through the phone. Not everyone will appreciate or even welcome such attention to facility detail, but as school leaders, it is our job to be the bad guy and give people extra work from time to time.

Sometimes It Takes Fresh Eyes

In my opinion, the longer we are in the same school system the more we fail to notice facility issues. Many times when I go into a new school system and point out something out of place or broken, the employees tell me that they have walked by something thousands of times and never noticed the issue. I truly believe them as I think back to a story from many years back.

I was driving a friend from out of town through my old neighborhood and pointed out a restaurant that I knew and loved my whole life. As we drove by he started laughing hysterically. When I asked him what he was laughing at, he told me that the word "restaurant" was misspelled in tall bold letters two different ways on different sides of the building. I just had to turn around and go back to look at the signs myself. Sure enough there they were, all this time.

He asked why this was such a big deal to me, and I then told him he just proved a point I like to make with people about their facilities: "Sometimes it takes fresh eyes to see problems." This philosophy is another reason to utilize the mystery guest from the Collect Reliable Information concept.

In my career I have probably removed over 100 signs and numerous dead trees. I have had dozens of rusty fences painted on my school campuses and have helped other schools and districts remove them when appropriate. Still, every now and then, someone new comes in and points out an eyesore I can't believe I've missed!

School Signage

My philosophy is, "If I would not see it posted at Disney World, I do not want it posted on our school campus." It takes some time to learn what is and isn't good signage. Below are a few examples of signs I've seen over the years that had no place in a public school, as well as my reaction. As you read them, imagine these rusty signs with poor grammar hung on an otherwise good-looking school façade or campus.

No Charging Allowed!!!!!!!!!

Kelly's Reaction: Do the extra exclamation marks really mean something? Is the sign also yelling at me? What if we change the wording to read: "In order to keep prices at the lowest level, we do not permit charging."

If you were not assigned a locker in this row, you better move. (In red letters): Your lock will be cut off!!!!!!!!!!

Kelly—Customer service 101 teaches to never threaten your customers. Wouldn't this be better? "We want to clean all lockers for our students next year. Please remove locks by [date] or we will have to remove them."

Refrigerator thieves you are being watched!!!
Do not take anything from here unless it is yours!

Kelly—I do not believe I would see this one at Disney World!

Persons coming onto this site before 8:00AM or after 4:00PM. Including students, do so at your own risk.

Kelly—Did I just enter a war zone?

Please use front door if you try to use this door we will not let you in.

Kelly—I was presenting at a district on customer service, and I was greeted by this sign upon trying to enter close to the stage area.

No skateboarding, bicycle riding or roller blading on campus

Kelly—How many "No's" can we place on one sign? Why not add, "No doing doughnuts in the grass in front of the school" or "No sex on the playground"?

In case of emergency (616) 729-7149
Dial 66211 Then call 911

Kelly—I really hope the robber is very slow as I try to dial all these numbers.

Maybe you've seen signs like these at schools. If not, start looking; they're everywhere. I make a game out of it, trying to one-up myself by finding one even worse than the last. I have to admit, I was not proud of one-upping myself on one occasion.

My elementary school was starting a campaign to increase student reading ability. Our school had been lagging for years and we were working hard to get our kids to read at grade-level. It was a schoolwide initiative, with teachers being told to hit this area hard and school staff helping out by putting up signage about our mission. I was admiring our staff's buy-in and looking around the school at all the reading positivity we had posted on the walls. And then I saw it: "We're on the road to proficientsy." I had to just roll my eyes and take the sign down. How can we get on the road to proficiency if we can't even spell it?

This speaks to a greater issue that public schools have with appearances. When it comes to first impressions, we don't exactly inspire confidence and excitement for new visitors. Remember the earlier example about passengers on an airplane being more likely to fear a plane crash if there was a coffee ring on their tray table? Research is replete with such evidence that it is hard to change a first impression. Facilities are the first thing you see when you enter a school. You cannot help, but come to certain conclusions about a school when you drive up to the parking lot, go into the office, or visit a school restroom.

Administrators must recognize that facility maintenance is a reflection on their leadership and their attention to detail. One of my favorite author duos, John A. Black and Fenwick W. English, states that, "Ineffective custodians work for administrative wimps. If they cannot keep the schools clean, chances are they are not able to improve the learning in it either."[101] I believe this to be true, which is why I have administrators remind themselves of what is most important when it comes to facilities:

- Is the interior and exterior of your school immaculate?

- What are the initial perceptions of people who enter your school?
- How do you hold custodial and maintenance personnel accountable?

Asking questions such as these will help guide you to making needed improvements to your facilities.

Accountability Is key

There should always be someone responsible when something goes wrong. If you haven't assigned someone to be in charge of it, that person is you. I learned this philosophy very early in my administrative career. I was walking through our school district inspecting various touch points. I got to the high school concession stand where many of our parents work in our booster organization to raise money for our athletic programs, and I noticed the popcorn popper had grease all over the glass from years ago. I looked closer and noticed dirt and filth everywhere, even dust all over the coolers and trash behind counters. I called a meeting and had the principals walk with us to all the booster club areas. Each area seemed to get worse, as now we had more eyes looking at everything. The low point came when we went outside to the football booster area and found chili left in pans from the previous year. When my leaders had to cover their faces from the smell, I knew they had seen enough. We all went into an area to discuss who was responsible for all this, and here are a few of the answers:

- The athletic director
- The head of custodial services
- Each booster club
- The coach of the sport
- All four groups are responsible

In my experience, if everyone is responsible for something then actually no one is responsible for anything. I told the principals they are responsible to me, and they are who I would hold accountable. It would be up to them how they handled it. My principals got on it, and soon every area was cleaned up and had written responsibilities for custodians and clubs posted. Once responsibilities were made clear, I noticed the area was cleaner and this was never a problem again. As a superintendent, I hold principals responsible for every touch point in their buildings and on their grounds, which includes recommending training or termination to any employee working in their building who is not holding up his or her clearly defined responsibilities.

Another story has to do with a baseboard in the kitchen that ran into the eating area. I was the assistant superintendent at the time. This particular baseboard was very dirty in the eating area, but somehow became immaculately clean once it ran into the kitchen. Knowing this is a continuously running baseboard, I just had to investigate further. I asked the cafeteria manager, and she told me her staff only cleaned the kitchen area. The custodian happened to walk into the cafeteria about that time so I thought I would get his opinion. The custodian was quick to tell me that this section of baseboard was the cafeteria manager's responsibility. By this time, word must have spread that I was in the cafeteria, so along came the assistant principal! I received a vague answer from the assistant principal and, while she was talking all around my question, the principal arrived. I knew I was the only one enjoying this moment, so I continued to have some fun! I had the school custodian, the cafeteria manager, the assistant principal, and the principal all looking at this one baseboard. As luck would have it, the food service director was in this elementary school main office, so I radioed her to join us in the cafeteria.

> **A Word of Caution About Renting Out Facilities:** When an event held by an outside group does not go well, it will be the school's fault in the public's mind! So a word to the wise, be cautious about who you let use your school as it will likely keep the stamp of your name with it.

So here we were, over a half million dollars in salary, looking at a dirty baseboard. I like to say: *if everyone is in charge, no one is in charge.* The mystery of the dirty baseboard concluded when we came to the agreement that it was the custodian's responsibility to clean it. I told the principal to make sure it was clean both before and after it runs into the kitchen. I held the principal accountable and he held his custodian accountable. This is the only way I know how to deal with such bureaucracy and organizational chart dilemmas.

Kelly's Tips and Best Practices

Earlier in this chapter, I shared some of the poor signage I've witnessed. The first step to improving facilities is recognizing the problems. Seeing your school grounds with new "customer service" eyes will help you spot eyesores to which you and your staff have gone blind.

> I always find signs hung on school walls that are no longer necessary. When I ask why they are there, I am usually told no one knows except maintenance and they have been there for years. People then seem surprised when I have such items taken down. If something is hanging in a school for no reason, it is taking up space for something positive to be hung!

Beyond spotting problems, we need to know how to *fix* said eyesores. Below are a few examples of school signs that actually get it right, along with my own thoughts on why these signs strike a customer service chord.

"No Skateboards Or Rollerblades, Please. It Breaks The Sidewalk!"

Kelly—While we could always make them better, I liked this sign because it tells everyone why and research says that students and adults are much more likely to comply if they are told the reason for a rule.

For Your Protection Property Is Under Surveillance

Kelly—The school might be spying on me but it is for my protection!

Please keep this door closed because of the heat and because of the noise from the bathrooms.

Kelly—I love this sign for many different reasons. The same administrative assistant who put up the "refrigerator thief" sign from earlier also created this excellent sign. The actual sign had a picture of a sun with a funny expression and students playing in the bathroom. This sign gives two reasons to keep the door closed. This is an uncommon sign in most schools!

At a local gas station I saw a sign that read,

"Cleanest restrooms in town"

Kelly—Might we choose gas stations based on cleanliness of restrooms? Could we say this about our restrooms? Can we use signage on our facilities to brag on our schools?

At Red Robin's take-out parking I spotted a sign that read,

**"Red Robin To Go Parking
Violators Will Be Dipped in Ranch Dressing"**

Kelly—Why not get your message across in a fun way?

A stuffed giraffe lay in a toy store just begging for a child to jump on it. The sign read,

"Please Don't Ride Me It Hurts My Legs and Back!

Kelly—I like the fun way the sign is sending a message to the customers.

Remember the Competition

Beyond the basics, such as having proper signage and general infrastructure upkeep, I would challenge all school leaders to consider using their facilities as a way to *entice students and parents into choosing and attending their schools.* What's your best feature? Your theatre? Your beautiful athletic facilities? Air conditioned school buses? Some schools have beautiful food courts with a diverse menu each day for students. I love to eat, and I can tell you that if I am choosing a school, the best cafeteria would be one factor in my decision. I'm not alone in thinking this. A friend and former college admissions office tour guide told me that one of the most common questions she got was, "How's the food here?" There's a reason the Princeton Review ranks the colleges and universities with the best food!

Highlighting your school's best feature can be a way to boost school pride and entice prospective students to enroll at your school. When thinking about your school facilities, try to use the Las Vegas philosophy of wowing each and every customer with facilities.

I've always loved the children's book *If You Give a Mouse a Cookie.* The mouse just keeps asking for one thing after another, running the little boy who's waiting on him ragged.[102] Sometimes I feel like my school is the mouse and I'm the boy. This was especially true when we got a new flag for the front of our school. The old one was starting to fray, and I'm a stickler for flag etiquette. Well, when we got the new flag up, it showed us just how badly the pole needed paint. So we put a new coat of paint on it. We looked at it again, pleased we had totally revamped our front lawn centerpiece. As the sun went down, I realized that we needed a light on it. So we installed a light on the ground in front of the flagpole. But to make sure nobody kicked or stepped on the light,

> When it comes to upkeep, like painting and structural upkeep, I invoke the law of referees: if people don't notice them, they're doing great.

we needed to put a circle of masonry rocks around the pole and light. So we did that. By the time we were finished, the flag had gotten ragged again! Just kidding, but all in all we spent several hours thinking about that one part of our facility. The before and after photos showed us just how big of a difference it made for the front of our school. Even though I felt pretty worn out from the ordeal, I had to smile when I remembered the boy in the book, run ragged by a demanding mouse.

Final Thoughts on Facilities

I once heard a story from a fellow administrator that a few girls at her middle school were kissing the restroom mirrors while wearing lipstick. The principal and custodian could not figure out which girls were doing it, so they gathered suspected girls into the restroom for questioning. The typical middle school girls, with their rosy red lips, all denied involvement. After no one came forward, the principal told the custodian to remove the lipstick like he does each night. The custodian took his squeegee, dipped it into the toilet, and cleaned the mirrors. The girls' mouths dropped in horror. Of course, that was the last we saw of girls leaving lipstick marks on the mirrors. I love this example because the principal and custodian thought outside the box together to solve an issue that did not result in the suspension of their customers. Now there's a custodian and principal who get it!

When it comes to facilities maintenance and overall school appearance, this concept seems to elude many public school administrators, but it is more important than they imagine. In fact, I've found that whether I'm looking at companies or schools, I can tell whether or not they value and practice customer service based on how good their facilities look. I don't recall pulling into a single school that had rusty jungle gyms or letters missing from their school sign and being pleasantly surprised with the staff's customer service attitudes when I walked inside.

Customer service is all about getting the little details right.

Once you start to find those details and fix them, you begin to notice them more. Just like with facilities maintenance, fixing one problem shows you the next problem; it's the *If You Give a Mouse a Cookie* phenomenon. Once you find yourself caught in that cycle, silently cursing your demanding mouse of a school, while being run ragged by it, you'll know you're really getting this concept. As we compete for students, facility maintenance becomes even more important to retaining and attracting students.

CONCEPT 11

Plan and Reflect on Customer Service Practices

*"Give me six hours to chop down a tree and
I will spend the first four sharpening the axe."*
— Abraham Lincoln[103]

My favorite ketchup has always been Heinz and, as a kid, I would refuse to try any other brand. I remember the glass bottles with the narrow neck and the effort it would take to get the ketchup to slowly roll out of the bottle. (Millennials may have to ask their parents, but this was a major annoyance!) One Heinz commercial played the song "Anticipation" by Carly Simon, mocking the slow-moving ketchup.[104]

I remember the many methods people used to speed up the ketchup flow. I used the "violent shake and pound with palm of my hand" method. Some people would insert a knife and scoop it out. A friend of mine said that if you tapped the "57" at the base of the neck it would come out faster, but the jury is still out on that one.

Heinz ketchup was invented in 1869, but Heinz didn't switch to a plastic, squeezable ketchup bottle until 1983. Still, people had difficulty getting that pesky ketchup from the bottom of the bottle. In 2002, they flipped the plastic bottle upside-down to create the incarnation we see today.[105] It only took 133 years to get there! We even got Go-GURT, the squeezable yogurt, before the proper squeezable ketchup bottle.

Why did it take so long for ketchup to progress into a more user-friendly vessel? I would argue that if Heinz had done more planning and reflecting, years of our frustration could have been avoided. How many minutes did we collectively spend in "antic-ipation," waiting for our condiment that now takes less than two seconds?

Some of the biggest issues I have dealt with in public educa-tion could have been avoided with better planning and reflecting on customer service. In this chapter, I'll talk about the importance of planning and reflecting and give some tips on how to do it well in the public school setting.

Sometimes events go smoothly on their own. Miracles do happen! But as a public school administrator, you know that there are no guarantees. Usually, there's some way an event could have been planned better, whether it's something big like not planning outdoor activities with the weather in mind, or the smoke detector going off while cooking, or something smaller like parents having nowhere to sit while waiting in the hallway for their time on par-ent-teacher night.

It is important for administrators and staff to plan before an event and reflect on what went wrong or right when the activity is over. From doctors and surgeons to the military and law enforce-ment (think TV shows like *NCIS* and *Criminal Minds*), debriefing is a long-standing method used to make sure an event or pro-cedure gets better with each repetition. Due to staff turnover in public schools, it is even more important for school leaders to teach staff how to plan and reflect with a customer service mindset. If the leadership doesn't value planning and reflecting on customer service practices, then it will be left up to the staff member in charge at any given moment. Planning and reflecting with a customer service mindset is not taught in schools of educa-tion, so it is on us as leaders to make sure this gets accomplished. In my opinion, each time an activity occurs, it should run more smoothly than the previous one, and eventually you'll have the event running like a well-oiled machine. Will there be problems? Oh my, yes! Problems are job security for all of us. Sometimes it seems like everything is going wrong, and we just have to shut our eyes, get the thing over with as quickly as possible, and reflect immediately on how it could be better next year. However, when an event is well planned, it's much easier to manage small problems that go awry.

Conducting An "Autopsy Without Blame"

I love Jim Collins's leadership tips! He hits the nail on the head with planning and reflecting. In his book *Good to Great*, he calls his method of getting together with staff to talk about an event after it has finished, "Autopsies Without Blame." Here's what he has to say about this idea:

> *When you conduct autopsies without blame, you go a long way toward creating a climate where the truth is heard. If you have the right people on the bus, you should almost never need to assign blame but need only to search for understanding and learning.*[106]

I have always found my "autopsies without blame" exhilarating because all members called to these meetings shared a common goal and attacked the issue with the focus and intensity of a group of surgeons reflecting on a real life autopsy. The key is that we are attacking the problem in order to give better service and not attacking any one person or team. In other words, we have "the right people on the bus," so there's no need to throw anyone under it.

I believe public schools should plan every school event with a customer service focus and, after major events, reflect on how customer service could have been improved. Regardless of the success of the event, a good reflection session will find ways to make customer service improvements for the next time. I've found that the urgency and intensity of these reflection sessions must increase when events are unsuccessful because, in order to get it right next time, we need to figure out more solutions and Plan Bs. I also like to keep a checklist of these reminders for each event to be revisited each year.

Why do this? It makes your job a whole lot easier. *Putting in the work up front is much easier than orchestrating damage control later.* A little bit of tweaking each year for five years until you've got a good system pays off in the long run in terms of time spent dealing with problems. Plus, you'll create successful events, which you should strive for in the first place.

What the Very Best Companies Do

The very best companies plan and reflect upon their customer service practices at every touch point. Going back to the chapter on touch points, there is a strong correlation between touch points and planning and reflecting. Looking at *every detail* of what an organization does is key to planning and reflecting well. Take professional sports teams and their coaches for example. The coach needs to be fully dedicated to planning and reflecting. The team doesn't just go out and play games. They have meetings, study tape, and look at every angle of what they do with an eye for detail. You don't find those little flaws and fixes in the game plan unless you analyze it. That analysis is planning and reflecting.

In the business world, that analysis can be the difference between another satisfied customer and a steaming mad one. Here's one example of planning and reflecting gone awry.

When it comes to food service, companies are under a lot of pressure to get it right. Low blood sugar or caffeine withdrawal will turn even the nicest, most understanding person into the customer from hell. I assure you, I was just about at this point when I stepped into an Arby's after a long day at a speaking engagement.

The Arby's franchise is well known for their roast beef sandwiches and, I've got to say, I'm a big fan.[107] As I ordered my sandwich, the cashier said, "We are out of roast beef." I couldn't help but laugh as I wondered how that was possible. I told the young man I am a school administrator and that would be like me telling students we were out of education! He apparently didn't see the humor in the situation and replied that I could have a turkey or chicken sandwich. I decided to leave the restaurant and at that exact time an entire bus of cheerleaders was unloading and entering the restaurant. I took great delight in announcing to all of them that Arby's was out of roast beef.

Fast food restaurants, like schools, are easy targets to pick on with their revolving door of young employees. However, if I was the manager, I believe I would have a procedure in place to make sure that my employees never have to look someone in the eye and tell them that Arby's is out of roast beef! I cannot help but wonder if this restaurant ever practices planning and reflecting.

I'm sure you have horror stories about companies that simply did not plan well enough and customers had to pay the price. Fortunately for us, there are some companies out there that are implementing Nostradamus-like plan and reflect practices. We can look at the foresight of Walt Disney for an anecdote. The developed area of Disney World makes up only about one-third of the total land that was purchased by Walt in 1965, showing how Walt had planned well into the future.[108] But enough about Disney (for now). Let's get to one of the leaders in the technology industry: Amazon.

Amazon is always trying to improve their customer service practices, especially when it comes to getting their products in the hands of their customers. It started with free, expedited shipping for Amazon Prime subscribers. But that wasn't good enough. Upon reflection, they decided that their products needed to get to people even faster. Since products were shipped countrywide from only a few mega-warehouses, products needed time to travel. So to cut down on wait time, they started to build more warehouses near major cities. These warehouses were smaller, but stocked the most-ordered items in the region, so people could get their products in a flash.

Again, it didn't stop there. For years, Amazon relied on outsourcing delivery to the likes of FedEx and UPS. However, in 2014, Amazon began delivering packages in their own white vans in San Francisco.[109] Today, in many cities, you can see the white vans marked with the signature lowercase "A" with the arrow on it delivering Amazon orders themselves, straight from the warehouse to the customer.

What happened next? You guessed it: they went back to the reflection phase, asking what else they could do. Now you can choose the option of having your packages delivered to a locker for pickup near your home.[110] Since there is one central drop-off for packages for the delivery van and not dozens of individual addresses, the van can deliver more packages per day and packages can arrive faster. Amazon lockers are also a more secure way to get packages to customers who don't want their orders sitting on their doorstep. The Amazon lockers are popping up like mushrooms across the country and are the company's answer to the post office box.

The newest addition to the delivery process is the Amazon Dash Button. This is a small Bluetooth button that affixes to a wall, cabinet, or just about any surface. It has the logo of a particular product like Bounty or Tide. When you start to run low on the item, all you do is tap the button and it places an order for that product instantly. No need to log in or get on your computer, tablet, or smartphone.

So what does the future hold for delivery at Amazon? Drones of course! The company has already flown its first unmanned air delivery system, called Amazon Prime Air, which will cut down even more on delivery time.[111]

I would be remiss if I didn't mention my local Chick-fil-A's planning and reflecting process. When management noticed that drive-thru lines got really long at mealtimes, they started having an employee walk through the line to take orders instead of having customers wait until they got to the order window. This "face-to-face" ordering, as the company calls it, allows customers to order and even pay via point of service devices, right from the drive-thru lane.[112]

After implementing this practice, Chick-fil-A found that the employees were getting overheated being outside taking orders in the hot sun all day, so they put tents up over the car lines. Now employees can stay cooler while making the customers' wait time shorter.

Whether it's retail or fast food, it's stories like these that show that the best companies are constantly tweaking their practices to improve customer service. Planning and reflecting is a cyclical process that never ends. Just like the model for giving great customer service, it is ongoing and always needs to be improved and updated. In the field of customer service, you never "arrive." Well, except if you're an Amazon package; then you arrive lightning fast!

What Schools Do and Don't Do

A colleague shared a story about a mother who was baking a ham while her inquisitive daughter watched closely. As the mother cut off both ends of the ham, the daughter asked why she would waste these parts of the ham. The mother said that is the way her mother cooks her ham. The next week at the family reunion the daughter, not quite satisfied with her mother's answer, went up to her grandmother to ask about why she cut off both ends of the ham. The grandmother gave the identical answer: "My mother always used to do it before she placed the ham into the pot." The next week the daughter was a little more excited than normal about visiting great-grandmother in the nursing home. As the daughter asked great-grandmother about cooking her hams and cutting off both ends, great-grandmother smiled at the question and gave her a different answer. She replied: "You see we only had one pan back in the day, and it was not large enough to hold the ham. I would cut it at both ends so it would fit into the pan." The little girl could do nothing but laugh at the fact that a lot of ham had been wasted through the years because no one thought to even ask the question, "Why?"

> If customer service was truly important in public education, there would never be a school improvement plan without a focus on customer service.

Let's address the elephant in the room: public schools are horrendous at planning and reflecting. We simply don't ask "why?" and it creates countless problems.

In my experience, public schools wait until a complaint is made before they consider fixing a problem. Even if the complaint is warranted, getting it fixed may still depend on who is actually making the complaint. "If it is not broken don't fix it" is an unofficial mantra in public education. After all, we have been doing things a certain way for hundreds of years, and generally parents put up with our methods because that is how it was done when they were in school, just like in the ham story above. The customer service bar is set very low in public education, so there is a lot of room for improvement for staff and leaders who want to excel at service.

Eventually though the complaints get loud enough for the issue to go to the school board, and it is only then that they say, "Okay, we will look into it." However, in order to be a school that focuses on giving great customer service, the school needs to be proactive. They need to find the problems *first* and solve them *before* complaints arise. Now, that doesn't mean you get it right the first time—in fact even the best companies don't do that. But over time, through careful planning and "autopsies," a school's customer service will evolve like the Amazon and Chick-fil-A examples above, and eventually gain the foresight to stop problems before they start.

It certainly takes time to get there. I was recently attending a high school graduation ceremony in another district that made me a nervous wreck. The ceremony was completely out of hand. While the superintendent and speaker talked, the graduates gabbed, laughed, and started hitting beach balls around. I personally had never witnessed such anarchy. The blatant disrespect did not end, as graduates danced across the stage to receive their diplomas. I have to admit that these situations cause me to cringe, whether they occur in my district or someone else's.

Of course, like John Maxwell, I believe "everything rises and falls on leadership." In the Arby's story earlier, the manager is the first person I held responsible. So, in this graduation story, if I was a parent or family member at the ceremony and saw beach balls flying around and general chaos on stage, above all else, I would hold the principal and superintendent accountable.

As a school leader, situations like these are a direct reflection on you, the person in charge. A lot of leaders don't realize this for some reason. Often, the cause of these problems is poor planning. After seeing this graduation debacle, I looked at the policies at my school. We have an X on the stage where students are supposed to stand. They're expected to shake with their right hand over the diploma and take the diploma with their left hand. We let them know ahead of time what is expected of them and the consequences of not following the protocol. A few police officers stand ready to remove unruly students. We shake hands with students all along the way as a safeguard to stop bad behavior before it gets too far. Without careful planning, students do not have the guidance they need to be successful during the event. Situations like this fit the old alliterative adage "prior planning prevents poor performance."

An Unplanned Grandparents' Day

If there's one thing I learned working in education it's that something will always go wrong. No school is exempt from the inevitable problems, no matter how much they focus on planning and reflecting. One day I found myself in a mess while at one of my elementary schools.

As the associate superintendent, I thought I would drop in on Grandparents' Day to talk with the grandparents and take some photos. As I pulled up to the school I noticed that the parking lot was full, and cars were beginning to park on our nicely manicured grass all around the school. There was no one coordinating the parking, so cars parked wherever they could find room. To complicate matters, it was raining ferociously, so our senior citizen guests were a wet, muddy mess walking into the front of the school to get their name tags. Only one person was manning the office, and she was handling several different issues at once. The line of grandparents down the hallway seemed endless, and they were slipping on the wet floor. All I could do was shake my head because I have learned that, once things are this poorly planned, there is just no way to turn the situation around. One phrase I like to use with my school leaders is: "Lack of planning on your part does not constitute an emergency on my part." I headed down the hallway and into the school cafeteria to see if it was any better there.

It was no surprise that things weren't better. Not only were the food and chocolate milk that were being served not conducive to the diets of the senior citizens, but neither was eating with sporks or sitting at low tables designed for elementary school students. In a movie called *Heartbreak Ridge*, Clint Eastwood had a term for such a messy, unsalvageable situation.[113] The first word started with a C and the second word started with an F. For the purpose of this book, we will just call it a Cluster. In my schools, Clusters are guaranteed to lead to autopsies!

The first home football game of the year is a major event in my school district. Besides everyone wanting to see the quality of the team, it is the first time the band gets to play in front of a large crowd. One year, as the band began to play the Star-Spangled Banner and everyone looked toward the flag, we all simultaneously realized there was no flag on the flagpole! Of course, being the highest ranking school official on hand, everyone turned and looked at me, waiting to see if I was going to stand and look toward the empty flagpole. I just had to laugh in the moment. But when I looked down at my phone, I'd gotten six texts from employees with their preemptive apologies. Afterward, we looked at the facility pregame checklist and added, "The flag needs to be on the flagpole." I have found that these readiness checklists are very fluid documents that can and should be revisited and possibly changed *each year*. Even though several people came up to me asking about the flag throughout the game, I was able turn this snafu into teachable moment.

When It Goes Wrong, We Just Blame the Students

As superintendent, I was asked to attend an awards day presentation for seniors who had scored well on the state test. The administrative team wanted to give the awards in front of all the students as motivation for the following year. Cake and punch had been ordered and slices of cake were already cut for all students to receive after the ceremony.

During the ceremony, the principal called the honored students to the floor one at a time, handed them their certificates, and had pictures taken with them. The honored students were seated all over the gym and had to step down rows of bleachers to get their awards, have their photos taken, and go back to their seats. Many students received multiple awards and had to keep going up and down to their seats to receive each award. Needless to say, this ceremony dragged on and, after a while, all the students seemed to lose interest in listening to the program or the principal. Students grew weary of clapping repeatedly for the same people and began to talk amongst themselves. Teachers tried to get the students to be quiet, but they soon gave up. Then the principal tried to get control, but to no avail.

When the awards presentation was over, the principal told all the students that because of their behavior they did not deserve punch and cake and sent them all back to class. Now we had an entire senior class going back to their classrooms mad at the school.

Later that day, I called an autopsy meeting with all my leaders and the high school administrative team, including the principal, assistant principal, and guidance counselors. I asked them all about how they thought the program went. Everyone felt that they had a great plan but the students just acted poorly. They even discussed a few additional ways they planned to punish these students. I let everyone have their say and then, at long last, I finally said what was on my mind.

I started out by admitting that I was also embarrassed by the conduct. I then asked some questions about how we might have done a few things differently. What about sitting the award winners together in the first row near the podium? What if each student was called up only once to receive all of his or her awards? What about taking pictures later, during the cake and punch activities? Looking around at my staff, I could tell that no one was going to take any responsibility. I then asked, "What authority have you all given the teachers who were in attendance? Did teachers have the authority to remove students? I could tell from their body language that the administrators were not happy, but I had to give them one final dig to nail the point home. "This assembly disaster was actually your fault and not the students'. I want you to go back and reflect on the questions that I have asked today, and I will follow up with everyone tomorrow." It's always easier to just blame the students when adults fail to plan. As a teacher, I always said, "If one kid doesn't get it, it's probably his fault, but if nineteen out of twenty fail, it's probably mine."

What the Best Schools Do

Let's go back to the Grandparents' Day debacle. After the event, we quickly held a meeting with the school principals, administrative assistant, food service director, and the head of custodial and maintenance. We immediately discussed and created our plan for next year's Grandparents' Day. We decided to have custodians and maintenance staff park cars. We would have people with umbrellas walking grandparents to their destinations in case of rain and more volunteers sitting at tables outside the office. We went on to discuss having students escort grandparents to the cafeteria and what food and drink we wanted to serve. We decided to set up additional rooms for crowd overflow with decorated tables. One out-of-the-box idea I loved was for teachers and staff to give up their own parking spaces to allow grandparents to park closest to the school. Now that's staff buy-in!

Planning and reflecting is essential for events like Grandparents' Day. But planning and reflecting is not just for major events. A cook or food service manager each day needs to think about food presentation. A bus driver might plan and reflect on how to better learn the names of the students on his or her bus. A teacher may need to plan and reflect on how to give great customer service at parent-teacher meetings. A coach may plan and reflect on offering a pregame meal alternative to country fried steak!

Autopsies in Public Schools— The When and How

I decided long ago that students are my first customers and top priority. While that thinking sometimes lands me in hot water, I do sleep better at night knowing I'm doing my job in accordance to my principles. Anytime I think a student has been treated unfairly, I reserve the right to call an autopsy meeting.

> Albert Einstein said, "The world will not be destroyed by those who do evil, but by those who watch without doing anything."[114] As administrators, if we sit and do nothing when events go awry, our schools will not improve.

In my opinion, there are no occurrences too small for an autopsy. I utilize them often, and my staff has come to expect them after events. Just like real-life autopsies, it's important to perform these as soon as possible after the event. If it's not immediate, people will start crafting plans to deflect responsibility or planning who they are going to throw under the bus. Here are some instances when I have called autopsies:

1. Major athletic event

2. Home Visit Day
3. Move-Up Day
4. First day of school
5. Preschool graduation
6. The school musical
7. Anytime a leader feels like there has been an injustice to a student
8. A major school discipline issue

Earlier in this chapter, I explained procedures we changed after an autopsy session about Grandparents' Day. With all the staffing changes that occur within our public schools, keeping organized records is important for the next time the event is run. I keep my notes for recurring events in binders labeled with the event name and store them in a bookshelf in my office. These binders go back many years for some events and come in handy when we have to go to Plan B (rain location, for example), especially when we haven't needed Plan B in several years. This material also is a great resource for new school personnel.

As I mentioned earlier, once you start to see your school with a customer service mindset, the problems reveal themselves, like a Magic Eye picture. Suddenly, you'll see these problems as clear as day. To help get you on that track, here are a few of my autopsy questions for school graduation.

- When and who tells students they are not on track to graduate? By what date? Who notifies the parents/guardians?
- Who contacts the graduation speaker? Who will introduce the speaker? Who will get the bio to read for the introduction? Will he or she receive a gift?
- What will go into the program? Who will create the program? Who will proofread?
- Who will make sure caps and gowns are ordered?

- Which students will speak at graduation?
- Who will check and clean all the seating for parents?
- Who will check all the restrooms before, during, and after graduation?
- Who will check or search students before they enter the ceremony?
- Who will make sure security personnel have been trained?
- Who will hand out the diplomas? Will the certificate be inside the diploma?
- Who is taking pictures? Who will place the "X" on the stage, designating where the student and the one handing out the diploma should stand?
- How many times will they practice the ceremony? When?
- When handing the diploma, do you handshake over or under the diploma?
- Who double-checks the spelling of all names on the diploma?
- Have we practiced pronunciation of the names with the students?
- Have we talked with maintenance staff about controlling the temperature in the gym?
- Have we landscaped the area where parents are entering?
- What is the procedure for students who act silly and need to be removed? What would happen if someone blows up a beach ball and starts hitting it during the ceremony?
- Who will park cars? Is there enough handicapped parking?
- Where will board members sit? Is there a sign on each chair for all stage guests? Do stage guests all receive water?
- Do chairs match? Are there floral arrangements?
- What will we do if a parent needs to be removed?

- Who will check the students' speeches? What is the plan if a student's speech turns vulgar? What is the signal to cut the sound?
- Are leaders or police placed throughout the crowd and in the stands to look for possible issues?

Final Thoughts on Planning and Reflecting

It takes time and effort to plan and reflect, but you get that time and peace of mind back in the long run by not having to address as many problems on the fly and after the event. By keeping records of events, you'll be able to refresh your memory during the weeks leading up to the event and tweak the details that need to run more smoothly. Adding "Autopsies Without Blame" will make sure no details are overlooked or forgotten for next year. Once you get rolling with planning and reflecting, you will find that it saves you time and frustration for future events. Yes, there will be days when it's raining cats and dogs on grandma and you have to throw in the waterlogged towel, but those days will be few and far between.

CONCEPT 12

Give Great Customer Service to Employees

"Motivate them, train them, care about them and make winners out of them . . . we know that if we treat our employees correctly, they'll treat the customers right. And if customers are treated right, they'll come back."
– J.W. Marriott Jr.[115]

One of my favorite Super Bowl ads from the 2000s was a Reebok commercial featuring Terry Tate, Office Linebacker.[116] In the ad, the CEO of an office tried to think outside the box on how to keep employees on task, so he hired a football player to use his skills of tackling and intimidation as the office enforcer. The linebacker, Terry Tate, would run up and tackle people, shouting "Woo!" like football players do during actual NFL games. He would then stand over the person pointing out what they did wrong, saying things like, "Break was over fifteen minutes ago," "You know you need a cover sheet on your TPS reports, Richard!," "You can't walk away from a K-22 paper jam. You must be out of your mind, son," "You kill the joe, you make some mo,'" and "That's a long distance call, *Doug!*" His presence in the office made employees fear him and the bodily harm that would ensue. Often, the camera would show Terry walking away after a tackle, leaving the employee huddled on the ground in pain.

While the "Office Linebacker" doesn't truly exist in the business world, the idea isn't far off from reality for many companies. As I mentioned in the Praise and Reward Employees for Great Customer Service concept, leaders having a "gotcha" mentality when it comes to keeping employees on task isn't a very productive policy among workers. Not only does it ignore all the positive things employees do, but it also creates an atmosphere of fear and anxiety for workers. Who wants to try to do their job when they are aware that at any moment they may be tackled by a literal or figurative office linebacker?

In psychology, we can see just how much of a problem this is by looking at Maslow's hierarchy of needs. His theory states that people cannot focus on a task like "putting a cover on a TPS report" when their more basic needs, like health, safety, and well-being, are not being met. Those needs must be sufficiently met in order for the person to care about or even be able to do anything else.[117]

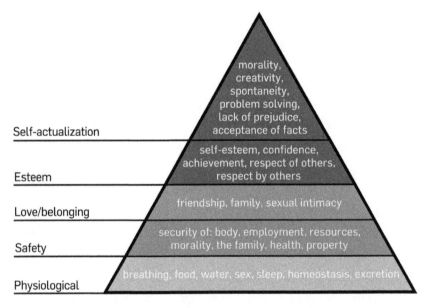

Photo Credit: Wikipedia

As you can see, from the graphic above, a lot of needs must be met before a person can truly be motivated to do his or her best with work tasks. In fact, work sits at the top of the pyramid in self-actualization. Without that motivation, employees will tend to do the bare minimum and, as you may recall from the *Office Space* example in the Confront concept, the bare minimum won't cut it with bosses.

So how does a leader go about motivating each and every employee? I've found that there are two important factors:

1. Employees need to believe that their boss cares about their health, well-being, and professional development.
2. Employees need to be comfortable and content at work.

In this chapter I will explain the importance of each of these factors and give examples from both business and public education. I'll also explain the importance of employees giving great service to each other, which includes ensuring that you've got the right culture.

Leadership

When we talk about giving great customer service to employees, just like with customers, it starts at the top and flows down through the organization like a waterfall.

In *Wellbeing—The Five Essential Elements* by Tom Rath and Jim Harter, we can see how important having a good boss is to our overall health. A study conducted in 150 countries looked at what makes us feel well when it comes to career well-being, social well-being, financial well-being, physical well-being, and community well-being. Of all of the interpersonal relationships that were studied, from friends to relatives to coworkers to children, the study found that participants rated the time they spent with their bosses as being the worst part of their day—lower than time spent doing chores and cleaning the house![118] That's not a ringing endorsement of leadership.

Another study found that if your manager ignores you, there is a 40 percent chance that you will be actively disengaged or filled with hostility about your job. If your manager is primarily focusing on your weaknesses, the chance you'll be actively disengaged goes down to 22 percent. If the manager is primarily focusing on your strengths, the chance you'll be actively disengaged is just 1 percent. These findings suggest that, contrary to what one might think, both positive *and negative* feedback from managers significantly decreases employee disengagement.

However, positive feedback is by far the more beneficial type of interaction between manager and employee.[119]

The American Psychological Association says, "Job stress is estimated to cost U.S. industry $300 billion a year in absenteeism, turnover, diminished productivity and medical, legal and insurance costs."[121] It seems the old model of the super-strict, over-rigorous workplace is incredibly shortsighted, sacrificing the health and well-being of their employees for ultimately no overall gain.

> Workers who deemed their managers to be the least competent had a 24 percent increased risk of a serious heart problem. For those who had worked for that manager for more than four years, the risk was 39 percent higher.[120]

So all this information tells us that bosses matter a great deal

The Benefits of Happiness to Employees
1. Three times more creative
2. Thirty-one percent more productive
3. Twenty-three fewer fatigue symptoms
4. Six times more engaged
5. Thirty-nine percent more likely to live to age 94
—Shawn Achor, *The Happiness Advantage*[122]

when it comes to worker satisfaction and well-being. Horrible bosses, take note!

In the 2011 movie *Horrible Bosses*, three friends commiserate over how badly they are treated by their bosses.[124] Nick, Jason Bateman's character, has been working overtime to get a promotion that he deserves. He gets called into his boss's office, hoping that this is finally the day. However, his boss, Mr. Harken, played by Kevin Spacey, has other ideas.

> "If you consistently mistrust all employees, you'll be correct 3% of the time. If on the other hand you trust all of your people all of the time, until they prove you wrong, you will be right 97 percent of the time!"
> —Wolf J. Rinke[123]

Mr. Harken (looking at the monitor displaying security camera footage of Nick coming in at 6:02 a.m.): See, this is what concerns me Nick. You're a punctual guy. You know the importance of being here right at 6 a.m., which is what leads me to think that there must be something wrong with the internal clock on our security system.

Nick: I may have been a minute late.

Mr. Harken: Well no, but according to this, you were two minutes late. So either you're a liar or this system is off by a full minute and if that's the case I'm going to have to fire Thomas, our longtime security coordinator.

Mr. Harken picks up the phone to fire Thomas.

Nick: No, I was lying. Sorry.

Mr. Harken: You were lying?

Nick: Yeah, I didn't mean to. It was more of a saying, you know? "Might have been a minute late." Literally, truthfully, I was two minutes late.

Now that's a horrible boss. Who would want to work for him? Unfortunately for Nick, this was just the tip of the iceberg, but I won't spoil it if you haven't seen the movie. Let's just say, Nick doesn't act like the model employee he would be if he had a boss who gave great service to his employees.

I have watched leaders who behaved much like Mr. Harken, watching every minute. In a school setting, there are times when we need our staff to stay longer than their work schedule or union contract permits. During a parent-teacher meeting after school, you don't ask your teacher to abruptly stop the parent when they are talking and say, "My time is up." Sometimes you need your administrative assistant to stay a little late to help you prepare for an important meeting. I have found that the closer you watch employees' minutes, the closer they watch the minutes they give you.

On the other hand, I have found that, if you are flexible with your employees' minutes, they will usually give you extra *hours*. This does not mean you will never have to confront someone who

> *The Paradoxical Commandments*
> **People are illogical, unreasonable, and self-centered.**
> *Love them anyway.*
> **If you do good, people will accuse you of selfish ulterior motives.**
> *Do good anyway.*
> **People really need help but may attack you if you do help them.**
> *Help people anyway.*
> —Dr. Kent M. Keith[125]

may take advantage of you, but I have found these confrontations to be very rare. After all, the threat of going back to watch time is all you need to encourage these employees to straighten up.

I've found that the vast majority of employees don't know what a good boss even looks like. They assume that breathing down their necks, chastising them for taking too long a break, or just generally being an unpleasant person to be around are normal, acceptable parts of "bosses being bosses." As you can see from the above data and from the Leadership concept, this model of the mean boss, the Office Linebacker boss, simply doesn't cut it in the real world. Whether we are talking about a corporate workplace or a public school, having a boss who cares about their well-being is vital to employees' motivation to do their jobs well and even to their overall health.

How the Boss Can Give Great Customer Service

So how does someone go from being a "horrible boss" to a leader who inspires employees to go the extra mile for them? It starts with having the right attitude. You can probably tell I'm about to talk about customer service. Well, you're right! The mentality that leaders must have toward customers extends to employees too. When we think about employee interactions with horrible bosses, then switch out the employee for a customer, we can see very clearly that it's a failing business model. You'll never walk into an Apple store and get tackled for touching their expensive devices with greasy hands. In the same way, you won't see Apple managers giving poor service to their employees. They know that when it comes to how they treat people, customers and employees are no different.

A great way to practice this mentality is by periodically walking around your school, pretending your employees are actually customers. Walk up to them, greet them, listen to them, care about what they have to say (whatever that may be!), and try to make their experience in the school more enjoyable. If they have a complaint, actually consider it, instead of dismissing it or saying you don't have time to deal with it. Likely, you don't have time to deal with it, but the best leaders at the best companies *make* time to deal with their employees' issues because they know that without happy employees, the company suffers.

> "Communicate downward to subordinates with at least the same care and attention as you communicate upward to superiors." —L.B. Belker[126]

When it comes to giving great service to employees, you don't have to break the bank or devote a whole day of your time. Sometimes, it's just that little extra that makes them feel appreciated and special. Below are some ideas that leaders can use to show employees they care about them.

- Attend major events in the lives of direct reports. Giving up nights and weekends for employees' funerals and weddings is the price you pay for being a leader. If you do not believe this is important, or you can't make this sacrifice, leadership is not for you.
- Something as simple as a handwritten personal note goes a long way with one's staff. Try to personalize the note as much as possible.

- Find out the favorite morning beverages of all your administrative assistants. If I'm out and purchase myself something to drink, I buy my administrative assistants their favorite drinks.
- Personally cook for your staff. The staff will appreciate that you used your personal time for them. I remember one cold winter day when many of my teachers were sick. I put on an apron and made chicken noodle soup for them. Our school administrative assistant went on the P.A. and announced that any staff members who would like a bowl of chicken soup could come get it throughout the day, courtesy of the principal. Many of my employees appreciated the gesture.
- Spend personal time with your staff—take them to lunch and just talk.
- Be flexible with time.
- Personally say hi to every staff member every day. It can be a tall task, but it's a great one to strive toward and one that no matter how far you end up from that goal, you're still doing more than a lot of administrators. You may actually save time by doing this, as you will learn about issues before they become a crisis.
- Be one of the hardest workers and always be one of the last to leave your school. Any school leader could go into her office, shut the door, and do paperwork all day. **Perception is reality** in customer service, and a shut door actually says, "I am too busy for you."
- Love your job and have fun!

Keep in mind, you're giving great service to employees "just because," not as a reward for doing things right. It's important to have these "just because" acts, as they will show employees that you truly care about their well-being and that your actions are not merely a result of them doing their jobs to your satisfaction. Praising and rewarding is a cause-and-effect model, whereas giving great service to employees—these "just because" actions—should have no direct cause and should ask nothing of employees in return (like asking them to put money in to help cover costs or asking them to work harder or longer because you did something nice for them). *It is important to remember not to hold it over your employees that you did something good for them.* Not only does that turn it into a cause-and-effect model (you've pre-rewarded them for future great work), but it will also take the specialness away from what you did and may even make employees feel manipulated due to your ulterior motives. That is not the positive work environment you want to create!

Work Environment

Speaking of creating a positive work environment, that is the second aspect of giving great service to employees. Beyond the leader's direct interactions with staff, there is a lot that leaders can do to make sure employees' basic needs are met so they can be motivated to do their very best work.

Have you ever walked into a business as a customer and noticed that it was a toxic work environment? You could feel the tension in the employees: no smiles on their faces or in their voices, not doing their jobs with any heart or enthusiasm, shouting or arguing with other employees or customers. Who wants to shop there, let alone work there? Leadership has not done its job in creating a positive work environment, so employees are not held to any standards.

On the other side are business leaders who create a work environment where employees feel cared about and thus motivated to work hard. In fact, the best companies are realizing the importance of having a desirable workplace that goes beyond competitive salaries and a great name to put on a résumé.

It's no surprise that millennials are driving this trend. They are looking for a different workplace than their parents and grandparents had and quality of life is at the top of their list. For example, young workers are saying no to working in a cubicle for eight to twelve hours straight with only bathroom breaks in favor of positions that allow them to do the same work from home. Top leaders in the business field are thinking outside the box about what makes a company a good place to work and how they can attract the very best candidates.

The gold standard in work environment is Google. In 2015, Forbes magazine ranked Google the best employer in America (and runner up in 2016 and 2017).[127,128,129] Not too shabby. So what do they do differently than other companies?

Employees at Google can take a nap in one of the many nap pods scattered across the Google campus. But it doesn't end there. In fact, the word campus is a great way to describe the Google workplace. Giving more of a college vibe than a work vibe, the Googleplex in Mountain View, California, offers employees a divergent experience from the typical cloistered corporate environment.

The Googleplex offers employees free laundry, three gourmet meals a day, yoga classes, massages, haircuts, parks and trails to walk, bike, or bring their dogs. The campus includes foosball and Ping-Pong tables, swimming pools, volleyball courts, a bowling alley, and over a dozen cafeterias.[130] They've taken the most important aspects of life for their employees and put them in the workplace. One look at the workers on their campus proves just how much Google has nailed employee happiness in the workplace.

> "If this is what being an intern feels like, I'd love to be an intern for the rest of my life."
> —Google intern[131]

Since 2000, the American Psychological Association has rewarded companies that promote healthy workplaces. They run an annual Best Practices Honors program that recognizes ten organizations, nationwide, that stand out in terms of employee involvement, work-life balance, employee growth and development, health and safety, and employee recognition. Russ Newman, APA's executive director for professional practice, says, "Many organizations are struggling to stem the forces that are whittling away at their employees' morale, productivity, and health. These Best Practices honorees are setting an example by creating strong, vibrant organizational cultures that contribute to both employee health and well-being and the company's bottom line."[132]

Don't Underestimate the Power of Fun

Some leaders believe that there is no room in the workplace for fun. Work is called work for a reason, right? Well, more and more companies are seeing the value of having a fun workplace. One reason is that it attracts better quality employees. As we mentioned in the Hiring concept, when a person applies for a job, the candidates are not the only ones deciding if the position is a good fit or not. The best candidates need to be wooed and one way to do so is by showing them that the work environment at your organization is fun.

Another value of having an enjoyable workplace is that it gets the right people on the company's team. Remember Southwest Airlines' philosophy of hiring attitude and training skills from the Hiring concept? That's what I'm talking about here. People who are naturally fun bring that enthusiasm to the workplace, and when the workplace encourages, rather than discourages, employees outwardly showing

> "If you want to bust a culture . . . Have fun in meetings that aren't supposed to be fun."
> —Gruenert and Whitaker[133]

their playful sides, morale and motivation improve. One great example where this idea plays out (no pun intended) is at the world famous Pike Place Fish Market in Seattle, Washington.

At Pike Place Fish Market, the workers there, called fishmongers or mongers for short, have realized that the shortest distance from point A to point B is through the air. And that's exactly what happens. Throughout the day you'll find them tossing fish to one another and even to patrons. When one monger is about to toss to another monger, he holds the fish up and those around chant "heeeey" until the fish soars through the air, and once it lands in the other monger's hands they shout "ahh!" like at the kickoff at a football game. It's a sight to see and both the customers and employees love it. This "flying fish" idea is what makes them unique, but it's also what makes employees love working there. Walking through the marketplace, you'll see employees laughing with each other, smiling and talking to customers as if they're old friends, being present when they are taking orders, and generally trying to brighten their customers' days.[134]

They're so inspirational, customer service icons Southwest Airlines use the *FiSH!* training video, based on the Pike Place Fish Market.[135] But it doesn't stop at videos. There are corporate trainings on "fish culture" too. They even offer a training specifically for schools.

FiSH! creator John Christensen relayed his "aha!" moment, which occurred when he took his three-year-old to the pediatrician. He was greeted with lackluster service from the receptionist and the nurse, then sat in a cold, sterile exam room. He said, "I thought: There's more love, more sense of being cared for, in a fish market than here—and if the fishmongers can do it in a cold, smelly work environment . . . why can't we do it in teaching, in ministry, in offices?"[136]

Good question. With the right employees and leadership who are committed to customer service, I've found that it is possible, by embracing the fun, playful side of work like at Pike Place Fish Market. You can even see for yourself on their live-streaming webcams, featured on their website!

School Culture

How can we incorporate giving great service to employees into public schools? I don't know about your school, but our school board would not approve a foosball table for the teachers'

lounge. Maybe we can't re-create the Googleplex college-esque
campus in our public schools, but
here's what we can do: we can
take the lessons we've learned
from companies like Google and
the Pike Place Fish Market and
re-create their *culture* in our schools.

> **Supreme Court Justice Potter Stewart, in a landmark pornography case in 1964, said that although he could not define pornography, "I know it when I see it."[137]**

"School culture" is the identity of the school. Dr. Kent D. Peterson, a professor in the Department of Educational Administration at the University of Wisconsin-Madison, defines school culture as "the set of norms, values and beliefs, rituals and ceremonies, symbols and stories that make up the 'persona' of the school."[138] School culture is a major customer service issue, so an infestation of negativity

> **"Culture is a social narcotic to which practically all of us are addicted. We feel good when we belong to a group." —Gruenert and Whitaker, *School Culture Rewired*[139]**

can keep a great school from meeting its potential. Whether we are talking about fighting amongst each other or simply apathy toward being at the school, negativity—even in small amounts—creates huge obstacles to success.

Have you ever worked in a place where people were always complaining about the boss or the work? That's a culture problem and it's contagious. Luckily a positive work environment is just as contagious and a whole lot more enjoyable for everyone, including your customers.

> **"The research is clear; being positive results in more resilient, adaptable and successful people and organizations. Furthermore, the research is also clear that positivity is contagious." —Shawn Achor, founder of "Orange Frog"[140]**

Shawn Achor's "Orange Frog" is a system that allows leaders to create a paradigm shift within their organization, transforming the dull, uninspired workplace into a positive, motivational one. In his book, *The Happiness Advantage*, Achor says,

> Conventional wisdom holds that if we work hard we will be more successful, and if we are more successful, *then* we'll be happy. If we can just find that great job, win that next promotion, lose those five pounds, happiness will follow. But recent discoveries in the field of positive psychology have shown that this formula is actually backward: Happiness *fuels* success, not the other way around. When we are positive, our brains become more engaged, creative, motivated, energetic, resilient, and productive at work. This isn't just an empty mantra. This discovery has been repeatedly borne out by rigorous research in psychology and neuroscience, management studies, and the bottom lines of organizations around the globe.[141]

I use Orange Frog as part of my staff training. I've found that this method creates buy-in with staff and positively contributes to school culture. In my experience, having a great school culture is the best way to recruit and retain school staff. But the benefits of having a positive school culture go beyond staff retention.

You may have heard this phrase before: culture trumps strategy. If your school isn't putting in the work to create a positive learning and working environment, all other school improvement initiatives will only be marginally successful.

Dr. Bill Daggett studied the best schools in the country. He found that, "The top 1% of these high achieving schools had a school culture that was noticeable when you walked in; you knew right away you were in a school with a strong culture based on respectful relationships."[143] So when it

> Traditional public schools don't command vast loyalty. If cost and location were not issues, just one-third of parents say they'd pick a traditional public school over a private school (31%), public charter school (17%), or a religious school (14%).—PDK Poll[142]

comes to improving student achievement, school culture must be a major part of that discussion.

Employees Giving Great Service to Each Other

Employees need to receive great customer service from their employer and to work in an environment where they feel comfortable, but to round out the picture and go from a good workplace to a great workplace, employees need to also *give* great service to each other. Yes, it seems there is no escaping the golden rule, and it's the final piece of the great work environment puzzle.

So what does giving great service to each other look like in a public school? It can be anything from smiling and saying hello to coworkers to planning a surprise birthday party for someone. I'd like to tell the story of a rose ceremony so emotional it would give the TV show *The Bachelor* a run for its money.

> For more ways staff can give great service to one another, consult "Giving Great Service Up and Down the Organizational Chart" in the Appendix.

As a principal, I inherited staff members that were fighting amongst themselves and creating a negative school culture. There was a lot of mistrust toward administration and between teachers. I called a meeting with my teachers and brought two-dozen roses. After everyone sat down and got settled, I said, "Let's talk about gratitude." I could see their faces twist up and their eyes roll. The last thing they wanted to do was be grateful; they wanted to complain! But I pushed on and said, "I want you to think of one person who's really helped you or done something really nice for you. Maybe you didn't tell them, so here is your opportunity to do that. Come up here, get a rose, and give it to that person and thank them for what they did.

At first, everyone just sat there. Eventually, hands went up around the room. It turns out, they all wanted to make things right among themselves. They just needed a kick-start.

As soon as one rose ceremony ended, I would say, "Next" and

all hands went up at the same time! After running out of roses, several teachers wanted to stay and say a few words of gratitude even without the roses. I even joined in and gave a rose myself. By the time we were done, there was not a dry eye in the room. I had just witnessed my teachers go from crossed arms and frowning faces moments before to crying and hugging each other. It truly brought us all together and improved the school culture afterward.

While this is a very powerful and effective example of employees giving great service to each other, there are many quicker, less grandiose ways to get employees to start executing the golden rule in school. Be creative and you may be amazed at how much your staff comes together over appreciating one another.

Final Thoughts on Giving Great Service to Employees

A leader who has his or her finger on the pulse of employees and is willing to think outside the box (think YUM! Hall of Champions) can really make a difference in employee attitude, work ethic, and overall positivity within the school culture. The best part is that, contrary to popular belief, you don't need to raise salaries to improve school culture. You just need a commitment to giving great service and some creativity. I believe this is especially true with public schools.

Once you start making it your daily goal to give great service to employees, you'll notice the infectiousness of that positivity on staff and students. Doing something like having school leaders sing the school announcements at the end of the day can raise morale by injecting some lightheartedness into the school culture. I have seen one school leader breakdance in front of all the students and teachers. While I have neither the skill nor the will to try that, it made everyone's face light up. As Justice Potter Stewart said about pornography, I will say about having a fun, productive workplace; I may not be able to define it, but I will know it when I see it!

CONCEPT 13

Give a Little Bit Extra

Lagniappe: (lan-yap)
noun
1. *Chiefly Southern Louisiana and Southeast Texas:* a
   small gift given with a purchase to a customer, by
   way of compliment or for good measure; bonus.[144]

I love using this term in my presentations to schools. Lagniappe is a very localized, regional word, but it is so fitting when talking about customer service. Giving a little bit extra is one of the cornerstones of business that ensures customers leave happy. Lagniappe is getting two cherries on top of your sundae. It's a website giving you free or expedited shipping. It's the doughnut shop throwing in an extra doughnut into your dozen-box. Anytime a person or company providing a service to a customer gives more than the person paid for, that's an example of lagniappe.

A Teacher Who Gave a Little Extra

I consider home visits an example of giving a little extra. My favorite home visit story, submitted by one of my excellent teachers, Kim Bryant, is an example of a teacher truly going the extra mile for her customers. Here's her story.

First, I went up a very narrow road to a house sitting up on a hill. The roof was caving in with a tarp covering the places where it was leaking. Out in the yard, five boys were racing on big wheels down the hill, just barely stopping before crashing down into a creek. They were having a blast. Mom came out of the house with a baby on her hip, two female Walker coonhounds at her heels and their twenty-six pups scurrying everywhere! After talking to Mom for a while and giving her the class list, supply list, and welcome letter, I went over to talk to the boys. Soon, I found out, two of the five boys were going to be in my class; they were cousins and lived close to one another.

One of the boys asked me if I wanted to race on the big wheel. Another boy replied, "She won't race down the hill, she is a teacher. She won't do it!" The boys began to argue about teachers and how they wouldn't do anything as daring as racing down a steep hill, on a big wheel toward a steep ravine full of jagged rocks.

I had looked at the cards for their last year's teacher before my visit to their home. Both boys had the reputation for being trouble-makers and being hard to handle. I knew this was my chance. "Sure, I don't want you guys to have all of the fun. Which big wheel do I get and who is brave enough to race me?" I asked them.

After a brief silence with stunned faces, the boys began yelling, "Me, me!" Shortly, I found myself racing down a steep hill, bottom bouncing up in the air, back aching, heart beating out of my chest, and looking at the sharp rocks ahead of me sticking up out of the steep ravine at the bottom. With cheers behind me, I slid sideways into a "big wheel doughnut," inches from certain death. I jumped from my big wheel, celebrating my victory. I MADE IT! I actually did not get killed and, best of all, I had won the race. All five boys came jumping and cheering to me with high-fives. They yelled, "Ms. Bryant, you won! That was sweet! Did you see her go?"

To this day, I have never had a bit of trouble from either boy. They work hard, always treat me with respect and even ask, "Ms. Bryant, when are you gonna come over and play again?" They are always eager to tell me about the new litters of puppies up for adoption. Who knows, I may end up with my very own coonhound from this unlikely bonding experience!

I love when my teachers are willing to take any opportunity presented to them in order to forge relationships with students. It shows a desire to go the extra mile for our customers. When Ms. Bryant told me this story I instantly knew it was one for the books (particularly this one!).

The Danger of Treading Water

On the other side of the coin, there's a business term for a company that isn't underperforming but also isn't wowing customers. It's called treading water. We all know a company with which we do business solely because of convenience or familiarity. We stand in line or walk the aisles in a state of semi-loathing, noticing all the little details that they can't seem to ever get right. Whether it's a fleet of shopping carts that all veer to the side or have one bad wheel, unswept floors, or rude, indifferent staff, these companies consistently underwhelm and underperform and, thus, are just treading water.

A friend recently bought a four-pack of fresh apple cider doughnuts from her supermarket's bakery department. As she ate, she looked at the nutrition information, which read: "Serving Size: one doughnut. Servings per Container: 6." Puzzled, she went back to the store and asked a salesclerk why it said there were six servings in the box when there were only four doughnuts. He said he had no idea and shrugged her off.

Unsatisfied, she went back to the display where she had purchased the doughnuts the day before, only to find the same display now had six-packs of doughnuts instead and were priced the same as her four-pack. Needless to say, she was furious about her package needing fifty percent more doughnuts! This company is clearly treading water with their service. Making a mistake like this and not correcting it before it got in the hands of customers was a managerial oversight. The fact that the person in charge of packaging the product didn't put in the correct amount was even worse. The nail in the coffin here was the employee not immediately fixing the issue when asked by a customer. No problem this large should be swept under the rug.

Let's face it, treading water doesn't work. Recall the "bare minimum" example from *Office Space* earlier in the book? When workers are just squeaking by, the whole organization suffers. Conversely, when workers chip in a little extra, like Ms. Bryant and her big wheel race, customers notice the difference. Whether we are talking about Fortune 500 companies or public schools, the concept of giving a little bit extra separates those offering great customer service from those simply treading water.

The Thirteenth Doughnut of Customer Service

As leaders, when it comes to how much we give, we want to be on the plus end of service by giving the baker's dozen, not shortchanging our customers by leaving them fifty percent short. I call this "giving the thirteenth doughnut." You don't have to be Homer Simpson to crave getting this extra doughnut. We all want to get that great, over-the-top service. In fact, the thirteenh doughnut may be more important than you think.

In JD Power's book *Satisfaction: How Every Great Company Listens to the Voice of the Customer*, customers were asked which companies they rave about and which they gripe about and why. The study found that going above and beyond what was expected was the most important factor in a person raving about a company. In fact, nearly fifty percent of these raving responses were rooted in the company giving "above and beyond service." Furthermore, customers who griped about a company did so because they felt that companies were trying to "maximize short-term profit potential of a transaction at the expense of customer satisfaction."[146] In other words, the company was cutting corners. That's a big no-no in my book! But you already know that.

Customers are more perceptive than many business leaders think. Many customers realize what the standard of service is for the particular business or industry that they are dealing with, and can see when they're getting a little bit more or being short-changed.

Back in the Forge Relationships with the Customers concept, I mentioned how I go to the same Waffle House all the time and my usual waitress brings me Splenda from the McDonald's across the street. That's a great example of giving a little bit extra, and one that we can easily see is above and beyond the call of duty. The waitress could have continued to let me pick from the sweeteners they have, but she chose to go a step further and offer me the best possible customer service. It also made me a loyal customer. Who doesn't love feeling like they're getting special treatment?

> "If a man is called to be a street sweeper, he should sweep streets even as a Michelangelo painted, or Beethoven composed music or Shakespeare wrote poetry. He should sweep streets so well that all the hosts of heaven and earth will pause to say, 'Here lived a great street sweeper who did his job well.'"
> —Martin Luther King Jr.[145]

School Staff Giving the Thirteenth Doughnut

Just like customers in the business world, students recognize when adults do a little bit extra for them or go beyond the call of duty. I remember a story from my high school days. I was on the tennis team and preparing for a very important tennis match. My physical education teacher, Coach Cook, knew about this important tennis match and offered to hit tennis balls to me during his planning period.

We ended up practicing all week during fifth period. I would go on to win the big match with Coach Cook in the stands, cheering me on to victory. To this day, I have the highest regard for Coach Cook and would be there in a minute if he ever needed my help. It was that little bit of his own time that he was willing to give me that was above and beyond his job description and meant so much to me. Even though Coach Cook knew very little about tennis, he did what he could to help me.

That wasn't the only time an adult gave me the gift of extra time. As a senior, I was able to take college English and high school English at the same time. My high school English teacher, Diane Ledford, helped me with the difficult college English class. Ms. Ledford seemed to take great pride in red marking the grammatical mistakes on my papers each night for both classes.

When I completed my first book, *Who Cares?*, I called Ms. Ledford and sent her a copy. I could tell she was both excited for me and surprised that I would ever produce a book! As fate would have it, I ended up being associate superintendent in her district during her last few years as a teacher. Ms. Ledford and I would laugh as she warned teachers, "You better be nice to your students as they might return to be your boss someday!" Thanks again Ms. Ledford for going above and beyond and taking my college papers home each night to help me get through college English. Without your help, I never would have tried writing.

Over the years, I've heard many stories like these from both students and coworkers. In fact, as administrators, when we think back to our favorite teacher or employee at school, chances are we are thinking about a time when they went above and beyond to give a little extra instead of just routine interactions. It really does just take one adult giving a little bit extra to make a difference with a student.

Fred The Mailman

In Mark Sanborn's book, *The Fred Factor*, he shares the true story of his mailman, Fred Shea. Fred goes above and beyond the call of duty by getting to know his customers and watching over their mail and their homes.[147] Some may describe being a mailman as monotonous or boring, but Fred sees it as a way to make a difference in the lives of his customers. He takes pleasure in seeing the surprise on the faces of those he serves as he gives a little extra compared to the typical mailman. When he was asked what moti-

Here are a few examples of public school staff giving the thirteenth doughnut:

- Teachers eating lunch with students even though by Kentucky law they are entitled to a duty-free lunch
- Teachers visiting students' homes to get to know them and their families
- Coaches getting paid next to nothing to coach after school
- Staff volunteering to tutor students after school or on weekends
- Staff bringing in extra clothes or coats for students
- Staff cooking meals or desserts for students
- Staff taking extra time to talk with students after school
- Staff truly getting to know students and take an interest in them
- School leaders being there in tough times such as funerals, death in families, divorce, etc.
- Teachers attending students' special events after school or on weekends
- Teachers packing snacks for hungry kids over the weekend
- Staff greeting kids at the front entrance and holding umbrellas on rainy days for them
- Teachers giving up parking spots for Grandparents' Day
- A school employee helping a parent change a flat tire
- Cafeteria managers letting students sample and decide on new foods for the cafeteria menu
- Any staff member seeing someone in person instead of using email or phone

vates him to go above and beyond, Fred gave this simple, powerful statement: "The impact you have on others is the reward."

Going Above and Beyond in the Business World

My favorite example of giving a little bit extra comes from *The Simple Truths of Service,* by Ken Blanchard and Barbara Glanz, about a grocery store employee. "Johnny the Bagger" is the true story of a teenager with Down Syndrome who takes it upon himself to brighten customers' days.[149] Johnny would bag each customer's groceries and, at the end, place a piece of paper into their bag with his "Thought for the Day" on it—an inspirational quote or interesting saying.

Pretty soon, customers would refuse to go through any other line but Johnny's in order to receive his "Thought for the Day." This way of giving a little bit extra spilled over to other departments, as the floral department started to take the broken flowers that could not be used for arrangements and pin them on elderly women and young girls.

Johnny inspired his customers to become fiercely loyal to his line and to his store, while demonstrating to his fellow employees that giving a little bit extra makes customers feel special. When one employee can inspire other employees or even the entire organi-

> "A sad employee left his job of many years
> Most days he worked were like the day before
> He wasn't disliked by colleagues, but he won't be missed
> And while he made good money, he felt quite poor.
>
> He always did what he was paid to do and nothing more
> And he did without having any fun.
> He performed his job the way he lived his life:
> He did it the way it had always been done."
> —Mark Sanborn, *The Fred Factor*[148]

zation, you know you've nailed customer service. As I mentioned earlier in the Give Great Service to Employees concept, this kind of positivity is infectious and can really energize school culture.

Ken Blanchard was hired to do the customer service training for frontline employees for the inaugural season of Petco Park, the baseball stadium for the San Diego Padres.[150] Before the games each night, managers would ask employees if they were "going to be a Johnny tonight." That season, Petco Park received 7,500 letters from fans raving about the service they received at the park! When leaders can motivate employees to give a little bit extra on as large a scale as this, great service is bound to happen.

Final Thoughts on Giving a Little Bit Extra

So why don't we see more public school employees going above and beyond the call of duty? I think it's because school administrators look at these as business concepts, not public school concepts. This is a mistake! Nobody talks about this concept. Nobody learns this concept in their schools of education; thus, nobody promotes it or enforces it. While some public school employees practice this concept, without involvement and commitment from the highest levels of leadership, a little extra will generally be given by only those select few employees.

Just as Johnny the Bagger influenced other employees and changed the entire culture of his company, I've found that when public schools make a group effort to give a little bit extra, it can change the entire school culture for the better. Every time your employees interact with a customer they should be thinking, "How can I give a little bit extra? How can I surprise and wow them?" Just imagine an entire school focused on these customer service concepts. Imagine a superintendent who goes above and beyond with the school board members. Imagine a school where a principal gives lagniappe to his staff and all the teachers try to be like Johnny the Bagger by giving a little bit extra to the students and parents. What about bus drivers, cooks, and custodians constantly thinking about how they can wow staff and students with the concept of giving extra? Consider giving "Johnny the Bagger" or "Fred the Mailman" awards to staff for giving service that goes above and beyond the call of duty.

As I've said throughout this book, public schools need to give great service in order to retain their students. Just like in the business world, it's the bells and whistles of customer service that keep students happy and coming back year after year. Let's face it, other schooling options are already doing this, so giving a little bit extra keeps public schools competitive with the status quo of twenty-first century education. With everyone pitching in and going above and beyond the call of duty, students will feel welcomed and special. Shouldn't this be the mission of every staff member every day?

CONCEPT 14

Under-Promise, Over-Deliver

"The best way to keep one's word is to not give it."
– Napoleon Bonaparte[151]

In an episode of the television show *Seinfeld*, Jerry and Elaine go to a car rental company to pick up a car.[152] When it is their turn, the woman behind the counter says they don't have the midsize car that Jerry reserved. Stupified, Jerry says, "I don't understand. I made a reservation. Do you have my reservation?"

She replies, "Yes we do. Unfortunately, we ran out of cars."

"But the reservation keeps the car here. That's why you have the reservation," Jerry says.

"I know why we have reservations," she replies, defensively.

"I don't think you do," Jerry says. "If you did, I'd have a car. See you know how to *take* the reservation, you just don't know how to *hold* the reservation. And that's really the most important part of the reservation: the holding. Anybody can just take 'em," he says, grabbing at imaginary reservations in the air.

After talking to her supervisor, she says there's nothing they can do. She offers him a compact car—certainly not what Jerry had asked for—and he reluctantly takes it. When asked if he'd like to purchase the insurance for the car, still fuming, he says, "Yeah, you'd better give me the insurance because I'm gonna beat the hell outta this thing!"

Nothing spoils a vacation quite like an unforeseen problem. What makes it worse is when it's a result of poor customer service. Unfortunately for Jerry, the car rental company in this example didn't get the memo about the art of under-promising and over-delivering.

Under-promise, over-deliver means that when you tell a customer what you are going to do, you surprise them by doing more. In this example, Jerry got a downgrade, which is less than what he expected. What they *should* be doing is giving him a free upgrade to a better car. In this way, they would be over-delivering on their promise of the midsize car.

At the heart of it, this concept is about expectations. Research shows that our enjoyment of something depends more on what we expect than what objectively happens.

A study conducted at the University College of London had twenty-six subjects repeatedly performing a task in which they were told that a positive financial outcome was either probable or unlikely.[153] Every few rounds, they were asked how happy they were in that moment. The study found that, "Ultimately . . . it was not the amount of total money or points won that mattered—it was how winning or losing stacked up to expectations." In other words, the subjects who beat the odds and won a nominal amount of money were happier than those who won the same amount of money but were told they would likely win a larger amount. The study concluded that, "Happiness depends not on how well things are going, but whether things are going better or worse than expected."

The practice of under-promise, over-deliver hinges on these expectations. If a day exceeds our expectations, we are happy; if it doesn't meet our expectations we are angry. So as a service provider, it is our job to ensure that we exceed our customers' expectations every day!

This concept is similar to the last concept, but differs in one key way. Giving a little bit extra is an effort to put a cherry on top, whereas under-promise, over-deliver is purposely setting the bar lower so that your customer's expectations are exceeded. The outcome for the customer may be the same—surprisingly great customer service—but the actions and ideas behind the outcome are different. They're two sides of the same customer service coin.

Examples and Counterexamples of Under-Promise, Over-Deliver

The *Seinfeld* example above is a classic case of *over*-promise and *under*-deliver, which can agitate our customers and turn them against us. I'll talk more about counterexamples of this concept later. Sticking with cars for a moment, one great example of under-promise, over-deliver that people may be familiar with is the car repair shop. We all know that having your car in the shop is a major project. Getting around can be a big pain without your trusty automobile. Great car repair shops know this and set you up to be pleasantly surprised. When they think a job is going to take a day or two max, they tell you it will take three to four days. Thus, when you receive a phone call forty-eight hours later that your car is ready to be picked up, you are filled with the excitement of getting a good surprise.

When a company decides to under-promise and over-deliver, there are a number of advantages. The first is that, when they deliver the finished product early, it pleases the customer, and the customer will speak well of the company in the future. Secondly, in the event that there is a problem or hiccup in the process, the company has a built in buffer, and it doesn't need to panic. In the example above, if they cannot get the part as quickly as anticipated, they might not be able to deliver by their internal target date of forty-eight hours, but the consumer will get the car in the four days it was promised and never be the wiser.

Not only does incorporating this concept help the mechanics get customers to keep coming back, but it also cuts down on headaches for them. The last thing they want is for people to come in three days later to pick up the car that was promised in twenty-four hours. Those customers are rightly fuming and will certainly give the mechanic a piece of their minds! Plus, they'll walk away with a bad taste in their mouths and no business wants that. For all of these reasons, under-promising, over-delivering is a true customer service expert's secret weapon.

Speaking of weapons, I always loved when Captain Kirk from *Star Trek* would command, "Fire photon torpedoes!" Those moments of suspense right afterward kept me on the edge of my seat. The crew of the Starship *Enterprise* taught me many life lessons. In fact, Scotty, the ship mechanic, knew a thing or two about under-promising, over-delivering. Here's a scene from an episode of *Star Trek: The Next Generation*:

Lt. Commander Geordi La Forge: Look, Mr. Scott, I'd love to explain everything to you, but the Captain wants this spectrographic analysis done by 1300 hours.

Lt. Commander Montgomery "Scotty" Scott: Do you mind a little advice? Starfleet captains are like children. They want everything right now and they want it their way. But the secret is to give them only what they need, not what they want.

Smart restaurant managers know that, if they are sure they can get you a table in fifteen minutes, they will tell you the wait will be thirty minutes so you'll be pleasantly surprised at how "fast" you got a table.

La Forge: Yeah, well, I told the Captain I'd have this analysis done in an hour.

Scotty: How long will it really take?

La Forge: An hour!

Scotty: Oh, you didn't tell him how long it would *really* take, did ya?

La Forge: Well, of course I did.

Scotty: Oh, laddie. You've got a lot to learn if you want people to think of you as a miracle worker.[154]

A miracle worker . . . that's a great name for someone who can consistently deliver ahead of schedule. I'll talk more about "miracle workers" later in the chapter.

We all know what it's like to be disappointed about a product or service. Whether it's a friend saying something is "the best ever," when, even if it's truly great, it cannot live up to the hype, or being told by a restaurant your wait will be ten to fifteen minutes and ends up being half an hour. Falling short of expectations is a sure way to ruin a person's day. These are counterexamples of under-promise, over-deliver. Here are a few instances where companies fall short of expectations:

- Hotels or resorts that look beautiful online and in brochures, but when you get there the rooms are smaller, the facilities are old, and the pool is closed. Talk about a let down!
- Commercials and the entertainment industry hyping a movie to the point, that when you go see it, you are expecting something amazing, and it is only okay or all the good parts were in the trailer.
- Airlines. They're a constant over-promise, under-deliver industry. With cancelled flights, late flights, having to check bags you don't want to check, lost luggage, gate changes, (the list goes on), they could stand to learn how to meet and exceed customer expectations. Hey, the bar's already pretty low!

Remember back in the Plan and Reflect concept when I shared a story about Arby's, the famous roast beef restaurant, being out of roast beef? That's a great counterexample; they were *over*-promising and *under*-delivering. It represents a form of under-delivering where the status quo isn't met. Arby's doesn't explicitly say they will always have roast beef, but one can reasonably assume that a place like Arby's would never ever run out of its flagship food — that would be like Starbucks running out of coffee! So when the status quo isn't kept, our expectations fall short of reality and we are faced with a company that has just under-delivered.

A few examples of this are the ATM being out of order, any business where you go for essentials (like a grocery store or bank) closing early, your cable or internet service going out, or the credit card machine being down at a store. Failure to meet the status quo is a very annoying form of under-delivering that companies truly must make every effort to avoid.

Counterexamples in Public Education

One day our cafeteria ran out of buns for hamburgers for the students in the last lunch period. The manager told the students he could give them a hot dog bun. The students smiled and took the hot dog buns. Later, a picture ended up on social media with the hot dog bun beside the hamburger. The caption read, "This is how we are treated in this school system." When we do not meet normal expectations we are actually over-promising and under-delivering. Here are a few more examples of under-delivering in public education:

1. The cafeteria running out of some of the students' favorite foods so that the last lunch period does not get to eat those foods
2. Schools not answering their telephones or having incompetent, rude people on the other line
3. Dirty classrooms: graffiti on desks, not well-lit, etc.
4. Teachers not grading classwork by the date they said they would or giving just a check mark on papers without any specific feedback
5. Restroom stalls without doors for privacy
6. Schools or classrooms that are too hot or cold
7. Teachers and leaders who tell students they'll do something but never follow through

8. Students who get on a school bus without a place to sit
9. Parents and students attending an event with a very poor sound system, dirty restrooms, or uncomfortable or insufficient seating

Being a "Miracle Worker" in Public Education

Public education can benefit from looking at the examples and counterexamples in this chapter to ensure that we are meeting or exceeding our customers' expectations. As you can see from the University College of London study, those happy moments come when people are pleasantly surprised. I've found that in our public schools, students, families, and community members are consistently underwhelmed by their experience with the schools. We can change these experiences by purposely telling our customers that something will take longer or be less impressive than in reality. Thus, when we deliver in less time they are pleasantly surprised, while at the same time making us look like miracle workers.

One of my favorite under-promise, over-deliver methods is having my administrative assistants tell callers that I will get back to them in two to three days. I have them say this because while my internal goal is to get back to callers within twenty-four hours, I always get back to people within two days, ensuring that their expectations are met. Either way, the response time certainly exceeds callers' expectations. Hearing back from me so much sooner than they thought not only leaves a positive impression on them, but it also works to diffuse some of their anger or disappointment if they happen to be calling with a problem or complaint.

I tell my staff to practice under-promise, over-deliver and have seen some truly inspiring and creative takes on this concept. One involved a teacher who had planned a wonderful class trip to the railroad museum. He thought that the students would really enjoy the trip, but was careful not to oversell it. When he told them what they would see, he spoke matter-of-factly and did not mention the cross-section of a locomotive that people could climb in and the steam engine demonstration, focusing solely on the more mundane things.

On the bus ride home from the trip, the teacher overheard the students talking about how cool the museum was, some even stating that they would like to come back and spend more time. The teacher

> "Exceeding expectations is where satisfaction ends and loyalty begins."
> —Ron Kaufman[155]

smiled, content that his under-promise, over-deliver strategy worked. He also enjoyed the positive mood that his students were in because of how pleasantly surprised they were with the field trip. And to think, he contemplated telling them it was going to be a spectacular trip, which would have surely produced a much different reaction.

Here are a few more examples of how to under-promise and over-deliver in the public school setting.

1. A coach knows he/she is supposed to have a great season, but does not promise a lot of wins.
2. The food service director promises staff and parents there will be at least four lunch choices every day, but really has six to eight choices.
3. The guidance counselor sets up a school tour for a new family; however, the principal or superintendent also shows up to welcome the new potential customers.
4. The principal or superintendent feels really good about upcoming test score results, but downplays his/her prediction.
5. The school district has a twenty-four-hour response-time rule for all employees, yet the administrative assistants have been instructed to tell everyone someone will get back to them within two days.
6. The finance department at the central office, located five

miles away from the schools, agrees to help staff members with the new insurance forms by actually going to all the schools during the day instead of having all the employees drive to the district office on their own time.

7. Staff members refer students to the office for discipline with a referral slip, but teachers complain they never know the outcome of how the discipline of the student was handled. The principal decides to not only provide the staff members with copies of the discipline referrals, but, when appropriate, has the students apologize to the staff member for inappropriate conduct.

8. A custodian tells the principal it will take several weeks to get all the floors ready for opening day and yet completes the job in one week. "A miracle worker."

9. A student or parent asks for directions from an employee and the employee walks the person or drives the person to the destination.

10. The school office helps new parents with all phases of moving into a school district, including information about water, gas and electric, important buildings in town, etc.

11. A teacher tells students their test papers will be graded by Friday, yet gives them back on Thursday, telling students he/she stayed up all night to get them finished.

12. A school leader sets the written agenda for the meeting to end at 4:00, knowing he/she will end the meeting by 3:30.

Final Thoughts on Under-Promise, Over-Deliver

As you can see from these examples, there really isn't a lot of work involved in under-promising and over-delivering. It's all in how you package information to students and families. Utilizing these tips in your school will turn mediocre events into positive experiences that will please your customers in the short term and improve school culture in the long term. What's not to love?

CONCEPT 15

Recover Well

"Apologizing does not always mean you're wrong and the other person is right. It just means you value your relationship more than your ego."
— Mark Matthews[156]

When I think about recovering well, I recall a story about someone notoriously difficult to please: my mother. I learned the importance of recovering well when I decided to spend a day Christmas shopping with my mom and dad. I was looking forward to a bit of rare "family time," and I had promised my mom that we would do anything her heart desired. The result? She wanted to go to the closest and busiest mall to return a purchase! Not the family time that I had envisioned, but it was what she wanted to do so I kept my promise.

As my parents and I circled the parking lot of the crowded mall, my mom asked my dad and me to return a shower radio to a popular department store, and said she would meet us after she picked up a couple of last-minute gifts. This should be a simple task for me to complete, and then we can move on to the next activity, right? Nope!

My dad and I waited in line, presented the bag to the young salesman, and told him that there was nothing wrong with the shower radio, but we wanted to return it. I looked in the bag for the receipt and realized it was missing. The shower radio was $9.99 but the salesman told me it was now on sale for $7.99, and that without the receipt, this lower price would be the amount my mom would be refunded. I shrugged but my dad said under his breath, that mom would not be happy about it. I reassured my dad that I would give mom the two dollar difference and she would be none the wiser. Just when I thought it would be over, the salesman counts out the refund to my dad and then the young man says to him, "The whole reason we cannot refund you the full purchase price is because without the receipt we don't know if you stole it or purchased it." Now, my dad is a big-hearted, former truck driver, who shoots from the hip with a quick wit. He looks the young man directly in the eye and says, "Son, if I was going to steal something from your store, it would be more valuable than a $9.99 shower radio. I can promise you that." He took the money and we headed to the car to meet mom.

Thinking that the event would be over and mom would be happy, she asked dad if there were any problems as he handed the money over to her. Praying that dad would just keep quiet, he looks at me and asks, "Kelly, you do all that customer service stuff ["*stuff*, right, dad!"]. What do you think about what that boy said about not giving us back all the money for that radio?" Oh no! I knew the very next thing that my mom was going to say as I edged the car onto the busy highway: One can guess the two words that came out of mom's mouth: "Turn around." Yes, we're going back to that store!

When we pulled into the parking spot, my mom was out of the car before I could put it into park. She was on a mission and she was in the right. She was going to prove a point and no one had better get in her way.

My mom entered the store and began the head-hunt for the young man who denied her the full refund. She kept looking back at me asking, "Is this him?" or "What about him?" My dad finally pointed out the young man, and when he saw us he ducked into the backroom. Mom finally located another lady and began to tell her the situation and voice her disappointment in what had occurred. The sales lady offered to give mom a ten dollar gift card and told her that is "the best we can do." It was obvious that she wanted the situation to go away and thought that her nonchalant attitude and half-hearted attempt to understand my mom's frustration would suffice. She did not know my mom! Mom went on to let her have it in the finest, good-old Kentucky fashion. Here I was thinking that she really got a great deal to have received the $7.99 *and* a ten dollar gift card, yet my mom was still not satisfied!

On our way out of the store and back to the car, mom turned to us and said, "I have been a loyal customer to that store for over thirty years and I will NEVER go back!" All this because a store employee did not know how to recover well.

I have used this story in many of my presentations because I feel it gets the message across about the importance of recovering well in even the most marginal of customer service situations. As you'll see below, it's also a reminder about how little effort is necessary to correct a mistake that may have big negative consequences.

> "Never ruin an apology with an excuse."
> — Benjamin Franklin[157]

What is Recovering Well?

We all know the old phrase "the customer is always right." While it has become something of a cliché, the idea behind it still rings true today. The best companies still practice this philosophy for several reasons. The first is customer satisfaction. When a customer has a complaint that gets resolved in their favor, that customer leaves with a smile on his or her face and is more likely to continue to patron that company. In other words, a satisfied customer is a recurring customer. But it doesn't stop there. Companies that consistently recover well inspire loyalty in their customers. That means that the customers won't just keep coming back, they will shop there exclusively. We all have a business or two that we are loyal toward. Whether it's our morning coffee shop, our favorite restaurant, or the place we go when we need laundry detergent, companies that consistently give great service have loyal customers.

Let's look at it from the other side. In the example with my mom above, we can see just how quickly a loyal customer can turn into a former customer. That one experience with a store that failed to recover well lost my mom's business forever. When it comes to recovery, a lot is riding on how a company responds to a complaint or customer service issue. The fact that we can all name at least one company that we have personally boycotted because of a bad customer service experience shows just how important recovering well is for a company.

Staying with the example above, I wonder what could have been done to make the situation go in a different direction and flip my mom to win her back. Let's begin with thinking how the case of not having the receipt began this whole situation. The young salesclerk was following policy, and I am most certain that he was doing as he was instructed. But the situation could have saved the store money and kept a loyal customer had the young man received training on good customer service practices. If so, he would have gone to a manager to ask to give the full refund. The saleswoman did offer my mom something on top of her refund, but it was too little too late, and she allowed my mom to walk away fuming instead of successfully resolving the conflict.

> "When you realize you've made a mistake, make amends immediately. It's easier to eat crow while it's still warm."
> —Dan Heist[158]

Most individuals see situations of conflict as "just a loss"; count it up and move on. I believe that the principles on recovery as set forth in the book *The One Minute Apology,* by Ken Blanchard, are a great starting point to recovering in bad customer service situations.[159] His book is very straightforward in explaining that a good apology must be: 1. Immediate, 2. Empathetic, and 3. Equal to the offense.

Many times, apologies are too little, too late. The longer an apology takes, one begins to wonder, *Why are they apologizing now?* or *I wonder what they are trying to cover up because it took him or her too long to come up with an apology.* A good example of that is the Tiger Woods infidelity accusation from November, 2009. A prepared statement addressing the situation finally appeared on

February 19, 2010.[160] It took fourteen minutes and no questions were permitted after it was issued. By that time, people were wondering why he even bothered, and it definitely appeared very insincere. Many years later, his career and popularity seem to still suffer.

Now, back to my mom. If the saleswoman had known of the one-minute apology concept and sensed that my mom was offended, she could have flipped my mom by apologizing and being sincere in the moment. Next, demonstrating empathy would be acknowledging that it was an aggravation. The manager could even share a lighthearted story about a similar situation that she may have dealt with herself. *Then, she could have allowed my mom's input in choosing an option that may have appealed to her as an alternative to remedy the situation.* This gives her some power over the problem, and we all feel better when we are contributing to the solution. To seal the deal, she could have given her a business card and told her to contact her if she ever had any problems in the store.

Now, my mom would probably never use the business card, but I know that she would brag to her friends about how she could help them should they ever have any problems at that store! People love the empowerment of having connections.

Mistakes are truly an opportunity, and I have found it is better to make mistakes and recover well than to never make mistakes at all. Most people understand that mistakes will occur. Recovering well gives us the opportunity to change a customer who may be lukewarm toward our organization into a customer who is extremely supportive. *We must see mistakes as opportunities to win favor with customers.* People will often become more loyal after a mistake if the recovery is positive and sincere.

A good versus a bad recovery is the difference between losing a loyal customer of over thirty years and impressing that customer enough to have her return the next day to spend more than her ten dollar gift card. In the business world, this is a *huge* swing. Furthermore, we have just been focusing on one instance of recovery. Imagine a company that does not buy into the philosophy that "the customer is always right." That company is repeatedly, institutionally recovering poorly. How long do you think that company will stay profitable in today's hyper-competitive business world? This is an example of treading water, which I discussed in the Give A Little Bit Extra concept. As I said there, a company that is merely treading water simply will not survive.

So when we think about the concept of recovery, even though making sure that any mistake on the company's part has been dealt with to the customer's satisfaction may seem like a small issue, the consequences of not recovering well in that situation and as an institution are monumental and can grow like a snowball rolling downhill.

Business Examples of Recovering Well

When I give presentations about recovering well, I always think of this Major League Baseball story from 2010. Jim Joyce, a well-known MLB umpire, mistakenly called a runner safe on a ground ball to first base with two outs in the ninth inning, which kept the pitcher from pitching a perfect game. As soon as the game was over, Jim Joyce gave one of the best, most empathetic apologies I have ever heard.[161,162] This apology may have saved his career, as he is known today as one of the best umpires in baseball.

Other examples of recovering well include Starbucks' policy that, whenever they mess up your order, they remake it for you and give you a coupon for a free drink.[163] And Zappos' free return policy, which gives customers a prepaid label to return their items (within 365 days!) even if it was not a Zappos error.[164]

A few years ago, I was driving to a hotel on my way to give a presentation in Louisville, Kentucky. I got in later than I expected and went to check in. Wouldn't you know, they gave my room away because they thought I wasn't coming! I was stupefied. I gave the confirmation number and everything, but there was nothing they could do. They sent me to one of their partner hotels fifteen miles away and deep into the city, which would make my commute the next morning hell.

The next day, I asked to speak with a supervisor from the first hotel and spoke with the general manager for about ten minutes. I explained just how crazy it was that my room was gone and how big of an inconvenience it had caused me. He was very apologetic, taking responsibility for their major gaffe. He ended up giving me a credit for three weeks at the hotel plus four passes for my family to go to the nearby theme park, Kentucky Kingdom. How's that for recovering well?

Of course, for every great recovery story, there's an example of a terrible recovery. Take this song that went viral in 2009.[165] Canadian musician Dave Carroll's song "United Breaks Guitars" is about, you guessed it, an experience he had with United Airlines when they mishandled his $3,500 guitar, broke it, then proceeded to "show complete indifference" toward his complaints. In the song, Carroll claims that for a year the company passed the buck and would not take responsibility for the broken guitar or offer any sort of compensation for it even though they did not deny that the incident occurred. Finally, when the customer service representative that he was speaking with denied his claim and closed his case, he made a claim of his own. He told her that he would write and produce three songs about his experience and put them on the internet.[166] His first song, "United Breaks Guitars," has received over eighteen million views on YouTube. It's worth noting that in the aftermath of the song going viral, the *Times of London* reported that United's stock plunged 10 percent, (or the value of 51,000 replacement guitars).[167] That in itself is enough to really drive home the message of recovering well, but imagine how many neutral people were influenced by this song and decided to go with other airlines over United? Likely, the full fallout was exponentially more costly. In the internet era, the stakes for recovery are higher than ever, so there really is no room or excuse for not making every effort to recover well.

The Chili Incident

The concept of recovering well can be applied daily in public schools. Problems are a part of every administrator's life, and I have always tried to look at problems as opportunities to flip customer opinions into a positive experience. A problem is like a small fire, and we and our employees can either throw water or gasoline on that fire. Without proper training in customer service, our employees are as likely to throw gasoline on this fire as they are water.

I want to come back to how my customer service concepts can be utilized throughout the entire school system by all departments. One example occurred in our food service department while I was associate superintendent. I had trained all departments in the art of recovering well, and this one training may have saved our school district and insurance company thousands of dollars.

It was chili soup day. The hot chili spilled onto a kindergarten-age little girl as she tried to carry her plate to the cafeteria table. Getting her to the nurse did not happen quickly enough, and it resulted in terrible burns on her leg and stomach. The child's parents were called and the little girl went home.

That evening, I received a text message from the parent of the child, and it contained pictures from the emergency room of our local hospital. The mother was very angry, and I knew with these pictures that we may be in trouble.

The little girl had third degree burns on her leg with terrible blistering. My mind went back to the $3 million lawsuit won by a McDonald's customer due to a hot coffee spill.[168] Since timing is very important in recovery, all items were removed from my calendar and it was all hands on deck. To quote country singer Luke Bryan, "This is a drop-everything kind of thing."[169]

The first question I had to ask as a school leader was, *Did we mess up?* In public school systems we never think that it's our fault. We seem so afraid to admit that we might have made a mistake. More often than not, we will be quick to blame another person or policy, thinking that by passing the buck we are saving our own hides. But, like the multi-headed Hydra from Greek Mythology, our customers see us all as one entity: as the school system. So no matter who we blame, to the parents, it's all the same. If a waiter gives us bad service in a restaurant, we blame the restaurant and more than likely we don't go back. When we pass the buck in public schools, we risk losing our customers.

Back to the chili incident, I contacted my food service director to ask her if this was something we had done, like if the chili was too hot. When she said that very well could have been the case, I called a meeting with the school principal, food service director, and cafeteria manager. Evidently, the little girl had worn some jeans that fit very tightly on her leg. The heat from the chili must have been trapped for a period of time and could have caused this type of burning. I also believe the chili may have been too hot. We all discussed how we could try to recover with this family and how we could prevent this from ever happening again. This was a situation that needed an apology that was immediate, empathetic and equal to the offense.

The solution? Later that night, the food service director and I went to the home of the young girl with three new outfits and a sincere apology. We were unsure of what would happen next, but one thing we were very certain of: *It was the right thing to do!*

We ended up on their living room couch having a pleasant conversation and apologizing to the girl and her mother. We showed the mother the new lids that would now be placed on the chili containers to help prevent such spills from happening again. It was clear that the mother was pleased with our effort to make things right. She thanked us for coming over and for showing concern for her daughter.

While this recovery took a lot of our time, we never heard about this incident again, nor was it ever in the media. She did not end up filing charges against the school, thus saving us countless hours of our time and likely a pretty hefty sum of money that we certainly did not have!

As education budget cuts continue throughout the country, public relations experts are usually on the chopping block in school districts. I deeply believe that a good public relations person who can train others and be a resource to school leaders is one of the most valuable employees to a school system. It was only through our public relations training that our school was able to narrowly dodge a bullet in this case. I'll talk more about public relations later.

In the long run, recovering well pays huge dividends for public schools. Why do you think every single top company retains world class lawyers who can squash any problems or lawsuits against their company? We can't afford such a luxury in the public school system, so we must rely on our ability to recover well and build great relationships with our customers in order to prevent the disasters of lawsuits and bad press from plaguing our schools.

Recovering Well in the Public School System

Most of my school administrative experience has been at the middle and high school levels. On one occasion I was asked by my superintendent to be an interim principal at our pre-K through second grade school, which had an enrollment of over a thousand students. Elementary, middle and high schools all have their idiosyncrasies peculiar to each of them. I quickly learned that bus calls were an extremely important time with this many little ones. I also noticed that the slightest deviation of a bus schedule would send parents into an extreme panic compared to middle and high school parents.

Little Johnny had already missed the school bus twice before I became interim principal. Wouldn't you know, within my first two weeks he missed the bus again. My administrative assistant had just been cussed out by the mother who was going to have to make an unexpected trip back to the school to get Johnny. I do not remember how Johnny missed the bus this third time, and I was not even an administrator in the building the first two times; but make no mistake, to Johnny's mother, all these faux pas were now completely on my shoulders!

My customer service mindset put me into recovery mode, and I decided how I could make the apology equal the offense. I had my administrative assistant call her back and apologize, and then told the mother that I was personally bringing her child home. As I drove Johnny seven miles to his home, I could see the inconvenience of such an unexpected trip.

> "A happy customer tells a friend; an unhappy customer tells the world."
> —Unknown

I recalled a concept I covered earlier, "Walk in the Shoes of the Customers," and found some insight into her anger.

It just so happens little Johnny fell asleep on the ride home. I tried not to wake him as I unfastened his seat belt and put him in my arms. Johnny stayed asleep, hugging my neck, as I brought him to his house. I noticed the mother's body language change immediately as she opened the door. I know that a parent will give you a break if they think you care about their children. I introduced myself as the new principal and apologized to the mother for any inconvenience to her family. I then told her that I would be talking to the teacher first thing in the morning. The mother told me to go easy on the teacher as she knows her son can be a "handful." I wondered if this could be the same mother that cussed at my administrative assistant an hour ago. I gave her my business card, circled my cell phone number, and told her to call me directly the next time this happens.

By recovering well, I was able to turn a mad parent who would have told many people about her displeasure into a parent that will at least now be neutral if not supportive of our school system. The next day I spoke with the teacher, as this is the monitoring and follow-up that must occur. I let the teacher know about using my time after school and giving the mother my business card. Sure enough, I did not have to deal with Johnny missing the bus again.

Examples of Recovering Well in Schools

Since we do not have the funds that companies have to give expensive gifts when we make mistakes, we must be clever when we try to recover well after we make a mistake. Of course we still need to be immediate or apologize as fast as possible, and we still need to be empathetic with our customers by trying to walk in their shoes. Here are a few ways you can try to make the apology offset the offense. As always, the quicker the better, and you must be empathetic.

1. Make a personal visit to their home and give a sincere apology.
2. Call and sincerely apologize over the phone.
3. Handwrite a sincere apology note.
4. See them at a restaurant and pay for their meal.
5. Once a parent I needed to apologize to was behind me in the drive-through line at McDonald's, and I wrote a quick apology and had the McDonald's employee hand them the note and tell them I paid for their meal. This was a low-cost way to win back a parent.
6. Personally pay for a parent's dry cleaning.
7. Acknowledge your mistakes in the media.
8. Place upset parents on a committee, and try to work with them in a positive manner.
9. Visit parents or students at the hospital when they are sick.
10. Write personal notes of encouragement.
11. Show up at their children's co-curricular or extra-curricular events.
12. Give someone your personal business card with your personal cell phone number on the card.
13. Bake or cook something for the person you have wronged.

14. If a policy needs to be changed, change it and give the person credit for bringing it to your attention.

Final Thoughts on Recovering Well

In order to see such results, public schools need to train personnel in the art of recovery. The best know how to apologize even if they did nothing wrong; they apologize for the situation that caused the problem. Be empathetic, timely, and do your best not to lose the relationship. As the competition for students continues to increase, recovering well when a mistake is made can help schools retain students.

CONCEPT 16

Keep Backstage Issues Backstage

"Your dirty laundry belongs in the basket, not on Facebook"
– Purex[170]

The first customer service concept I ever learned occurred when I was very young. While I may not have been able to give it a title, I became proficient at using it early in life and would teach and implement this concept with my own children. I remember as a kid being somewhat confused by my parents' inconsistency. It seemed that behavior that was fine at home was not tolerated out in public. Furthermore, there was a much higher price to pay for misbehavior outside the house, especially when in the company of other people.

I think many of us can relate to this difference in standards from childhood. Most families want their kids to be "on their best behavior" in the grocery store, at restaurants, during religious services, or anywhere out in public. After all, at some basic level we understand that our children are a reflection of us. We want to put our best foot forward in the presence of others to demonstrate we are a good family and we have good parenting skills. We all know there are some unsightly moments to raising a family, but why publicize them?

Having a professional outward appearance that puts our best foot forward is a great asset for any organization. You wouldn't wear a T-shirt and shorts to an interview on Wall Street, so why would a company allow the public to be subjected to the messy inner workings of their business? As I mentioned earlier, in the Facilities concept, first impressions matter. But beyond that, what people see on *any* given day can be just as important.

This concept is about keeping those unsightly aspects of running an organization out of the public's view. Anything that may cause a negative impression or evoke a negative emotion should be controlled and kept away from the customer, just like how parents teach their kids to be on their best behavior around company or in public.

When thinking about this concept, it can help to look at the five senses. What smells are you subjecting your customers to? Are they pleasant or foul? How can you keep the foul ones out? The same goes for unsightly objects like trash receptacles, cooking equipment, heating and ventilation units, and other machinery.

But more than just objects, keeping backstage issues backstage is also about interactions the customer sees. Are staff fighting amongst each other or with customers? Having these confrontations in front of other customers can create a negative buying environment and influence their buying behavior or even scare them away completely.

Examples from the Business World

Hotels are a great example of an industry that keeps backstage issues backstage. Even at mediocre hotels, you won't see trash cans where customers congregate and those giant, noisy heating and ventilation units are hidden by carefully placed trees and shrubs behind the building. Similarly, you won't see hotel employees on break hanging out in the lobby, eating or drinking or out front smoking. They have designated areas for employee breaks that are away from the customers. The end result is that the face that we see, as guests at the hotel, is their best face, and all the unsightly components that must exist to run their business are concealed. Every organization has blemishes but anyone can learn to use makeup.

One great example of keeping backstage issues backstage comes from, you guessed it, Disney World. The Disney employee who was playing Snow White was in her dressing room with her staff, getting into wardrobe. She was venting to her colleagues about a recent breakup with her boyfriend. Then, when it was time for her to go out and greet the guests, she switched off her personal life and instantly transformed into happy, cheerful Snow White.[171]

It's that type of *professionalism* that companies need when it comes to employee-facing aspects of their business. The character Snow White needs to be happy and pleasant when a child comes up to her. If she lets her personal problems affect the way she does her job, she will let down a lot of kids that day and possibly turn what could have been the highlight of their trip into the bad story that they tell everyone for years to come.

All it takes is one bad story to get out and a company's reputation can be severely damaged. Remember the example from the last concept about the singer who wrote about United Airlines breaking his guitar? The song went viral and the company's stock dropped ten percent in the aftermath. They had several opportunities to make things right, but didn't. The singer even told his claim person at United that since they would not pay for the damages they made to his equipment, he would write three songs about his experience with United and put them on the internet. Right there, a great customer service employee's red flag has to go up, and he or she should find a way to keep such a potentially disastrous act of bad publicity from occurring. In that moment, when the United employee chose to hang up and not tell the singer that she would talk to her supervisor and try one last time, she failed to keep this issue backstage. *Allowing an issue to get out of hand and then to go into the media—whether it's the internet, the news, or simply a person's blog—is a critical customer service mistake and one that lets a backstage issue go public.* I'll talk more about the media later on in this concept.

Here are a few examples of businesses not keeping their unsightly issues backstage:

1. Employees fighting amongst themselves in front of customers or worse, employees fighting *with* customers.
2. Employees using inappropriate language within earshot of customers.
3. Restaurants with flies, bugs, or rodents. Call an exterminator and get that under wraps!
4. Terrible media stories from data breaches of restaurant employees doing bad things to food.
5. Stores that have bad smells in them. There's no reason customers should be subjected to foul odors. The best companies get them under control before they open their doors and have protocol for how to handle them when they arise during business hours. Chronic issues like dumpsters too close to entrances or so poorly maintained they can be smelled by a customer are inexcusable.
6. Cleaning while customers are eating around them. I have been asked to raise my feet so an employee could sweep and mop. When emergencies happen, clean quickly and covertly. Hearing "Clean up on aisle 7" may be a funny line, but it's one that ought to be kept backstage.
7. Employees picketing in from of the establishment. Picketers know the importance of this concept!

These are just a few examples of how businesses fail at this concept. One great TV show I watch to learn about keeping backstage issues backstage is *Bar Rescue* with host Jon Taffer. Taffer has a keen eye for these kinds of issues, and in each episode he works with the owner of an underperforming bar to change its image, spruce things up, and get it on track to success. If you haven't seen *Bar Rescue*, I recommend watching a few episodes. Try spotting the problems in the beginning before he does; it's a great way to train your eye to see problems, and you may even find some solutions to your own backstage issues.

Keeping Backstage Issues Backstage
in Public Education

So how can we apply this principle to public education? We certainly need it. In fact, this concept may be the one that has hurt public education the most. I've seen so much airing of dirty laundry (both figuratively and literally!) in public schools that it's clear we don't really understand this concept. I'll start with my absolute biggest pet peeve, and one that blows the minds of a lot of administrators when I present.

It's the front office. You know, the place where your guests come to check in and the place where you send the kids that got in trouble to wait for the principal. Why anyone thought this was a good idea in the first place, I'll never understand, but it drives me bonkers. Can you think of any other business that deals with their problems and their new customers in the same place? I didn't think so. And yet, public schools do it, and have done it, for years without putting two and two together. If we are trying to make a good first impression on our new students, our parents, and our guests from the community, the last thing we should be doing is having them sit and wait next to a couple of kids who just got into a fight at recess and are scraped up, bruised, and looking pretty darn ornery.

The solution? Separate the two. Put our best foot forward when it comes to what customers see at the front office. Discipline and all other issues belong somewhere else: somewhere backstage. It might take some creative thinking and some rearranging, but believe me, it's not only worth it, it's essential. In my experience, a school can be doing all of these concepts: hire the best, train well, employ great leaders, monitor touch points, etc., but if someone walks into their school and sees the worst parts of that school, they will instantly be turned off. How that manifests itself varies, but the end result is that the school fails to pass the first impressions test. To undo that first impression will involve some serious time and energy in the art of recovery—time and energy that staff doesn't have and that should have been used to make adjustments to avoid the problem beforehand.

School Board Meetings in Public Schools

While we are on the subject of personal pet peeves, I'll just keep rolling with another: school board meetings. Some of these meetings remind me of the 2016 presidential election: a circus. The candidates acted more like they were on an episode of *The Jerry Springer Show* than in a political debate. Now to be fair, not all public school districts have problems with school board meetings. But those who do know what I'm talking about. This is where your school's problems take center stage, right in front of the media. Because of this, schools need to be extra careful about how they act at these meetings. I've seen actual physical fights break out at these meetings. Hopefully you're not at that level, but the verbal fighting can be just as damaging.

In this era of sensationalism in reporting, the media are always looking for a juicy story and public schools are easy pickings for them. Even when there is no actual fighting at school board meetings, reporters find a way to make a scandal out of a scrap. As public school leaders, the philosophy is simple: don't make it easy for them. Don't air your dirty laundry right in front of the cameras or the reporters; don't let petty issues or personal vendettas cloud your judgment and

> Would Disney World allow Mickey Mouse and Snow White to be at the entrance of their theme park smoking? Sometimes it helps to ask "What would Disney do?" in order to realize an issue needs to be kept backstage.

affect your behavior. We are school leaders because we are passionate about public education, but it's important to keep those emotions in check when interacting with our own people—whether it is with other administrators, board members, school staff, parents, students, or community members.

For schools that aren't keeping their dirty laundry out of sight, this negative portrayal in the media means private schools and charter schools don't even need to advertise! They can simply sit back and wait for students and families to go looking for another education alternative and, when they do, these options will be there to reel them in.

Let's have a rule that we can disagree behind closed doors but treat each other with respect while on stage. The best companies, including the military, do not tear one another apart on camera. I have heard it said that even rattlesnakes do not use their venom when fighting other rattlesnakes. School board meetings should take a page out of that book.

Another epidemic I've seen at schools is sharing information that should be kept private. Whether it's a school employee sharing something inappropriate on social media (Facebook has become a school administrator's nightmare), teachers openly talking about how they have failed certification tests, school staff discussing failed drug tests or DUIs, or any school personnel talking with the media about something that paints the school in a negative light, keeping backstage issues backstage means not airing our dirty laundry for the world to see, and any chance we get to catch these problems before they go public ought to be taken.

Infighting

I'd like to go back to infighting because it is such a major issue in public education. It's not just at school board meetings; it can be anywhere. Teachers complain to friends about the principal or superintendent, administrative assistants complain about each other, food service employees complain about facilities maintenance, and so on. One winter, I dealt with an employee who got on Facebook and questioned the district's decision to not call off school because of snow. This employee basically said the district, and thus her superintendent, did not care about the teachers.

While I understand the need for all people to vent about their work frustrations, it is important for us as public school employees to understand the effects of our words when talking with those outside of our school. While some people may see it as just talking badly about one decision or one person, others may see these comments as reflective of a wholly terrible school system or may reinforce an already existing negative impression.

That's because people tend to generalize. Whether it's one bad customer service experience at the department store that causes a person to never go back there again, like with my mother in the last concept, or hearing from a friend that a scene from a movie was so unrealistic that we do not to go see it ourselves: when we talk badly about anything, we run the risk of that person generalizing that criticism to the entity as a whole.

In this age of competition, public schools simply cannot afford to take these risks. Even outside of work, it is important to treat jobs with professionalism and not badmouth our coworkers and bosses. The fallout from public school employees criticizing their coworkers to friends and family can result in those listening simply passing on the gossip, or even families finding a new schooling option for their children. When negative gossip about the school goes around, you can bet it affects how many parents volunteer for school functions, how many parents support school sports, and how many parents speak highly of the school to others. As I mentioned earlier in the Give Great Customer Service to Employees concept, school culture is an immensely important part of a school's success and, when the parents and community lose faith in the goodness of their school, the school culture suffers. And when it comes time to vote on issues affecting the school, whether it's a tax increase for educational spending or a motion to expand charter schools in the district, there's a good chance they won't be on the public school's side. At the very least, we need to ensure that our employees' words and actions are not the reason for our customers jumping ship.

There Is Hope!

Thankfully, there are some bright spots when it comes to keeping backstage issues backstage. I've consulted for schools and districts that worked very hard to improve their public image and put their best foot forward in the presence of students and families. During one training, a group of custodial and maintenance staff came up with ideas they wanted to implement immediately. They decided they would remove any graffiti *as soon as they saw it.* This would require the necessary supplies and paint to have on location. They also wanted to hide the trash bins located in a high-traffic area by placing a metal fence around the bins and wind screens around the fence. I was so impressed by the initiative these employees showed towards improving their customer service and their school's image. I could tell they took a lot of pride in making these changes. They could now see how they and their department were an integral part of the school's customer service plan.

> If you hear that the manager of a local restaurant mistreats the employees, that will probably not be your first choice when deciding where to eat!

> Public schools are so bad with this concept, the competition does not even need to advertise to recruit our students. They can just sit back and watch us self-destruct.

When we can get *everyone* thinking like this group of custodial and maintenance personnel, we will conquer the concept of keeping backstage issues backstage. While it takes time, commitment, and effort, the payoff for public schools can be significant. Great customer service can improve every aspect of a school or school district. If we are going to be successful in this age of competition, every department must value customer service.

Final Thoughts on Keeping Backstage Issues Backstage

Let's go back to the impression that the best companies give their customers. Their staff are friendly and happy and their facilities are immaculate (remember the study about the tray table with the coffee stain on it in the Touch Points chapter?). If we model these companies and remember that not keeping backstage issues backstage will prevent us from being like them, we can cut down on instances of people being turned off by our school. As with all of these concepts, it starts with awareness and then continues with efforts to correct and adjust. By walking through your school with an eye for what should be backstage, like Jon Taffer on *Bar Rescue*, you can improve public perception of your entire school district.

CONCEPT 17

Don't Do Dumb Things!

"Common sense is not so common."
– Voltaire[172]

Panasonic, one of the largest electronics companies in the world, got in some hot water over the branding of their first touchscreen computer. The company named the computer's touchscreen capability "Touch Woody" (after the character Woody the Wood-pecker, the device's namesake). Now, I'm not sure who was on the committee to make this decision, but whoever it was lacked some serious common sense. But it doesn't stop there. They went on to name the automated online support function "Internet Pecker."[173] I'm not making this up.

Funny blunders are going to happen in the business world as well as in public education. Sometimes we just have to shake our heads and laugh, but we can't always count on our customers to see the humor in the situation.

This is a fun concept for me, as I get to reach deep into the customer service gaffe bag and pull out some of the biggest bonehead decisions that occur in the business world and in public education.

There is no shortage of dumb things companies do with the best of intentions. For the purpose of this concept, when I use the term "dumb things," I am not talking about breaking the law, I am talking about *preventable* mishaps that have the opportunity to turn off and possibly scar customers for a very long time. These mistakes can even cause customers to want to get even with the institution. Training in the concepts in this book will greatly diminish these mistakes. In my experience, most dumb things occur for two reasons.

The first reason is because institutions fail to make customers their top priority, thus forgetting why they exist in the first place. The second reason is because institutions operate with the "I am the boss" mentality. In other words, they say to customers, "I am the boss and I am right. I have the power and I am in charge." Many dumb things that occur in the business world and public education have both these tentacles working together at the same time.

No Shoes, No Service

In 2009, a woman walked into a St. Louis Burger King with her baby, ordered, and sat down with her food.[174] Shortly after she began eating, she was approached by a store employee who informed her that, due to Missouri state regulations regarding shoelessness in eating establishments, she would have to leave *because the baby in her stroller was barefoot.*

Now you may be thinking, okay this employee was just doing his job. But the real head-scratcher here is that, first of all, the "No Shirt, No Shoes, No Service" signs on Burger King's stores are simply policies and not based on actual laws. In fact, in the state of Missouri, shoelessness is not grounds for removing a person from an eating establishment. So, this uninformed employee was citing a nonexistent law when kicking the woman out.

The second problem is that, beyond the technicalities of the law, this employee did not exercise what Voltaire called "common sense." What harm was this child's shoelessness doing for the establishment? The child's feet were completely contained in the stroller. There just isn't any need to boot a paying customer here, no pun intended.

This is a great example of both the "I am the boss" mentality and workers forgetting why their company exists in the first place. Burger King was demonized by news outlets, nationwide, as well as on blogs and Facebook over this one dumb mistake. Apologies and free meals were offered by the owner, but articles and blogs continued for many days. A lot of time and effort was spent recovering from this one dumb mistake made by someone who wanted to show he was the boss and who had forgotten why Burger King exists in the first place. In my experience, dumb mistakes made with no common sense are the hardest to defend and to recover from.

Doing Dumb Things Can Create Saboteurs!

As a school administrator I create enemies without even trying or sometimes without even knowing. The one thing none of us wants to create in the customer service world is a saboteur. These are people who try to figure out how to cause your school or business great harm.

The best companies minimize blatant errors, unforgivable gaffes, and any other customer service nightmares. In the last two concepts, I've mentioned the plight of musician Dave Carroll when his guitar was severely damaged by an airline. I'll bring it up again because it's such a perfect customer service disaster. It's a great example of not recovering well and not keeping this issue backstage, but before any of these happened, someone did a dumb thing and somehow managed to break a guitar. However, the dumb mistake was compounded by an even dumber mistake when United Airlines refused to pay for the damages, even after the hit song "United Breaks Guitars" was viewed over 18 million times with over 100,000 likes on YouTube. Dave Carroll became a saboteur to United Airlines and, if offered the opportunity, United would probably like a "do over."

We can blame such mistakes on a bad hire or insufficient customer service training. We can blame leadership for not providing sufficient oversight so as to catch employees not following protocol, or for leadership putting its employees in a position where they have to cut corners with luggage in order to stay on schedule. Maybe the company did not monitor well enough to see that this problem keeps happening with people's personal belongings. I could keep going, but the point here is that when a company doesn't follow the previously covered customer service concepts, they make dumb mistakes that we all collectively shake our heads at when we see them in the news. These headlines cause terrible public relations issues, affect personnel decisions, and require apologies or some other type of financial offerings, sometimes ending in a court case. When people tell me they do not have time for customer service trainings or to plan and reflect, I always wonder how they have time to provide on-the-spot damage control when employees make these inevitable dumb mistakes.

We all have personal stories from the business world that cover a wide range of minor faux pas. There are the funny stories, like when I went through the drive-thru line at KFC and ordered a Diet Coke only to be asked if I wanted a bucket of chicken with it. Hmm. If I wanted a bucket of chicken, wouldn't I have ordered it? If I am watching my calories with a Diet Coke, what makes you think I forgot a bucket of chicken? This example made me laugh, gave me a good story, and will probably go down as the most unusual upselling job I ever experienced. People hate upselling! Then there are the serious stories, like when LG celebrated a phone release by holding an event where they put vouchers for free phones in balloons and allowed people to shoot them down with BB guns, resulting in nearly twenty people being shot and injured.[175] How dumb can you get?!

Will You Go to the Prom with Me?

On a calm spring night in Shelton, Connecticut, high school senior James Tate and his two friends, Andrew Boretsky and Christian Lombardi, walked onto their school campus with a ladder, a helmet, and twelve-inch cardboard letters. James's mission was to impress Sonali Rodrigues by asking her, in dramatic and public fashion, to the prom by taping the letters on the front of the school. His message read: "Sonali Rodrigues, will you go to prom with me? HMU—Tate." (HMU stands for hit me up, or, call me). Much like how couples go to great lengths to ask their loved ones for their hand in marriage, James wanted to impress Sonali, and he wanted the entire student body to know his heartfelt convictions. Sonali accepted and it was shaping up to be an amazing prom for the two. That is, until administrators found out what he'd done.[176]

What Tate thought was a "harmless, fun, thoughtful, and creative way to ask a girl to prom,"[177] the school saw as trespassing and a safety risk for climbing up a ladder. Headmaster Beth Smith suspended James Tate for one day as a result. She also cited a rule that stated that any student who receives a suspension after a certain date would not be allowed to attend the prom. In another instance of "just carrying out orders," the principal washed her hands of her responsibility to do right by her students, her customers, and to make a judgment call using common sense.

When we think about this story from the "I am the boss" perspective, it certainly fits the profile. The student does something out of the ordinary that is technically against school rules, so we need to apply the rules, regardless of whether the punishment fits the crime. Just like in the Burger King example, there was no judgment involved here on the part of the administration, only a sentence carried out without any wiggle room.

Over 200,000 people rallied to support Tate on Facebook and Twitter, which led to his appearance on *The Today Show*.[178] Even CNN picked up the story, interviewing one legislator who said, "I do think punishment is necessary but I don't think the punishment fits the crime."[179] The mayor of Shelton also spoke out in criticism of the rules, stating, "We put regulations in place that are inflexible and that do not allow for us to apply some common sense or have flexibility."[6] There it is, straight from the horse's mouth.

There is a happy ending here, thankfully. Headmaster Smith reversed her decision after all the media attention her mistake garnered. This case also pushed legislators to consider an amendment that would force schools to provide an alternate means of punishment rather than banning students from school-related activities. Not only was James Tate allowed to attend the prom, he was selected prom king.

Besides Headmaster Smith refusing to admit she'd made a mistake, I was also surprised by her statement that she could have never predicted one decision could garner such national and international attention. *In my opinion, when such an injustice occurs to a student who has been a good customer for twelve years in our school system, it should garner this much attention!* Think about it from his perspective: you just courageously and publicly asked a girl to go to the senior prom and she said yes; it's a big deal to take that away due to terrible school policy. I believe school leaders must make many tough decisions that do not always fit exactly into some type of school policy. Do we want school leaders or someone who just carries out policy? As I've said earlier, if a person has the power to change an injustice and does nothing, the person is as guilty as the one doing the injustice.

Public School Strip Search

One of the more blatant cases of dumb things occurred in Arizona in 2003 when school officials strip-searched thirteen-year-old Savanah Redding, an honor student at Safford Middle School in Arizona.[180] Savanah, having no prior disciplinary record, was searched because another student said she might be hiding ibuprofen in her

In public schools, do we have higher expectations for students than we do for our staff?

underwear. Savanah was asked to remove her clothes in front of school staff, as they searched her for the ibuprofen.

No drugs were ever found. Savanah and her mother eventually sued school officials, contending her constitutional rights had been violated. The U.S. Court of Appeals ruled that school officials violated Ms. Redding's Fourth Amendment right to be free from unreasonable search and seizure, acting contrary to all reason and common sense. The school district lawyers appealed and it finally took the Supreme Court to rule that the school district went too far.[181]

Justice John Paul Stevens called the school's strip search "outrageous conduct." He went on to say, "I have long believed that it does not require a constitutional scholar to conclude that a nude search of a 13-year-old child is an invasion of constitutional rights of some magnitude."[182]

Amazingly, strip searches were common in public schools before this decision. Had school leaders walked in the shoes of their customers, they would have asked how they would like to be strip searched. What if this had happened to our children? Common sense should have prevented this situation from escalating to a strip search. Just like in the Burger King example, what goal is going to be accomplished by calling out the customer? It couldn't have been so important that the school officials humiliated a young girl within the confines of her school. Do you think Disney would strip search suspected shoplifters? That just *sounds* ridiculous. If the best companies wouldn't do it, maybe public schools shouldn't either.

This case garnered a lot of media attention for six years and, in my opinion, it's stories like these that fuel the fire of school choice. I know we like to bury the past and act like we are nothing like the public schools of yesterday, but strip searches had been a common practice until just recently. Even as a lifetime educator, I am bewildered at how a school could continue to defend a policy that is so clearly morally wrong throughout several levels of judicial systems, all the way to the US Supreme Court. If we don't learn our lesson and stop doing dumb things like this, we will continue to add to the list of dumb things public schools have done to hurt themselves and bring about school choice. But of course, there's always more.

Bus Driver Takes Wrong Group of Students on Field Trip

In presentations to school bus drivers, I like to tell a story about a bus driver who failed to use common sense. In a bizarre mix-up, the bus driver

> **A Good Rule:**
> **If you would not do it to a teacher—you should not do it to your first customer, the student.**

picked up a group of thirty middle school students and instead of bringing them to school—where they were supposed to go— she brought them to Six Flags Great Adventure theme park, miles down the highway.[183]

The children on board were shocked and scared to see the bus driver going out of town and asked her to stop, telling her that they were supposed to go to school and not on a field trip. Then the children asked her to call the school and double-check. But the bus driver did not listen to their pleas. At this point, some of the children feared they were being abducted.

Without a single adult on board to reason with the bus driver, the students had to take matters into their own hands, calling their parents and the school to inform them of what was happening. One child had the principal on her cell phone and tried to give the phone to the driver. The driver told her she was not allowed to handle the cell phone while she was driving the bus. Eventually, law enforcement caught up to the bus and stopped it from going to the theme park. An officer boarded the bus to inform the bus driver to go back to the school and stayed on to ensure they got back safely.

There are many obvious red flags that the bus driver missed. One that amuses me is that there is just no way a group of middle school students—or any minors—would be going on a school field trip *without any adult chaperone*, especially to a huge theme park. Even if she didn't notice right away that there was no adult, with the protests of the children, she should have put two and two together. The driver showed a clear "I am the boss" mentality by not listening to the entire bus of students saying something was wrong.

A Common Sense Clause

Every school policy should contain a common sense clause that goes something like this: "The school principal and/or superintendent may override school and district policies after reviewing all facts of a situation." This clause generally scares weak leaders who like to hide behind school policies. The mantra of the weak leader goes something like this: "I am sorry. It's our policy/school policy/school board's policy." The student or parent might ask, "If it is a bad policy, why don't you change it?" Strong leaders recognize that policies generally put you in a box. Leaders must also give all staff the ability to make commonsense decisions without fear of reprisals. Perhaps if it is not against state or federal law, a better mantra for public education might be "Common sense trumps policy." Now that's a mantra for which I can get on board!

Ramifications of Poor Decision Making
in Public Education

We all make mistakes; they're unavoidable in business and in education. But working to minimize the errors you make by using common sense and rethinking the policy and red tape that dominate decision making can have a huge impact on your school. Think about this: If you were to read the local newspaper each week and consistently find stories about commonsense mistakes that the school makes, what would your opinion of the school be? Would you lose respect for the people in charge? Would you want to send your own children there? Would you support tax increases that would fund this school? What about ballot items that would build charter schools, which promise to end the shenanigans that public schools perpetuate?

It's questions like these that we must ask ourselves when we look at the impression our actions give to the community. The stakes are higher than ever for public schools, so why not make every effort to minimize these gaffes?

An important component in decision making in public education is policy. Policy is the red tape that prevents common sense from being exercised by many employees for fear of being disciplined or even fired. In situations where policy is responsible for public school employees doing dumb things, it doesn't matter how well the school has hired, how thoroughly they've trained employees, or how closely they monitor their schools: these types of blunders are bound to occur when rules tie our hands and leaders adhere to policies that do not make sense. I struggle with the term "zero tolerance." I think that zero tolerance puts leaders in a box and may cause people to lose common sense. Here's an example of a zero tolerance policy that now seems quite ridiculous.

> Coaches—throw out your list of team rules and use this one Common Sense Clause: "Athletes, don't do anything that will embarrass you, your family, or your school. If you do you may be removed from this team." Now you have the freedom to make the punishment fit the crime in any student discipline situation.

Back in the early 2000s, we saw the explosion of cell phone ownership among school-aged children. Prior to the mid-1990s, this was a completely absent issue. So when all of a sudden the whole student body seemingly had cell phones, schools had to act fast. One way to curb the problems of student cell phone usage in class was to enact a zero tolerance policy. That meant that "If I see it, I own it," was the law of the land. I recall having boxes upon boxes of student cell phones in our principal's office. Storing them became a problem in itself. We'd lose track of whose phone was whose and had a heck of a time trying to give the phones back.

Of course, we received endless phone calls from irate parents for taking these expensive devices, often used by children to call their parents for a ride home or to receive a call as to when and where to meet for pickup. Naturally, we had to rethink the rule and ended up revoking the zero tolerance policy in exchange for a system of rules that were taught to the students and which were fair and uniformly enforced by school employees. Students were involved in helping us find a solution and we ended up allowing students to use their phones at lunch and during breaks.

> In a Thanksgiving episode of the TV show *WKRP in Cincinnati*, the radio station manager released hundreds of live turkeys from a helicopter, only to see them plummet to the earth instead of flying away. In the last line of this episode, he says, "As God is my witness, I thought turkeys could fly."[184]

Have you ever been at an event—a school concert, a movie, a play, a meeting—and all of a sudden you hear the unmistakable sound of your phone ringing in your pocket or your bag? The embarrassment of being "that person," is enough to learn your lesson (hopefully). But even if it's not, have you ever been approached by an usher afterward and been told to hand your device over to them? Of course not, that's just ridiculous! So why would we do this to students, especially when they are our primary customers in public education? Yes, we need rules and we need to teach students what is appropriate. But we don't have to go out of our way to punish them. We must stop operating with this "I am the boss" mentality and treat our students as the customer.

When thinking about how to incorporate the cautionary tales in this concept into your school policy and training, consider the following:

- Do we train our employees to use common sense when making decisions?
- Do we spend any professional development time role-playing past mistakes or scenarios such as those in this concept?
- Do we discuss how to alternatively handle school situa-

tions that may lie in the gray area of our rules and could lead to major problems?

- Do we consider the political ramifications of the outcomes of our decisions? In other words, do we look beyond the moment to see the potential long-term and large-scale consequences of each decision?
- Leaders should ask themselves, "Do I feel good enough about my decision that I could defend it on national TV?" Our job as leaders is to pass this philosophy on to our staff.

Final Thoughts on Don't Do Dumb Things

I have made my share of dumb mistakes as both a teacher and administrator. I could have filled an entire book with stories that I have either been a part of or have witnessed. To paraphrase Voltaire, in education sometimes common sense is not so common. When we lose sight of the fact that the students are our first customer and we operate with the "I am the boss" mentality, we open the door to doing dumb things that hurt our students and eventually hurt ourselves.

Without the philosophy espoused in this chapter, we will end up in bloody time-consuming battles that do nothing but help our competitors. The solution is for public schools to immerse employees in the concept that the student is our first customer, and that we have jobs because they (and their parents) choose to walk through our doors each day.

CONCEPT 18

Everyone Is a Public Relations Agent

"Advertising is what you pay for, publicity is what you pray for."
– Unknown

Muhammad Ali once said, "It's not bragging if you can back it up."[185] In the business world, leaders know that it's not enough to be successful; they must shout their successes from the rooftops. While many of us may have learned about modesty as a positive personality trait growing up, that idea applies better to personal life than to business life. In any highly competitive market, modesty gets you nowhere. Customers have come to expect and even appreciate companies sharing their successes; it gives them confidence in the brand.

When it comes to confidence, the best companies exude it out of every aspect of their service. Employees of Southwest Airlines get really creative, bragging about their service. One flight attendant (or an operations agent as they're called at Southwest) boarded a plane and put a fun spin on the idea of "shouting success from the rooftops" when he shared the company's slogan, "Bags fly free."[186]

> Ladies and Gentlemen, can I have your attention please. My name is Jay, and I am the Operations Agent for your flight to San Diego today. I want to give a shout out to my math teachers for teaching me how to do the following math: I show 137 passengers had 125 bags checked in today for this flight ... with what the other airlines are now charging for luggage, I come up with at least $3,250

that you all did not have to pay EXTRA today to travel. Thanks for flying Southwest Airlines.[187]

Southwest's free checked-bag policy keeps them out of a multi-billion dollar revenue stream. So why do they continue to keep this policy? Southwest CEO Gary Kelly says it's part of their company's identity and part of what keeps their customers coming back. In short, it's great public relations.[188]

What Is Public Relations?

You may recall earlier in this book I said that when it comes to customer service, it's all about relationships. At the very core, public relations, or PR, is about relationships. It's building trust—one person at a time—that what you represent is a good thing to customers and to the community.

PR is also storytelling. It's spinning your brand in a way that appeals to the public and enhances your brand's reputation, whether your brand is computers, catering or public education. In other words, sometimes, *you simply gotta brag* to survive in a competitive market. The Southwest example above is an instance where an employee talking up his company's policy is meant to maintain customer loyalty by reminding the customers of what Southwest does for them. For many businesses, this is a key PR move that helps give them the edge in customer satisfaction. If public schools are going to compete in today's educational climate, we are going to have to do a much better job at selling ourselves. Leaders cannot do this alone; we need all school employees tooting our school district's horn, delivering our message, and if necessary singing our songs: We're About Kids and We Are Free!

Revisiting Johnny the Bagger

The best companies know the importance of public relations. That's why they have a department or an agency handle it for them. When you make the big bucks, this is one of the luxuries that comes with the territory. Along with a team of lawyers on retainer, the PR team is an essential part of the success of the best companies. But PR success is not all about money.

Remember the story of Johnny the Bagger from the Give a Little Bit Extra concept? One employee thinking outside the box and delivering a level of service unheard of in the grocery bagging department caused a massive buzz about the supermarket in which he worked. This is the kind of story that draws news reporters, creates positive word of mouth amongst customers, and builds a lasting impression on the community as a whole. People think, "Oh that's the store that gives you inspirational quotes with your groceries." Even after the quotes stop being given out, that's how people will remember this store; it will be its legacy.

> Blogging and social media are two easy, cheap methods companies use to endear the audience to their brand.

Whether we are talking about a grocery store bagger or the operations agent in the Southwest Airlines example above, it's amazing how much of an impact one employee can have on creating positive PR. But imagine if instead of just Johnny, *every* employee regularly created positive publicity for an organization. When an organization can get most or even all its employees to work as PR agents, that positive public response increases exponentially, and can even drive business away from its competitors.

Employee Advocates

In the business world, there is a term for employees who do not work in PR but who act as PR agents. They're called Employee Advocates.[189] Companies have discovered that designated PR people are not as believable to customers as "real people"; that is, employees who aren't being paid to tell everyone and their mother about their amazing company.

Employee Advocates further their company's brand by breaking the mold of "leaving work at work." In their spare time, whether it is in conversation with friends, on social media, or in their buying choices, they make sure they are supporting their brand. It can be as simple as a person talking about something great their company is doing or sharing an article about a new advancement or technology they are pioneering. But it can even be more subtle, as the Employee Advocates of the following company show us.[190]

> On Black Friday, 2016, Patagonia decided to donate 100 percent of sales from the day (over $10 million dollars) to grassroots nonprofits around the world who work to conserve our natural resources. *Fortune, CNN, Forbes* and *Business Insider* lauded the company for its commitment to its cause, despite huge losses on the biggest shopping day of the year. This is the kind of PR that companies who *get it* are doing.[195,196,197,198]

The outdoor/adventure company Patagonia has been a making athletic gear for over fifty years. Named after the rugged, mountainous land that covers much of southern Argentina and Chile, Patagonia has developed a reputation for being the clothing choice of the eco-conscious adventurer. While their official social media accounts are well-followed and filled with information that is relevant and exciting to their customer base, the real gold is in what their non-PR employees do. The company sends employee advocates on trips to far-off locations with Patagonia gear, sometimes with camera crews.[6] And of course these real people—not the brand—share their photos and stories on the internet via their personal blogs and social media. Having real people share their experiences with a brand with their friends and followers has enormous benefits.[191] According to everyonesocial.com, the number of people reached via an *employee's* social media sharing is 571 percent greater than the number people reached via a company's *official* accounts! So not only is this great content reaching more people, but it's from what customers consider "real people," which makes the impact much greater than if it had come from a PR person.[192] Business magazines like *Forbes* and MIT Sloan's *Sloan Review* have chronicled the employee buy-in that has propelled Patagonia into social media superstardom.[193,194]

PR Nightmares

Of course, on the other side of the coin, we have those moments when a company's employees actually create problems. Since I have more from the "Don't Do Dumb Things" bank, here are some PR nightmares for your entertainment and education.

- US Airways tweeting a customer an explicit photo, then saying it was "an honest mistake."[199]
- Bud Light's 2015 "Up for Whatever" campaign, printing "The perfect beer for removing 'no' from your vocabulary for the night" on cans. Customers took to social media claiming that the beer company's message undermined the "no means no," national anti-sexual assault campaign, not to mention the phrase's meaning when it comes to saying no to drunk driving.[200]
- Lululemon, the yoga clothing giants, installing a tile floor in its Buffalo store that spelled out "Wide Right," referencing their team's recent Super Bowl loss.[201] Why on earth would they do this in the losing team's city? Lululemon's other PR disasters include realizing too late that its pants were too sheer[202] and defending its decision to not carry plus-sized clothing because "some women's bodies just don't work" for their pants.[203]
- Urban Outfitters selling a Kent State sweatshirt with fake blood spattered on it, referencing the 1970 Kent State Massacre school shooting.[204]
- Play-Doh selling a cake decorating toy that looked more like an adult toy.[205]
- An ESPN sportswriter tweeting a link to an adult video in a post about college sports. Then, instead of apol-

ogizing, he simply deleted the post and ignored any comments about it.[206]

You can imagine the field day the press had with these PR snafus. In fact, many of these stories made year-end lists of worst PR disasters. Imagine if such a list existed for public schools! I have a feeling that list would be even more cringeworthy than the one above. Here's how to prevent your school from ending up on the year-end fail lists.

Public Relations in Public Schools

Each employee in every job code should be a public relations agent for his or her school district. Not only should school employees understand that they are the face of their school district, but like the Southwest Airlines example, now everyone must intentionally look for ways to promote their school. They must understand that their job, their benefits, and their retirement depends on how well their school competes with other educational organizations that are trying to attract their students and families.

The job of public schools is to provide a service to everyone; they're institutions of relationships. Meanwhile, public relations is the deliberate act of building relationships. How much more perfect a match could there be? The only obstacle is understanding how they go together, which can be tricky. Navigating that path starts with realizing that every school employee is a PR agent.

Best Practices

The first rule is to remember that every school employee is a PR touch point, whether they mean to be or not. They all participate in PR whenever they interact with parents, students, other employees, or the community. Like I mentioned earlier in this book, employees represent their employers in the minds of others. A bad experience with a checkout clerk causes customers to generalize about the whole business. The same goes for school employees. Keep this in mind when you think about how to implement PR practices in your school, and remember that you can't hide your bad PR agents, so either train them, trade them, or let them go.

Below are some ideas for implementing PR practices in your school. The more staff you can bring on board with this, the more positive buzz you'll create about your school, which can in turn influence your school culture by energizing the community and bringing them on board with your mission. For example, who wouldn't want to go to the big rivalry game that the whole city or town is talking about on social media? Don't underestimate people's FOMO—fear of missing out!

- Administrators and staff use social media to highlight good information about the school. Remember, in the chapter on keeping backstage issues backstage, that airing our dirty laundry for the community (and world!) to see can have serious detrimental effects on how our schools are perceived. Keep it as positive on social media as in real-life conversations.

- Connect with parents and students via social media: friend or follow them. This not only helps build community and trust, but also allows you to share your school victories with them in real time.

- Administrators should use their own voice, not automated voices, when interacting with parents and students. My rule in terms of best to worst: Face to face, ear to ear, handwritten note, email, automated voicemail. Using this rule helps build relationships that are the foundation of customer service. When a robot calls to say my child missed school, it doesn't send the message that the school cares about my child the way a real person calling does.

- Highlight school and student achievements at school board meetings and any time press is present.

- Banners, trophies, and awards should be displayed prominently to celebrate achievements and to remind the staff, students, families, and community of the excellence that exists in the school.
- Visit students and parents at their homes and have a strategic plan for positive phone calls home and positive handwritten notes.
- Use ads in newspapers, the school website, social media, editorial columns from a local news outlet, etc. to share college acceptance letters and the total amount of college scholarships offered to your seniors each year. The competition is already using this strategy, so why do we rarely talk about these major victories outside of our school walls? Shout it from the rooftops: your students go to college!
- All leaders must get involved in city government. Each leader takes a different organization: chamber of commerce, town business association, Kiwanis Club, Rotary Club, etc. As part of the organization, leaders can give important school updates and build relationships. It's also an opportunity to explain your school's reasons behind, say, needing a tax increase. Make it so people can't go anywhere without seeing a school person. "If you're not at the table, you're on the plate." Don't leave things to chance. Don't let public opinion be made without someone from the school there to get them to understand the school perspective. Know what's going on with your community and kids. We can't put our heads in the sand; we need to have a finger on the pulse of our customers.
- Superintendent and principals offer "See For Yourself" tours to get parents, community leaders, and prospective families in the schools to view your departments and to see the good things that are occurring. Feed everyone if possible!

- Use parents as PR agents—especially when it's parent-to-parent communication. There's great value in having parents sing praise to their peers because they tend to be more trusted than school personnel.
- Keep an up-to-date website and have an interactive Facebook page where families can get good information out about staff and students. This is free PR. Use it!
- Every *department* must have a page on your website and a social media (Facebook/Twitter) account to promote their department's events, awards, victories, and overall good news.
- All departments are evaluated on their PR initiatives and must find ways to promote their departments in the school community.

I'm a big fan of banners. Not just banners in the school, like in the gymnasium showing the year the school won the state championship, but also banners *outside* the school. Don't we want the whole world to know about our great school? Why hide all the good stuff inside when many schools have great big exterior walls that face the street where a banner could be hung to brag on the school? We've all seen a great billboard on the highway that made us laugh or smile. We can do that with our schools too. Our building facades can be used as free advertising space. But it's not just sports teams and test scores that deserve banners. Every department can be used as part of a great PR plan. Here are two examples you might not have considered:

- A school transportation banner that reads, "We transport students safely over one million miles each year. Riding a school bus is the safest way to get to school."
- A food service banner that reads, "We serve two million healthy meals to students each year!"

Mix it up and have fun with them. Give parents something

good about your school to stare at every day while they wait to pick up their children. It's perfect advertising!

How Employees Can Promote Their Schools

I encourage every department to create a brag book. A brag book is like a scrapbook for your organization, highlighting the best moments and accomplishments over the years. Here's what a brag book in public education would contain.

- Positive comments received from supervisors, parents, and students
- Pictures of before and after facility improvements
- Pictures of students and staff working together
- Evidence of any successes or awards won individually, by department, or by school/district
- Evidence of time given to a particular project
- Evidence of money spent on projects
- Positive newspaper articles, blog posts, and Facebook posts

It is very easy to forget all that has been accomplished each year, so a brag book is a great way to ensure everyone in the school sees—and remembers—all that hard work for years to come. If you do not work consistently on your brag book, you will forget and lose great material that can be used at future events. But its use goes far beyond this "remember when . . . " practice.

How I have used Brag Books:

1. As evidence to parents, students, and school board members of what has been accomplished
2. As evidence to site councils on how the school board has spent money for their school
3. As evidence to new school board members of what improvements have been made in the schools and districts
4. Pictures and articles used for awards for staff or when honoring retirees

Going back to social media, there is a lot of potential value that I think many schools miss out on for fear that getting on social media will create more problems than it solves. As you can guess, I disagree! If you look at the best companies, *every single one is on social media*. I challenge you to find one that isn't. The reason? That's where their customers are. Imagine sending out a tweet and your whole customer base sees it? That's power! We can do that in public education and reap the benefits that these best companies have been enjoying for years. Below are some examples of how employees can practice PR at the school, out in the community and even from home.

- The district finance office takes pictures of some of the great student work that is displayed on the walls and posts the pictures on their Facebook page.
- The custodians, who are extra vigilant in picking up trash both before students arrive and after students leave the building, stop to talk with parents about all the school improvements.
- The cafeteria manager and cooks, who tweet today's lunch specials to all the students, also take time to tell parents how well their own children are doing in the school system.
- The teacher who once sent her children to private school tells all her friends how well her children are doing now in public school.
- The Parent-Teacher Association highlights school and district success stories in all their publications. They regularly help build their own follower base and add followers to the various school employee social media.
- The transportation department posts directions to sporting events on Facebook, takes pictures, and tweets the scores of the games.
- Employees help gain community support for ballot measures affecting the school or district by educating the

public on the school's stance on the issue.

I regularly post positive information about our school and district. I also encourage all of my school leaders to do the same, and then we share and retweet each other's posts to expand our reach to a wider audience. Because of this, our followers are constantly bombarded with positive school information. We also try to increase our number of followers to keep that range of people we reach growing until, with the click of a button, we can reach the whole community. And, yes, I believe in allowing students to follow me on Twitter and parents to do the same on Facebook. I take any chance I get to make a connection with one of my customers and build our relationship. Public education is about caring adults helping young people succeed, so why not take that opportunity to interact with students? Additionally, it allows me to keep my finger on the pulse of what is going on with my students. What are they talking about? What do they care about? Knowledge is power, and being in the loop via social media is an opportunity I think all school leaders and staff should take.

> Have you ever had your server at a restaurant explain that he or she took an item off your bill? The best companies train their employees to inform you when they have given you great service, ensuring that you do not forget how well you were treated. We can do the same in education.

PR as Damage Control

But PR isn't just for sharing the good news. It's also damage control. In a crisis, be prepared to field questions and frustration from the community. The media may very well pick up the story, so be prepared for that too. This is another value of making strong connections with media personnel; a friend can be more forgiving than a stranger.

It may not seem like the best idea, but I believe administrators should notify press when something bad happens that is related to their school because it guarantees they can put their own spin on it. Or better yet, write the article yourself for the paper, saving them time. It's a win/win!

One note about speaking to the media. When it comes to administrators dealing with the press, there is great value in bringing a staff member with you to a news briefing. Let's say something really bad happens in the cafeteria. Instead of the principal or superintendent speaking to the press, a cook or manager talking about it is better because people will believe a worker or a person closest to the issue over a leader. Leaders get paid to spin and the public knows that, so if you have a trusted employee close on the front lines when a potential PR disaster comes up, try giving him or her the microphone. You can control PR damage by briefing all staff when an issue occurs at the school, making sure they have the pertinent facts so that when they go out into the community, they can represent the school in the correct manner and dispel any negative rumors themselves. *This speaks to the importance of all employees knowing how to be a PR agent.* You'll learn the value of having your school staff helping out with PR as you enlist them. It certainly lessens the burden of being the "voice" of your school. However, at the end of the day, yours may be the only voice that matters in some situations.

When rumors are going around, the strategy of "One Clear Voice" is helpful.[207] This PR strategy is about leaders taking control of situations by being the voice of the organization. By issuing an official statement, whether it's at an assembly, a schoolwide voice-mail or email, or a letter home, having One Clear Voice speak on a matter may be necessary to diffuse a situation or dispel false information. When the superintendent speaks up, it stops the rumors because the public has the facts. It cuts down any future noise or news reporting.

One time, there was a rumor that a kid got shot at our school. Stories like this spread like wildfire on social media and then get picked up by the local news. As superintendent, I was able to use the One Clear Voice strategy to clear it up quickly by sending out a message about what really happened and what didn't. Hearing an authority speak about an issue that people only hear about via word of mouth quickly stops that gossip from spreading. This is why having a social media presence and connection with families is important for school administrators. If I hadn't made connections with parents on social media beforehand, I would have had to take the time to call or email everyone. But sending out one simple tweet got the information out faster and easier than other methods. For this reason, connecting with families and students in the forum that they prefer saves time on the back end and shows how invaluable social media can be in a time of crisis.

Some administrators see social media as a nightmare and something to avoid. But my philosophy is that it's already being used the wrong way, so we might as well find ways to use it to our advantage. Yes, social media is rampant with haters, but once we get past that noise, we can see the true benefit of having our entire school community in one place when that final bell rings for the day. Being connected with the students and families helps leaders find problems before they start. How many inter-student fights start at home on social media and carry over to the next day and week at school? Being on social media keeps us in the loop and, though we may not be able to stop it, we can at least be prepared to handle the situation when we get to school.

> Before you send a statement to the media, always send it to internal staff first. You never want employees to see news about their school on the TV instead of from you.

Another way to control PR damage is by using an internal One

Clear Voice strategy. By briefing all staff when an issue occurs at the school, we can make sure they have the pertinent facts so that when they go out into the community, they can represent the school in the correct manner and dispel any negative rumors themselves.

So if you haven't already, I suggest tapping social media in order to quash nasty, untrue rumors before they go too far. While you have their ears, take a moment to share some of the triumphs and successes of your school that make you proud and that may inspire pride and enthusiasm in your customers. Hey, you might even have some fun while you're at it!

Sometimes School Public Relations Go Awry

For every PR success story, there are several PR snafus. Here are a few examples of stories that ended up in the media:

- A school PR employee got fired for a DUI. Talk about irony!
- A teacher came to school drunk
- A PR employee at a public school sent her kids to private school. You can imagine the field day the press had when they found out that the person in charge of endearing the public to her school didn't value the school enough to send her own kids there.
- A teacher stealing books and materials to start her own private school
- A public school principal sent a voicemail to all students' parents to announce the school dance. However, he didn't pay close enough attention to detail and set the phone message to call out at 5 a.m. instead of 5 p.m., waking up every family! Even the best intentions can have a negative outcome, so carefully plan your PR and guard against backfires that can hurt your credibility.
- Teachers, coaches, and principals found guilty of having sexual relations with students

- A teacher called in a school bomb threat to get out of having to attend a meeting
- A cook cussing at students when they go through the lunch line
- Staff selling drugs to students
- Teachers caught cheating on state tests
- School staff embezzling money
- A superintendent suspended for pulling a board member's pants down[208]
- Principals and teachers receiving DUIs

A Key Communicator List

My leaders and I maintain email lists, text threads, and social media groups with what we refer to as key communicators. Included in these lists of key communicators are high profile city and community members and businesses from the community. Members might include the chamber of commerce, the town council, mayor, city manager, police officers, insurance agents, real estate agents, librarians, shop owners, religious leaders, and local barbers and stylists. I can then distribute positive stories to key people and media contacts with the click of a button. I will also try to friend such personnel on Facebook and follow them on Twitter. I suggest school leaders update these lists regularly and send out positive information each week. The more people hearing your praise, the better the odds someone will sing it, and that's the point of a good public relations plan.

Final Thoughts on Everyone Is a Public Relations Agent

In an earlier concept, I mentioned that people will judge the entire organization based on their interaction with one employee. There is a lot riding on what we all say and do. It's not the responsibility of one person or department. If we, as school leaders, are truly doing our job, our entire staff will be PR agents and will spread the word to others, who will also become positive PR agents. *If your school is successful in any area, whether it's sports, academics, or facilities, you're not doing your job if you're not bragging about it to your community until you're blue in the face.* We must challenge each school employee to promote their school and district. Everyone must know that being a positive PR agent is essential in this age of competition if we want to survive and thrive.

Customer Service Micro-Concepts

"There is a spiritual aspect to our lives—when we give, we receive—
when a business does something good for somebody,
that somebody feels good about them!"
– Ben Cohen, Cofounder, Ben & Jerry's[209]

This chapter is dedicated to concepts or that have been touched on briefly in other chapters but not completely, so the full weight of their point was missed.

Customer service is such a huge subject, and this book could have easily been twice as long! There's always more I want to say, but these last few "micro-concepts" on customer service round out what I think are the most important foundational components of a great customer service system. Though these concepts are small, they are still important to consider when creating a well-rounded customer service system in your school.

CONCEPT 19

The Importance of First Impressions

I've mentioned first impressions in the Facilities Maintenance concept, the Touch Points concept, and the Keep Backstage Issues Backstage concept, but I want to emphasize a few more key aspects of this idea.

First off, the importance of first impressions goes beyond the tangible things like signage and airplane tray tables. Even when it comes to interactions with the customer, there is so much more riding on first interactions. They play a tremendous role in what a customer thinks of an organization. To quote a Head and Shoulders commercial from the 1990s, "You never get a second chance to make a first impression."[210]

I was speaking in Chicago, and I heard about a certain McDonald's at the convention center that gave exceptional customer service. Normally I like to eat at establishments that are not germane, but I decided to make an exception. I was not disappointed.

As I turned the corner, I saw this huge line of people and could not tell what the line represented. I looked down and there were painted feet to show people where the line went. I walked around the line to see what was going on and, to my surprise, it was for this particular McDonald's. The painted feet seemed to extend for a hundred yards or more from the entrance to the restaurant.

Part of me wanted to go elsewhere, but my curiosity would not allow me to do anything but stand in line. The line moved very quickly and, before long, there was a gentleman waiting to greet me. This nice gentleman was the manager, and he shook my hand and welcomed me to McDonald's. He complimented my clothes and even asked me about my day. This guy had to do this hundreds if not thousands of times each day for his customers. As I ordered my meal, the employees spoke to me and told me to have a nice day. There were signs up in this restaurant that stated: "If we do not say hi or hello to you, your meal is on us."

After I ate my meal, I talked with several locals in the restaurant and they said they eat here every day. Some seniors told me it was the best part of their day, because the manager always found a way to complement them. When there was a break in the line, I was able to talk with the gentleman and he told me that he greets his customers every day. He told me that without the customers, he does not have a job. I snapped a picture with this manager and the people in line to show in my presentations. The short conversation with this gentleman and the experience have honed my customer service philosophy regarding first impressions.

There is plenty of research on first impressions (some of which I've mentioned in earlier concepts), but forget about what the experts say for a moment. We inherently know the importance of a first impression, and we also know how hard it is to change a first impression. Take these common first impressions for example:

- A first date
- Meeting your in-laws for the first time
- Attending a new place of worship
- A job interview
- Your first day of school as a student or teacher
- Starting a fitness class or joining a sports team

When you look at this list, do you recall how it felt to be seeing people for the first time? It's often nerve-wracking, because we don't know what to expect and we want to make a good impression. This is where it starts, on the very basic human level.

At the business level we have Walmart, the nation's largest retailer. They brought back greeters to their stores. Dressed in those blue Walmart vests, they say "Hi, may I help you?" to everyone who enters the store. Walmart did away with greeters in 2012, but their research indicated customers appreciated being met at the door by a smiling worker, happy to have their business.[211] From this example and the McDonald's example above, we can see the power of having a positive first encounter with a person at an organization. Now, how can we apply this concept to public schools?

Public Schools and First Impressions

With all the research about first impressions and how hard it is to change a first impression, why do public schools struggle with this concept? One might think we *try* to give a negative first impression! Our motto might be, "Public Education: We enjoy starting out in a hole with parents," or "We like walking uphill in public relations." How about "You are here, we are here, deal with it"? This is a far cry from the greeters at Walmart and McDonald's.

In public education, how likely is it that a parent will hear something negative from the school before they hear something positive? Here is a test. Ask one hundred parents their first thought when they hear the school has called their home? I bet more than 90 percent will believe the reason pertains to something negative about their child. How likely is it that a middle school or high school student will bring home an F on a report card without his or her parent ever having had a pleasant one-on-one conversation with that teacher? I believe in this rule for public schools: *The parent must have a positive experience with the school and with each of his or her student's teachers, before they have a negative experience with the school or teachers.* While it sounds quite simple, the devil, or magic, is in the details.

When writing my second book, *Simply the Best: 29 Things*

Students Say the Best Teachers Do Around Relationships, the students' answers to our questions correlated with first impression research.[212] They told us they love it when staff smile at them, speak to them, say hello and goodbye. These are the four most important aspects of making a great first impression. It really is that simple when it comes to first impressions, but school personnel are not trained in this concept. So now the challenge is to train staff and implement these practices throughout the school district.

As leaders, we must figure out every school and district touch point and then make sure we have the ability to make a good first impression at each touch point. Below is a list of a few of the very best techniques used by schools to give a great first impression.

1. Move issues like student discipline and head lice out of the front office and make the office a warm and inviting place for new and existing students and parents.
2. Have a good customer–service driven school employee greet all visitors at your school and district.
3. Have excellent customer–service driven administrative assistants in front offices and answering your phones.
4. Make sure every parent receives a positive phone call from the school during the first few days of school.
5. Make sure every student receives a home visit by a school employee before the school year begins.
6. Ensure the entire district has a Move-Up Day where students get to meet their next year's teacher and school before the start of the next school year.
7. Every day have a customer–service driven employee greet and help parents get students out of cars at the elementary school.
8. Have principals and teachers greet students every day as they enter the school.
9. Ensure that bus drivers and monitors welcome students

by name onto their bus each day, and say a positive remark like good-bye or see you tomorrow when students exit the bus in the afternoon.

10. Make sure cafeteria workers speak to students each day as they are going through the lines and when they are paying for their meals. The manager should walk around the cafeteria to talk with students.

11. Teachers should be well-dressed and well-groomed at the beginning of each class. If possible, they should greet students at the door as they enter the classroom.

12. Guarantee that students and teachers celebrate when new students enter the classroom for the first time.

13. Ensure that new students are paired with a buddy to each lunch with and spend time with during their first day.

14. Have superintendents, principals, and teachers use their voice on the One Call system to say hello to parents and students.

15. Send hand-written letters or postcards from staff to students.

16. Have greeters meet everyone as they enter for school board meetings. This allows staff to help angry parents before the meeting starts and solve issues before they become newspaper headlines. I always like to start off with a student and staff spotlight to get the meeting started on a positive note.

Not as Easy as It Sounds

While many of the practices listed above sound simple, this is actually very difficult to implement in public schools. Many of these practices are subjective and thus hard to track and document on employee evaluations. It is easy to fire staff for being inappropriate with a student, but it's not so easy to bring in a teacher and tell them they need to learn how to smile! I have had teachers who I thought had to be the most miserable people on earth by the way they carried themselves. Sometimes they were actually very nice, good-natured employees who just had terrible dispositions. I've seen other teachers who always dressed in dirty jeans or were not well groomed and, not surprisingly, they were not respected by students. They gave a bad first impression and many times that first impression was the correct impression. In instances like these, leaders must make the challenging call to retrain an employee on customer service principles such as giving great first impressions.

Thinking about the first impressions our customers may have when they interact with our school personnel will help you understand just how vital these exchanges can be. While it's not always easy to correct and adjust people, we as leaders have to try. It's these customer service skills that are sometimes hard to address that contribute to public schools falling short in their quests for great customer service.

CONCEPT 20

Give Great Customer Service
Across Generations

Entire books have been written about the characteristics of the various generations and how generation gaps are impacting our world and our workplace. I chose to leave out this micro-concept from previous concepts, even though it had a place in just about every one, including the Walk in the Shoes of Your Customers, Collect Reliable Information, and Give Great Service to Employees concepts, to name a few. Not all customers are alike and it is up to the organization to know each subgroup of its customer base and cater to each group's needs. This micro-concept will explain just how important it is to understand the generational differences between customers and how ignoring one group can be the downfall of an organization.

When it comes to defining the different generations, there are widely divergent viewpoints. I suggest doing some research on influences, attributes, and belief systems for each generation. I believe there is enough data on generational differences to now say we must at least acknowledge that our customer service practices may appeal to our customers and employees differently depending on when they were born.

Below is just one example of titles and timelines.[213]

- The Silent Generation: 1925–1942
- Baby Boomers: 1943–1964
- Generation X: 1965–1980
- Generation Y/Millennials: 1981–2000
- Generation Z: 2001–Present

We know that human beings do not fit so neatly into categories and timelines. However, we can see certain generational trends in our students, parents, staff, and our communities. The savvy customer service professional will look for ways to tailor these customer service concepts to the generational needs of his or her customers and staff.

One way retail companies are recognizing the generational gaps between their customers is by catering to how each group shops. What do Apple, L.L. Bean, Target, and Nordstrom have in common? Not only are they some of the best customer service companies, but they are also able to cater to both the older and younger generations' shopping styles by offering customers the ability to shop in stores (like traditionalists and baby boomers prefer) or online (like millennials tend to prefer). These companies put as much effort into their cyber-selling as they do their brick-and-mortar stores, offering the same merchandise and the same discounts.

> "The millennial generation is 80 million strong and already outnumbers baby boomers in the workplace. According to the US Bureau of Labor Statistics, by 2020 millennials will be the new majority and by 2030 they could dominate the workplace with a 75 percent majority."
> —Cara Silletto, "The millennial mindset: why today's workforce thinks differently"[214]

A few years ago, many companies would have never thought that shoppers would stop visiting their stores in favor of shopping exclusively from home. Years back, Montgomery Ward met their demise because of their catalog-only sales method. When people started to shop more at department stores, Ward's stuck with their mail order system instead of following what the customers wanted, only to be surpassed by the likes of Sears in a matter of only twenty years.[215]

Today, there are many people, typically of the younger generations, who value their time so dearly that they overwhelmingly prefer to shop at home on a computer over going to a store. The companies that allow for online shopping in addition to in-store shopping are reaping the benefits and staying relevant to younger shoppers now and for years to come, unlike the late Montgomery Ward.

Of course, offering both buying options alone isn't enough to make a company great at customer service. Walmart owns over 5,000 stores in the U.S. and offers shoppers the option to purchase any of their merchandise on their website, but it also ranks among the worst customer service companies in the world, according to the blog *24/7 Wall St.*[216,217] That's because Walmart's business model is based on low prices rather than giving great customer service. No wonder Amazon has eclipsed Walmart as the largest retailer in the US.

Walmart's struggle also underscores the notion of how important it is for an organization to build a model based on service above all else. Picking and choosing one or two customer service concepts to adopt won't help much, and in fact may get you on those dreaded "worst-of" lists.

What this Looks Like in Public Education

Being a baby boomer myself I remember growing up listening to music on records. My children make fun of the fact that I still keep my old vinyl albums! Although many young people today never had records, in many millennials' short lifetimes, they've seen cassettes make way for CDs, which made way for digital music purchases, which made way for streaming music services like Spotify, and their "non-ownership" model. Today's young adults are experiencing music change at such a rapid pace they share little to no history with older generations. This disconnect between people, even in the same generation, is occurring worldwide in many facets of life, but especially in the technology sector.

Schools are encountering this generational gap as well. We have teachers who never knew a world without typewriters and encyclopedias teaching students who have never known a world without iPads and the internet. These students interact with the world in an entirely different way than baby boomers, so it makes sense that we would adapt and incorporate our students' methods into our education system.

In my experience, interacting with the younger generations, especially millennials, it's all about technology. Young students, teachers, and parents want to use the internet for everything. Parents want to find out about school field trips not from a piece of paper that their kid will likely lose in his or her backpack, but from the school's website, social media page, or even a personal email. I have young teachers who utilize distribution lists for each of their classes. These distribution lists have the email addresses of all the parents of students in the class, so that with the click of a button, a memo can be sent to all parents and be sure to get there!

Young parents and young teachers tend to be tech savvy, but it's really the students who truly need us to utilize technology to get on the same page as them. They want fewer textbooks and more PDF readings. They are right at home emailing a teacher, when previously, students had zero contact with teachers outside of class time. This also speaks to

> I've found that millennial staff are much more likely to quit—even mid-school year—than older generations, especially if the school has outdated or archaic methods and protocol.

the social differences between generations. Students today do not subscribe to the old teacher-student hierarchy. While they see teachers as adults and authority figures, they're not ruler-wielding, silence-demanding, nobody-leaves-their-seat authoritarians that many baby boomers had growing up. They don't fear adults, and there's a need to be treated more like a younger peer than a child.

Knowing how students of today differ from students of the past is important because it dictates expectations. We simply cannot expect our students to behave like previous generations did in school. It's not because they're bad kids or because they're disrespectful, per se. It's simply a cultural shift. Like anything else in customer service, we can either adapt and accept it or try to paddle upstream against it.

CONCEPT 21

Always Look for Ways to Improve Customer Service

I'd like to end with a forward-thinking micro-concept. While I've tried to be exhaustive about customer service in this book, remember that no matter what you do, you can always do more. Knowing that fact, respecting it, and always chasing it will put any organization in a great position to succeed in customer service. The companies that are always looking for ways to improve their service are the innovators, industry leaders, and the most beloved by customers. When a company stops looking to the future and rests on its laurels, it is only a matter of time before something new comes along and takes that company's customers.

One example of this is Blockbuster Video. Up until the early 2000s, Blockbuster was the hottest video rental company. People I know were always jealous when a friend announced that they'd opened up a Blockbuster in his town. They were the kings of the video rental game because they always had the newest movies and video games and often had a larger number of them than the local chains or the mom-and-pop video stores. A new movie would come out and everyone would want to rent it, leaving many to wait weeks to see the movie. I've even witnessed people staking out the store or standing outside first thing in the morning in order to get their hands on a newly returned movie they wanted to rent. Even though some of their policies were widely hated and criticized by customers nationwide, Blockbuster was able to fill the supply and demand need better than anyone else.

We all remember being nickeled and dimed with late fees, rewind fees, and fees for scratching a DVD, to name a few. These were the annoying prices we paid for getting to see a movie the week it came out on video. For years people put up with it. Video rental, it seemed, would never die.

Then a little startup called Netflix came around. They offered movie rentals by mail on a subscription-based system and boasted no due dates, no late fees, no shipping and handling fees and best of all, unlimited rentals for no extra fee.

Customers caught onto this customer-friendly business model, rejoicing the end of late fees and having to operate on someone else's schedule to watch movies. But Blockbuster did not adapt to the changing market needs. Even after Netflix took off and offered to be bought out by Blockbuster, the video chain passed on the deal.[218] Little did they know, they'd just signed their own death warrant. Netflix solved the customer service issues that plagued Blockbuster customers, so when this better option came along, people jumped on it. Eventually, Blockbuster started a video-by-mail service, but it was too little too late.

Meanwhile, Netflix has continued to look for ways to improve their customer service. In addition to solving the problems that plagued video renal stores with its DVDs by mail subscription service, Netflix began offering streaming video in 2007, while Blockbuster was still heavily promoting its movies-by-mail service, a strategy that was already becoming out of date. Once they were able to offer streaming services, Netflix was able to expand to 190 countries.[219]

But of course, Netflix didn't stop there. In 2013, they began their own production company, which creates "Netflix Originals"—movies and TV shows that can only be watched by Netflix subscribers. This move to creating exclusive content has kept competitors like Amazon Video and Hulu from taking away the competitive edge Netflix has built. In 2016, Netflix had a combined total of 126 original series and films—more than all other networks and channels.[220]

Blockbuster went bankrupt in 2010. Netflix is currently worth $70 billion[221] — ten times what Blockbuster was worth in its heyday and more than CBS is worth today — all because they kept finding ways to give better service than their competitors.

More Examples from the Business World

Sometimes, looking for ways to improve customer service is more in the details than the overarching structure of an organization, like Netflix. I've already mentioned the Chick-fil-A drive-thru in my town that I've personally witnessed transform because of their commitment to customer service. Other companies that are looking to innovate, and even push into new territory, are Uber, with their foray into food delivery called UberEATS[222] and Amazon with their first grocery store — which as you can expect breaks all the rules because it has no checkout lines.[223] People simply put items in the cart and walk out the door! It's innovation like this — thinking outside the box of a company's limitations — that is key to success in today's competitive climate. Organizations better be looking for the next big move — or at least keeping up with what competitors are doing — or else they'll be doomed to the Blockbuster fate.

> Amazon is not afraid to push the boundaries of technology. In 2017 they announced a new delivery method called Amazon Key, which would allow delivery personnel to leave a package inside the customer's home through the use of a smart lock and short-term unlock code.[224,225]

Applying this Concept to Public Education

For hundreds of years, public school was about passing information from textbooks to the minds of students via reading, lecture, worksheets, tests, and papers. That's been the model for longer than any of us can remember. When you think about how few companies today are still doing things the way they did hundreds of years ago, you can see why public schools are struggling to stay afloat and why alternative forms of education are growing at such a rapid rate, nationwide. Like Netflix, public schools' competitors are solving the problems that have plagued their customers for years; problems that most people would put up with because there were no other choices. The inflexibility of the way students are taught and the reluctance to adopt new technology that their students are using outside the classroom are the late fees and lack of streaming video of the educational world. Below are some innovations that public schools are adopting to keep up with and even get ahead of what private, charter, and home schools are doing.

I've already mentioned home visits and, while this may not be a new idea, it's one that I find many schools are still not incorporating. When it comes to customer service, face-to-face, one-on-one conversations are the building blocks to success. Beyond home visits, schools are now offering more options for students to work and learn from home. At such schools, when a student is sick and has to stay home, he or she can still access lectures, homework, and notes from class via the school website and the teacher's sharing of lesson materials online. Some schools are even offering online classes, similar to those used by homeschooled students. It's not a far leap to say that in the future we can offer 100 percent online education to our students so they can attend their virtual classes on their own schedules. This would allow our high school students the ability to pursue meaningful employment and still complete their education, in turn making them eligible to go to college when previously their only option was to drop out of school and work to make ends meet.

Remember the Google campus description from the Give Great Service to Employees concept? Well it turns out that public education is right on their heels! Three public schools in southern New Mexico have started using nap pods to help students who are tired, have headaches, or are agitated from confrontations with peers or teachers.[226,227] Recent research has even shown that these nap pods show great health benefits for students.[228]

Staying in the Southwest, the University of Phoenix was originally scoffed at for being a campus-less, online-only college. However, they opened the door for the online learning that is integral to most college experiences, including Yale, Stanford, and Harvard to name a few. Not only do these schools offer online-only courses to their enrolled students, but they offer free online courses as well that are open to the public. You simply click on a class and get started! Open Yale, which has been around for years, offers anyone the ability to watch recorded actual Yale classes and even do homework and take exams.[229]

This is just the tip of the iceberg of what is being offered to college students today. Maybe as public school educators, we can look to what our students are doing *after* they leave our walls and try to set them up for success by adopting some of higher education's innovative practices. Colleges understand competition because each student that they admit has *chosen* their school. Modeling college practices in public schools would not be a bad idea, don't you think? Hey, we've come a long way from the days that even I can remember when it was "okay" to beat students with paddles in public schools. But we are not there yet. In customer service, the rule is that you never arrive. We must always strive to find new areas of improvement.

Final Thoughts on Customer Service Micro-Concepts

In this chapter, I've shared three micro-concepts for public education that were just too important to leave out. First impressions are really the start of customer service. They're the welcome mats at the front door of our schools that show our students, families, and community that this is a safe and friendly place. When we can commit to making great first impressions, we get bodies in the door. What we do once they're inside will determine if they stay.

Giving great service across generations is another key to success. In business, not all customers want the same thing, nor are they marketed to in the same way. But the best companies find ways to target customers to reel them in and get them excited about the brand. When we can do this in public education—really know our customers—then we can not only communicate more effectively with them, but also make them feel at home with our methods. Whether those customers are students, parents or staff, understanding each person in the context of his or her generation can keep them from feeling disconnected and, in turn, moving on to competing schools.

The final piece to the customer service puzzle is striving for more. The best companies never rest on their laurels, and public schools must do the same. Our schools must change with the times and the changing clientele by offering services that are up to par with and even surpass our competitors. When we look at what other types of schooling are doing and we see that we are falling behind, it's on us to catch up or else get left in the dust. The competition is here, whether we like it (or accept it) or not. The future of our schools depends on how we adapt to the changing landscape of education.

In this innovate or die world, the choice is ours and I hope that these concepts have given you the tools to choose to adopt new customer service practices and fully commit your school to giving great service to your students, families, and staff. After all, it's what they deserve.

Epilogue

Excerpt from *Who Cares: Improving Public Schools Through Relationships and Customer Service* (2007):

Educators who have retired or are nearing retirement may think they don't have to worry about what happens in public education. However, one should remember that retirement funds may not be as safe as one would hope. *The New York Times* published an article entitled "Once Safe, Public Pensions are Now Facing Cuts." This article examines the false sense of security among workers who "have enshrined the view that once a public employee has earned a pension, no one can take it away" (Walsh, 2006). Many states have retired teachers and public employees who are either losing pay or benefits or seeing an increase in retirement age or years of experience, or maybe all three. Whether it is rising health insurance costs or a reduction in benefits or pay, public employees' retirement programs are being increasingly targeted in city and state budgets. If public education continues on a downward spiral, retirees may find that their benefits will parallel the plight of public schools.[230]

I wrote this over eleven years ago not knowing how relevant it would be for me later. As of the writing of this book, my personal retirement has been impacted by changing legislation. In 2018 the state of Kentucky passed Charted School Legislation, changed pension plans for all new Kentucky teachers, and stopped allowing sick day accumulation to be figured into retirement pay for all teachers.

Also in 2018, our nation saw teacher strikes and bus loads of teachers descending on state capitals. At the writing of this book we currently have a president and a secretary of education who are pro-school choice. And in our state of Kentucky we have a governor, state board of education, and educational commissioner who are all pro-school choice. As paraphrased earlier from the *Wizard of Oz*, "I've a feeling we're not in 1987 anymore." Competing For Kids is our new reality!

Appendix

Appendix Contents

1

Reflection Questions and Training Activities

"Sometimes the questions are complicated and the answers are simple"
– Dr. Seuss[231]

Introduction:
The Competition Is Here
Customer Service Reflections

1. In your opinion, why did the market for homeschooling and charter schools grow so quickly?
2. Is anyone in public school totally safe from losing their job due to competition?
3. Are public school teacher retirement systems totally safe?
4. Which states offer the most school choice? How are public schools doing in those states?
5. Does school choice lead to more segregation? What value comes from school choice? What problems does it create?
6. Does it hurt the perception of public education when those who work in public schools choose to send their children to private and charter schools?

Introduction:
The Competition Is Here
Customer Service Training Activities

1. How many forms of school choice exist in your community? Are they gaining or losing students? Chart five to ten year enrollment trends.
2. When students leave your school or district, where are they going? College? Work? Unknown? Make a K-12 five-year list

of where students are going when they leave your school or district. Any noticeable trends?

3. What do schools of choice offer students that we are not currently offering? What can we do? For example, have we checked to see how they feed their students compared to how we feed our students? In other words, have we checked out our competition? Be a mystery guest and go observe school choice options. Interview new students to your school or district; what can we learn from our competition?

4. Name some local companies that went out of business in your community. Did their departure surprise you? Currently, are there some companies you know that are struggling? In your opinion, what happened in most of these companies that led to their demise? How about other national companies that went out of business? Do you see similar trends in public education?

Concept 1:
Customer Service Must Be the Top Priority of Leadership
Customer Service Reflections

1. A school bus driver has a terrible relationship with students on his/her bus. The driver does not make any attempt to learn the students' names, nor does he speak to the students as they enter or leave his bus. The driver also refuses to communicate with parents in a timely manner. Is this a training issue? Is this a transportation director issue? Is this a superintendent issue?

2. A high school cafeteria worker is working the register when a student asks to charge her lunch. The worker tells the student that she is over the charge limit and must take a cheese sandwich for lunch. The cafeteria worker then takes the tray of food and dumps it into the trash can. Is this a leadership issue? Is this a training issue? Who is responsible for changing

this? The cafeteria manager, principal, food service director, and/or superintendent?

3. Why should school boards make customer service part of the criteria for hiring and evaluating school superintendents?
4. Why should principals be hired and evaluated by superintendents based on how well they perform customer service?
5. Should customer service be a major component of evaluations for directors of food service transportation, facilities, and special education? Should every employee be evaluated on customer service?
6. How could customer service be incorporated into all staff evaluations?
7. If customer service is important, how might this shape the interview process as it pertains to interview questions and role-playing?
8. How will customer service standards fit into school and district improvement plans? How will customer service fit into long-range district plans? Refer to "Possible Customer Service Objectives for School Improvement Plans" in the Appendix.
9. Think of your favorite sports team. Do you believe the leadership of the coach and the organization truly make a difference?
10. Who are some of your favorite leaders you have worked for in the past? Why are they your favorites?

Concept 1:
Customer Service Must Be the Top Priority of Leadership
Customer Service Training Activities

1. Look up leadership quotes or use the quotes below. Choose your favorite quotes, and tell why you like and/or believe it.

   "I am not afraid of an army of lions led by a sheep; I am afraid of an army of sheep led by a lion." —Alexander the Great

"The quality of a leader is reflected in the standards they set for themselves." —Ray Kroc[232]

"The supreme quality for leadership is unquestionably integrity. Without it, no real success is possible, no matter whether it is on a section gang, a football field, in an army, or in an office." —Dwight D. Eisenhower[233]

"A leader is one who knows the way, goes the way, and shows the way." —John C. Maxwell[234]

"Everything rises and falls on leadership." —John C. Maxwell[235]

"No man will make a great leader who wants to do it all himself or get all the credit for doing it." —Andrew Carnegie[236]

"The task of the leader is to get his people from where they are to where they have not been." —Henry A. Kissinger[237]

"A good leader takes a little more than his share of the blame, a little less than his share of the credit." —Arnold H. Glasow[238]

"I suppose leadership at one time meant muscles; but today it means getting along with people." —Mahatma Gandhi[239]

"Leadership is about taking responsibility, not making excuses." —Mitt Romney[240]

"Leadership Is Influence: Nothing More, Nothing Less" —John C. Maxwell[241]

2. Work in Groups—Chart how current leadership could give better customer service to you. Compare answers among group and post. Give chart paper to leadership. See "Giving Great Service Up and Down the Organizational Chart" in the

Appendix to see how giving great customer service flows through an entire school system.

3. Create Customer Service SMART Goals for your schools and districts. Specific, Measurable, Achievable, Realistic, and Timely.

4. Research YouTube video clips and movie clips that might be included in a school or district customer service training program. Make a list of how clips might be used and for which work groups the clips might be utilized.

5. Look at school district evaluations for various work groups within the school or district. Determine if customer service can be infused into the current evaluation system. Is there a way within the current system to infuse customer service into the current growth plans?

Concept 2:
Every Touch Point Matters
Customer Service Reflections

1. What are the issues if more than one person is responsible for a particular touch point?

2. How well does your school or district monitor these various touch points? Why might some touch points be more important than others?

3. Looking at your district, school, and/or programs, where are your worst coffee stains (touch points) and how can you clean them?

4. Think of a few places where you do your personal business. What are the touch points of these businesses? Where and how would you make improvements?

5. For parents enrolling their new student at your school, what are some of the most important touch points for the parents and student during this process?

Concept 2:
Every Touch Point Matters
Customer Service Training Activities

1. List as many school or district touch points as possible. Take some time to walk around your school with a critical eye and view some of the places listed. List one and only one person who is responsible for each touch point.
2. List some of your school's or district's best touch points and some touch points that need improvement.
3. The superintendent wants a survey form developed for new parents and students to fill out about their first-day experience. This form will go directly to the superintendent. Develop questions for this survey. You can start by creating a list of all touch points a student encounters from the time they first arrive at your school or campus until they arrive at their home.
4. List all touch points under your direct purview. Examples: school bus, classroom, cafeteria, gymnasium.
5. Think about a major program in your district, such as a major high school sports contest, senior trip, the hiring process, grandparents' day, or graduation. List all the touch points for this event.

Concept 3:
Hire the Best
Customer Service Reflections

1. Have you ever been part of an ineffective hiring process as either a member of a hiring committee or as an interviewee? What specifically made this hiring process ineffective?
2. What are the customer service ramifications about the perceptions of a school when the interview process is effective? Ineffective?
3. Are there any hiring processes public schools can borrow from the best customer service companies?

4. Do you think the success of the entire hiring process falls on leadership? Why or why not?
5. What are the customer service qualities a school or district should look for in a potential staff member?
6. How often does your school recruit great candidates and how often do you think about customer service in this process?
7. How can you use the interview process to set the expectations for new hires?
8. How often does politics trump quality in the hiring process in your school or district?

Concept 3:
Hire the Best
Customer Service Training Activities

1. Review the customer service interview questions for staff and teachers. Choose and chart ten of your favorite questions. Then develop three additional customer service questions that will help you to hire the correct person for your customer service-driven school.
2. Discuss and develop two customer service role playing scenarios and two performance events around customer service that can be utilized in the interview process.
3. Make a list of ten ways a school or district can ensure that applicants receive good customer service during the entire hiring process.
4. Read through the "Interview Committee Checklist" in the Appendix and make adaptations for your school and or district.

Concept 4:
Forge Relationships with the Customers
Customer Service Reflections

1. Do you include relationship building and getting to know students in your school improvement plan?
2. Should all district staff attend graduation? What obstacles might we face when trying to implement such a plan?
3. Do you believe home visits are important to students and families? Do any teachers do home visits? What obstacles might we face when trying to implement such a plan?
4. Do you believe eating lunch with students is a good relationship-building practice? Would you pay for staff members' meals who are willing to eat with students? How can you find relationship-building time within a school day?
5. Should all employees be trained each year in how to establish relationships with children?
6. Do staff members attend professional development on relationship building?
7. List a few attributes of your favorite teacher or school person. How many attributes are relational?
8. Why are coaches generally listed by students as people who make a difference in their lives?
9. Do people call home when students are absent, or do you allow a computer to do it? Might parents have a different view depending on which process is used?
10. Do you allow the students' favorite teacher to hand graduates their diplomas?
11. At the end of the year, do you have a Move-Up Day where students go to their next year's teacher or school? Why might this be important?
12. Do the elementary, middle, and high schools incorporate relationship-building time into the school day?

Concept 4:
Forge Relationships with the Customers
Customer Service Training Activities

1. Find a large space such as a cafeteria, gym, or library. Have counselors place the name of each student in the school on poster paper. Each teacher is to place two significant noneducational facts about each student on the poster paper.

   Afterward, think about this:
   How many students (customers) do we not know anything about who come into our schools and choose our services every day?

2. Develop a system where every student has an adult advocate who knows them and can be the one contact for the parents or guardians.

3. Load staff on buses and drive them into the poorer sections of the neighborhood. Develop a list of reflection questions for staff members to answer and share with the group after this trip.

4. Get a test group of teachers to do home visits and recruit more teachers to participate each year. How can we reward these teachers for doing these visits? Money? Extra personal day? Other ways to reward? How can these teachers share their stories with other teachers? How can leaders model these visits?

5. Organize a "Move-Up Day" where each student gets to visit their next year's teacher and school before the end of the school year.

6. Create a one-page relationship form of things next year's teacher needs to know about every student in each classroom. Teachers lose valuable time each year relearning this information.

7. Name staff that have the best relationships with students. Chart what they do well.

8. Find evidence of relationship-building initiatives in the school or district improvement plan and/or the school or district professional development plan. Evaluate current relationship initiatives and discuss how current programs can be improved. Create new customer service and relationship initiatives and required training programs. Who will conduct these trainings?

Concept 5:
Train for Customer Service
Customer Service Reflections

1. How much will training help a bad hire? Why?
2. Who in the district should provide customer service training?
3. Do you have some employees that could use public relations training? With whom would you start?
4. What trainings have school leaders had in the art of customer service?
5. Do you have school leaders involved in state and national school public relations conferences?
6. Is customer service training part of your school or district improvement plan?
7. If customer service is important, how often do you think you should train staff in customer service practices?
8. Why is it important for leadership to be involved in the school and district customer service training? What impact will poor and/or ineffective leadership have on training employees in customer service?

Concept 5:
Train for Customer Service
Customer Service Training Activities

1. Your school or district has decided to train all employees in customer service. Chart answers to the following questions.
2. What are the objectives?
   • How do you break the staff down into various work

groups? (For help, refer to "15 Thoughts on a Customer Service Training Plan for Public Schools" in the Appendix.)

- Can you do one session with all work groups, and what might that training look like?
- How do you provide great customer service for all the trainees?
- How do you make the trainings fun and informative?
- How will you publicize the trainings?
- How will you monitor your customer service objectives after the trainings?

3. Look at the training guide brochure created for office staff in the Newport Independent School District in Kentucky. Allow staff to create similar guides for various work groups within the school or school district.
4. Go to YouTube and find video clips you would want to use in your district customer service trainings. Some examples I've mentioned earlier include the Seinfeld Car Rental clip in the Under-Promise, Over-Deliver concept and the United Breaks Guitars clip in the Recover Well concept.
5. List 3-5 specific training topics that should be included for each work group within your school or district.

Chapter 6:
Walk in the Shoes of the Customers
Customer Service Reflections

1. How many times do school and district leaders ride the school buses? Eat in the cafeteria? Sit in classrooms for an entire period?
2. Are teachers, administrators, and board members allowed to choose the teachers for their children? What would it be like to have no control when your children are placed with a bad teacher?

3. Have you ever punished a group of students because of the behavior of a few students? What would happen if we punished all teachers because of the behavior of a few teachers?

4. Evaluate how your extracurricular programs cut students during tryouts. Would we allow the same cutting methods for adults in our system?

5. Do we implement policies and procedures that adults within the school system would not tolerate? For example:
   - Do we confiscate cell phones from students for the very same mistakes adults make with their cell phones?
   - Do we give staff members cheese or peanut butter sandwiches when they forget their lunch money?
   - Do we make uncooperative staff members sit in a cafeteria or on a bus in absolute silence?

Chapter 6:
Walk in the Shoes of the Customers
Customer Service Training Activities

1. Review current discipline code, lunchroom procedures, bus procedures, etc. Which policies and procedures would adults in the system struggle to adhere to within your school system.

2. Be a mystery guest and go through the lunch line like a student, ride a school bus, etc. Create a mystery guest form to fill out during and after the mystery guest experience. Discuss findings.

3. Ask coaches for their procedures on cutting players for their respective programs. Walk in the student's shoes and choose some of the best strategies that could be employed by all coaches.

4. Review and list some of the biggest student and parent issues over the past several years. Interview school administrators for help.

5. Could the school or district have handled these issues differently, which could have led to a more positive outcome?

Chapter 7:
Collect Reliable Information
Customer Service Reflections

1. Assuming that students are your first and most important customer, how often do you ask for their honest feedback about food service, transportation, teaching, learning, etc.?
2. Discuss the quote, "What gets monitored gets accomplished."
3. What methods of feedback are you currently using in your school or district for students and parents?
4. How can you improve your current methods to collect reliable information?
5. Are you currently using focus groups to get reliable information? Who should lead the discussion? What can you do to make sure these focus groups give honest feedback?
6. What focus groups would benefit your school or district? Who should lead the focus groups?
7. How likely is it that people will give honest feedback to those who evaluate them? How can you tweak your evaluation system to ensure that you get honest feedback?
8. Name a time when you, your school, or your district asked and received good feedback, changed a process, or made a decision based on the feedback?
9. How could you use a mystery guest in your department, school, or school district?
10. Do you allow students to do truly anonymous surveys on their teachers, their cafeterias, their bus drivers, etc.?
11. What are a few areas in your school or district that could use more monitoring for customer service?

Concept 7:
Collect Reliable Information
Customer Service Training Activities

1. Recruit a random sample of substitute teachers who have worked at your schools to be a focus group, and ask them how each of the schools in the school district could improve upon their customer service to substitute teachers and the customer service offered to students, staff, and parents.
    *   How might you reward the substitute teachers for their time?
    *   How might you go about building trust?
    *   How will you use the information?
    *   Create a list of questions for these substitute teachers. Create an anonymous form for substitute teachers to rate their subbing experience at each of the schools each day they substitute teach.
2. Pull a random sample (focus group) of students from each school and ask them how you can make improvements in the school lunch programs, transportation programs, or other school initiatives.
    *   How can you build trust with the students to get their honest opinions?
    *   What are the similarities between adult and student responses?
    *   What can you do to improve the initiative(s)?
3. Think of a major school issue, and list how to get reliable information on helping to make the issue better.
4. Have a school leader serve as a mystery guest for a day and go through school lunch lines, ride a bus, etc. Create forms to be utilized.
5. Have a school leader be a mystery guest substitute teacher for a day.
    *   Follow up with a same-day reflection

- How does this reflection compare to what was said by the substitute teachers (#1 above)?
- How can you make improvements?

6. Your school or district wants to get some community input on how to improve customer service. It has been decided that every school leader as well as assistants will personally and randomly call ten parents or guardians.
    - Develop the questionnaire that will be utilized by all leaders.
    - Create a survey to ask all parents about how to improve upon the school and/or district customer service.
    - How can you assure everyone that answers are completely anonymous?
    - How can you assure parents that their responses are valued?
    - To gather more responses, who else can be recruited to make the phone calls?
    - Create a student and staff exit survey. This survey could be given to students as they leave each school in the district to attend another school in or out of the current district.
    - Create an exit survey for all staff, by department, to be filled out before their final day.

Concept 8:
Praise and Reward Employees for Giving Great Service
Customer Service Reflections

1. Recall a time when you received excellent recognition from a supervisor. What made it meaningful?
2. Recall a time when you received general nonspecific praise from a supervisor? How did it make you feel? How could the general praise have been improved?
3. As a supervisor of students or adults, what are some awards you could give? How can you personalize the rewards either from you or to the receiver?

4. How can you use recognition programs to promote customer service initiatives within your school or district?
5. Why is timing important when giving recognition to students and staff?
6. Discuss salary as a form of recognition in a public school system.

Concept 8:
Praise and Reward Employees for Giving Great Service
Customer Service Training Activities

1. Get into groups and chart everyone's favorite ways they have been recognized in their lifetime. List and discuss your personal favorites.
2. Borrowing from the business world, list forms of recognition that might work in a public school setting. List why it may or may not be more difficult within a public school system.
3. List forms of recognition and give examples of why some forms of recognition do not work with employees within a school system.
4. Create your own personal award that could be given to staff members for going above and beyond in giving great customer service to students and parents.
5. Interview other school administrators and business leaders about giving recognition to their employees.
6. Research articles on companies rated the best places to work. Make a list of reasons employees love working in these organizations (you can start with examples from this concept). How could some of these ideas be implemented within a public school system?

Concept 9:
Confront Poor Customer Service
Customer Service Reflections

1. How does a leader navigate having to confront bad employee

customer service, but avoid creating a sentiment that poorly affects teacher morale and culture?

2. Are school employees more protected from being terminated than employees in the business world? How can we hold staff members to high levels of customer service?

3. Explain how customer service standards and training can help remove bad employees.

4. Think of a few ways leaders should not confront poor performers. Example: Do leaders send blanket emails to staff to correct the actions of a few? What should they do instead?

5. Is it harder for leaders to confront employees when they are close friends with the leader? What methods could be employed to make such confrontations easier?

Concept 9:
Confront Poor Customer Service
Customer Service Training Activities

1. The principal brings a new student to a teacher's classroom. The teacher has bad body language, seems disgusted, and states she does not have a desk for the student. How should the principal handle this situation? Role-play a discussion with this teacher.

2. List times when you have been confronted by a supervisor. List and discuss the best and worst techniques utilized by the leader.

3. Interview school leaders and business leaders and discuss their best methods of confrontation. What have been some of their confrontation mistakes?

4. Compile a list of resources on confronting poor performance. The resources should include books, YouTube videos, and movie clips. Discuss how these resources can be utilized.

Concept 10:
Facility Maintenance Is a Top Priority
Customer Service Reflections

1. Can you think of a time you chose to eat at a restaurant based on the condition of the facility?
2. Might clean restrooms help you decide your gas station of choice?
3. Name and list some places of business locally and nationally that do a great job with facility maintenance.
4. Name a few local places and national companies that could stand to have some training with facility maintenance.
5. How can leaders model the importance of facility maintenance?
6. Why is it hard for some custodial staff to notice facility issues that need to be fixed without first being told to do so? How can this be corrected?
7. In the age of competition, how might a school use facilities as a way to attract students?

Concept 10:
Facility Maintenance Is a Top Priority
Customer Service Training Activities

1. Look over "A Sample School First Impression Checklist" in the Appendix. Adjust the checklist for your school or district.
2. Find a local business within the community that does a great job keeping their facilities immaculate and well maintained. Bring a leader from that business to speak to your staff. Record lessons that you can apply to your school system.
3. If you were going to develop a customer service training program for your custodial and maintenance crew, what elements of customer service need to be provided in the training?
4. Look at the list of facility items that might cause some concern

or cause one to have a negative first impression. Look at your school and district; what else can be added to this list?

5. How can you train staff to see facility issues before they are so obvious to guests? Have appropriate staff take pictures of well-done facility maintenance and facilities that need improvement. Then reconvene together to compare the good and the bad aspects of your facilities. See how many people took pictures of the same facility issues!

Concept 11:
Plan and Reflect on Customer Service Practices
Customer Service Reflections

1. Name an event (in or out of school) you have attended that was very organized. What made it go so well?

2. Name an event (in or out of school) you have attended that was unorganized. How did it make you feel?

3. Name an event that you have personally been responsible for organizing? What did you learn from the experience? What went well and not so well?

4. Why are schools notorious for not doing a good job with planning and reflecting on their customer service practices at major events?

5. How do your new staff members know how to run school and district events?

Concept 11:
Plan and Reflect on Customer Service Practices
Customer Service Training Activities

1. In this chapter, I mentioned keeping a checklist of to-do items for an event. List five to ten events for which you think your school or district could use a checklist.

2. Create an event checklist for your next school or district event. Remember to revisit your checklist after the event to make changes for the next time the event is held.

3. Create an event evaluation form to receive feedback on how to improve the event. Discuss how to encourage everyone to give feedback after the event.
4. List characteristics of well-planned events and terribly planned events.
5. Interview school leaders about their largest events and how they plan for such events. Ask about things that have gone wrong at events due to poor planning and make note.

Concept 12:
Give Great Customer Service to Employees
Customer Service Reflections

1. Discuss some positive qualities of your favorite boss. What do you think made him/her great?
2. Discuss some some qualities of your least-favorite bosses.
3. What actions from your school leaders might positively impact your colleagues' attitudes at work?
4. What are a few ideas you could implement to improve your school culture?
5. Discuss having fun at work. How can more fun be incorporated into daily tasks?
6. If culture trumps strategies, why do you think schools don't make improving school culture a priority?

Concept 12:
Give Great Customer Service to Employees
Customer Service Training Activities

1. Think about all the leaders you have worked for in your life. List positive and negative customer service examples from these leaders that you experienced or witnessed.
2. Survey staff and leaders from other schools to get ten examples of how they have been provided with great service from their school or district leaders. Survey staff and leaders at private and charter schools within the district boundaries. Make a list of similarities and differences.

3. Survey new staff members, and ask them how the school and district could have provided them with better customer service. What did the school and district do well and not so well?

Concept 13:
Give a Little Bit Extra
Customer Service Reflections

1. Think of a business example of a time when you received a little extra.
2. Discuss receiving good customer service from a business. Was "giving a little bit extra" part of any of your answers?
3. Discuss a school experience where you received a little extra from a teacher or staff member.
4. Give examples of what a little extra might look like for various school administrative positions.
5. Give examples of what a little extra might look like from school secretaries, cooks, custodians, and instructional assistants.
6. How might school leaders monitor and reward "giving a little bit extra" within the school and district?

Concept 13:
Give a Little Bit Extra
Customer Service Training Activities

1. List some of the best and worst customer service experiences you have received. Which examples included getting a little extra.
2. Make a list of departments or work groups within a public school system, such as business office, coaching, transportation, food service, etc. Write out how each group could do a better job in the area of giving a little extra customer service?
3. List examples of how the best teachers give a little extra customer service to their students.

4. Develop a school and district method for recognizing staff members for giving a little extra.

Concept 14:
Under-Promise, Over-Deliver
Customer Service Reflections

1. Discuss examples of under-promise and over-deliver from either education or the business world.
2. How can a school or district leader use this concept with his/ her staff?
3. How might staff members use this concept with school leaders?

Concept 14:
Under-Promise, Over-Deliver
Customer Service Training Activities

1. Make a list of various work groups within a public school system. List a few examples of how under-promise and over-deliver could be utilized within the work group for students, staff, and parents.
2. List a few examples of *over*-promise and *under*-deliver in education and the business world.
3. List several examples of how a teacher can use this concept with his/her students.

Concept 15:
Recover Well
Customer Service Reflections

1. How can you train all employees in the art of recovery?
2. Would school leaders and school board members receive a lot fewer phone calls if everyone were trained in customer service recovery?

3. Think of a time you could have tried to make an apology equal the offense. How did you do?

4. Can you recall a time you saw an employee turn an upset customer into a supporter?

5. Can you think of business examples of both good and bad recovery attempts?

Concept 15:
Recover Well
Customer Service Training Activities

1. Research five to ten major mistakes made by companies in the business world. How did these companies try to recover? In your opinion, how well did these companies recover?

2. Research five to ten major mistakes made by schools or school districts. How did these schools/districts try to recover? In your opinion, how well did these schools recover?

3. You are the school principal and it's the first day of school. Your elementary school is trying a new dismissal procedure for all students. This new system has some unforeseen issues that cause the buses to leave your school 45 minutes later than the previous year. This faux pas causes every student in the district who rides a school bus to be 45 minutes late getting home. The superintendent's office receives many calls from concerned, angry parents wanting to know why their children are not home. Walk through your entire recovery process.

4. Interview food service directors, managers, transportation directors, principals, assistant principals, superintendents, etc. Ask them about major mistakes and how they recovered well or not so well.

Concept 16:
Keep Backstage Issues Backstage
Customer Service Reflections

1. Why is this concept more important today than in the past for public education?
2. How is this concept important to individual staff members in a public school?
3. Can a public school district be too transparent?
4. What new problems has social media brought to keeping backstage issues backstage?
5. Generally, how effective is the conduct at school board meetings between superintendents and the school board? What can you do to ensure that backstage issues remain backstage.
6. How can schools improve their main office to keep backstage issues backstage?
7. How do you maintain a good relationship with the newspaper while trying to keep from promoting bad information?
8. Should the staff/faculty lounge be considered a sacred place for staff only? Why or why not?

Concept 16:
Keep Backstage Issues Backstage
Customer Service Training Activities

1. Generally, how well is your school or district keeping backstage issues backstage? In which specific areas are the school or district doing well and not so well?
2. Imagine a parent asks a school employee about their elementary school and where they should place their first grade child. What would be some good answers? What about some bad answers? Should we train school employees on how to answer such questions?
3. What are the main areas within a school or district where it is

most important to keep backstage issues backstage? How do we get staff to not talk about negative school issues in public?

4. How can the main entrance of the school and school office be more customer service friendly. Can the main entrance and front office areas be rearranged and redecorated to make sure that they are a pleasant place for students, parents, staff, and guests?

Concept 17:
Don't Do Dumb Things
Customer Service Reflections

1. Give an example of a dumb customer service moment you have experienced in the business world.
2. How could we do a better job preventing schools and staff from doing dumb things to students, parents, and each other?
3. Recall one dumb moment you experienced as a teacher or staff member.
4. Discuss dumb things you believe most schools and school systems do.
5. Can good training help prevent new teachers from doing dumb things? Why or why not?

Concept 17:
Don't Do Dumb Things
Customer Service Training Activities

1. As a principal of a middle school you noticed your basketball coach had posted the students who made the basketball team on the windows of the school. You asked the coach about about his discussions with the players who did not make the team. The coach said there is no discussion, and that this is how he lets everyone know who made the team. Is posting the names of players who made an athletic team on a wall an acceptable method for communicating with students? Create a more

customer-service-based method for all coaches to use to let students know if they made or did not make an athletic team.

2. Research five major mistakes made by companies or their employees. How could these mistakes have been prevented.

3. Interview various school administrators, and ask them about some of the dumbest mistakes made by their employees (without using names) and how these mistakes were handled.

4. Think back to the time when you were in school, and try to remember a dumb thing that was done to you. How was it handled? What are some policies and procedures at your school that must seem quite dumb to parents.

Concept 18:
Everyone Is a Public Relations Agent
Customer Service Reflections

1. Why does bragging on ourselves, thus advertising, seem like a foreign concept for public education?

2. How might keeping a brag book or Facebook page help you change negative opinions of your school district, school, or individual departments?

3. What ideas in this chapter have intrigued you to possibly try in your area of work?

4. Do you believe in allowing parents to follow you on Facebook? Twitter? What are the positives and negatives?

5. How can you better promote yourself and your department?

6. How can you encourage your staff to promote the school and the school district?

Concept 18:
Everyone Is a Public Relations Agent
Customer Service Training Activities

1. Create a video to highlight positive aspects of your school

or district. Your audience is current and new students and parents. What should the video include?

2. Create a list of some great strategies used by staff in various groups (coaches, transportation, teachers, food service etc.) to promote their work area, school, or school district. If you don't know any, think of examples that employees can use at your school.

3. Survey various school leaders and public relations professionals about some of the best strategies to promote schools and school districts.

Concept 19:
The Importance of First Impressions
Customer Service Reflections

1. Discuss a time you had an incorrect first impression of a company.
2. Is there a difference between a relationship first impression and a school or business first impression? Why or why not?
3. How might a good first impression assist you in making a good recovery?
4. Should a principal handle a student being disruptive in a teacher's classroom if the teacher has never made a positive contact with the parent or guardian?
5. How do schools foster bad first impressions?
6. How can schools and teachers overcome bad first impressions?
7. How do you try to make a positive first impression?
8. What types of training can be provided to help school personnel make good first impressions?

Concept 19:
The Importance of First Impressions
Customer Service Training Activities

1. Place staff into various groups and send them to a designated

area within the school or district (gym, cafeteria, etc.). Staff should go to areas other than where they work. Have staff list every touch point in this area that could cause a negative first impression. Next, have staff discuss if items listed are noticed by employees who work in that area every day. Do you think we sometimes need a fresh set of eyes to look at areas within our school or district? Why?

2. Develop a system or school/district policy that ensures a parent or guardian will always have a positive contact with a teacher before they have a negative contact with a teacher.

3. Role-play how to properly give negative information to a new parent over the phone or in person.

Concept 20:
Give Great Customer Service Across Generations
Customer Service Reflections

1. Discuss how hiring practices might be changed for millennial teacher applicants.

2. How might you want to collect reliable information differently for each generation? Do you need to break respondent answers down by generational categories?

3. How might baby boomers and millennial teachers work together to utilize their various strengths to improve customer service for students?

4. How might leaders look at employee recognition programs differently to maximize benefits for generationally different staff members?

5. How might millennial leaders differ from baby boomer leaders? What are the possible implications?

Concept 20:
Give Great Customer Service Across Generations
Customer Service Training Activities

1. List ways schools may need to change to meet the generation-specific needs of students and parents.
2. List changes schools and school districts will need to make to meet the needs of generationally different staff members.
3. Review current board and staff policies to see if some items need to be changed to meet the needs of new staff members. For example, should any tattoo be allowed to be visible to students?
4. Research hiring practices of millennial-run companies and see if there are any practices you could implement into your school system.
5. Find some company surveys that differentiate the wording and/or group responses by generation. Why do they do this? Compare this strategy with how public education looks at survey data.
6. Research millennial companies and how they give great service to their employees. Look for strategies that public schools might want to borrow.

Concept 21:
Always Look for Ways to Improve Customer Service
Customer Service Reflections

1. What are some new customer service ideas that you would like to try in your job description, your school, or your district?
2. What are some methods for selling new customer service initiatives? Why is being a good salesperson important for school leaders?
3. Besides ideas mentioned in this book, what are some other positive customer service changes that are emerging in the business world?

4. Why are customer service ideas seldom listed in school improvement plans? Think of a few that your improvement plan could utilize.

Concept 21:
Always Look for Ways to Improve Customer Service
Customer Service Training Activities

1. Write three to five new customer service objectives for your school or school district. List steps necessary for full implementation.
2. Create a few customer-service-based responsibilities to add to various job descriptions within your school district. Example: School bus drivers should greet each student each day with a hello.
3. List how a school system could reward employees for coming up with new ways to improve customer service to students, staff, and parents. Rank methods and list pros and cons of each reward system.
4. Make a list of methods you can personally use to improve how you give customer service to employees, students and families.

2

A Sample School First Impression Checklist

Applicable Concepts: Touch Points, Facility Maintenance, First Impressions

This checklist can be utilized to see if your school or district is creating a positive first impression. I suggest you use some of these ideas and create your own document for your school or district.

- ☐ Main office entrance is clearly defined by structure and signage.
- ☐ Good signage directs everyone from parking lot to all areas of the building. Signage is one consistent color and always directs with very positive language. There is a light on important outdoor signs when it is dark.
- ☐ There are designated spaces for visitor parking—lines and numbers are freshly painted.
- ☐ Grounds are well mulched (I prefer dark rubber mulch). Grass and weeds are not growing up through the mulch.
- ☐ Curbs are freshly painted once a year.
- ☐ Concrete or blacktop is in good condition and sealed.
- ☐ Fences are painted with no visible rust or disrepair.
- ☐ All fence poles are perpendicular to the ground—not leaning or damaged.
- ☐ The entrance to each facility is well marked (gymnasium, auditorium, main office, central office, elementary school, middle school, high school, preschool, etc.).

☐ Marquee is updated using proper grammar and spelling.

☐ There is ample, clearly marked parking for handicapped customers.

☐ The grounds are well maintained and there are no dead trees or shrubs.

☐ There is no visible trash or graffiti on grounds.

☐ If there is brass, it is polished regularly.

☐ Hardware on doors matches.

☐ Athletic facilities are well maintained—i.e., nets on basketball hoops and tennis courts are in great shape.

☐ Quality trash cans placed every forty to fifty feet and routinely emptied.

☐ Ensure every sign has a purpose and is worded in a positive manner. Rusted, old, and damaged signage is removed.

☐ Playgrounds are in working order and no missing parts.

☐ There are no missing or stained ceiling tiles.

☐ All lights work, not flickering. No bugs in the lights!

☐ Flags are not torn, tattered or faded, and the size of the flag is appropriate for the size of the pole. The flagpole is nicely painted.

☐ If the flag flies at night, it is well lit.

☐ Rails, steps, etc. are nicely painted.

☐ Doors are clean, and scratches are minimized by Murphy's oil soap and wood pens. Hinges are clean and kick plates cleaned and repaired if necessary.

☐ All glass is cleaned regularly and free of handprints, smudges, etc. Any glass with a broken seal is removed. No visible cracks, holes, or chips.

- [ ] Hallways are filled with current student work.
- [ ] One can tell the subject taught in each classroom by how it's decorated.
- [ ] Discipline and sickness are not in the main office "welcoming" the visitors.
- [ ] Guests are welcomed as they enter the main office.
- [ ] Front office provides an inviting setup that promotes positive interaction for visitors and guests.
- [ ] Office looks professional and is free of clutter and bad smells.
- [ ] No dust on tops of lockers, furniture, ledges, etc.
- [ ] Student desks and tables are clean and free of graffiti.
- [ ] Cafeteria is well lit. Cafeteria tables cleaned thoroughly between lunch shifts.
- [ ] A light, comfortable scent is acceptable, but remember too much scent can be worse than no scent at all!
- [ ] Walls are painted. Fingerprints and handprints are cleaned daily from walls and glass.
- [ ] Carpet and tile are cleaned regularly with no stains. Grout is cleaned regularly. Carpets are free of wrinkles and bulges. Cracked floor tiles are quickly replaced.
- [ ] Secretaries are well trained in customer service and speak and smile to everyone who enters the building.
- [ ] Guests are walked to their destinations.
- [ ] Restrooms are clean, fully stocked, and free of graffiti.
- [ ] New student information is available and easy to read. All forms are easy to read and there is ample space to fill them out. A clipboard and pen or pencil are provided.

☐ Personnel are "in the moment" with one customer at a time.

☐ Umbrellas are available at the main office for guests upon request.

☐ There is plenty of parking for visitors close to the entry.

☐ There are canopies or something to protect students and parents from the weather.

☐ Birds' nests and beehives are routinely removed under canopies.

☐ Offices are all well lit, clean, organized, and smell good.

☐ Pictures are hung with a theme. They are all hung straight on walls. Every item in the school office should have a purpose.

☐ TVs, computers, printers, cables, and other technology are all clean and dust-free. Wires are neatly bundled.

☐ Classrooms, hallways, and offices are free from clutter.

☐ All vents are clean.

☐ Window shades are uniform and in good working condition.

3

Possible Customer Service Interview Questions by Job Category

Applicable Concepts: Hiring

Consider adding some of these customer service questions to your job interviews. Also, decide what a good answer might look like. Can you think of better customer service questions to ask? Do you have job categories where you can add customer service questions?

Customer Service Interview Questions
General (Appropriate for Various Job Descriptions)

1. Do you believe customer service is part of your job? Explain your answer.
2. Why should schools be concerned about customer service?
3. Who would you identify as your customer and how would you develop a positive relationship with this individual?
4. How would you provide great customer service in this position?
5. Describe the customer service you've received at this office from the moment you were contacted for the interview until arriving and waiting for this interview to start. Based on your experience and observations, what are one or two ways we could improve our customer service?
6. As a school employee, working with the public is an important part of your job. Do you agree? Do you have concerns?
7. Give an example of a time in your life when you had to

deal with an angry customer. Have you ever been an angry customer? What could have made the situation better? What could have made the situation worse?

8. Identify what you believe are the key elements in handling a complaint.

9. How might you show a customer that you value his or her complaint or comment, even if you are unsure about what can be done about the situation?

10. Describe a problem you faced at your last workplace. How did you resolve it?

11. Provide two or three examples of situations when you showed initiative by doing something that needed to be done without being asked.

12. How would you make someone feel welcome in your position at your school?

13. How would you be a positive public relations agent for this school and district? Name 2 specific actions you could take.

14. How would you keep yourself informed on key issues within the school district?

15. What would good customer service look like coming from your direct supervisor to you and what would good customer service look like coming from you to your supervisor?

Customer Service Interview Questions
Position: Teacher

1. How will you get to know your students? How will students get to know a little about you? How long will this process take?

2. Describe how you will communicate to parents. What if a student is struggling in your class? How and when would you communicate?

3. You have a helper or assistant in your room, and she yells

at students or treats them inappropriately. How would you handle this situation?

4. Provide us with examples that support the following:

   a. Your ability to be positive even when others are negative

   b. Your ability to put students first in decisions and show you care

   c. Your commitment to improving your professional skills

5. What would you do if . . .

   a. you have a student in your classroom who is consistently disruptive?

   b. you have a student who makes fun of the assignment you are giving?

6. Do you have a problem with visiting the homes of your students before the start of the school year?

7. How do your ideas align with our district priorities and philosophy? *(If applicant is unaware or fails to mention priorities or philosophies like "ask student connections," "home visits," or "relationships," then share a couple of these directly with applicant and have her or him respond.)*

8. Identify two to three essential elements for a positive school culture. How would you foster those as a teacher new to the district?

9. How will you work with students after school? Will you coach, lead an extracurricular group, or do after-school tutoring?

10. How will you provide great customer service to your principal?

Customer Service Interview Questions
Position: Food Service Director/Manager/Cook

1. You are at the cash register when you realize a student is over

his or her charge limit. The student has a full tray and has handled some of the food. What do you do?

2. A student asks for a little more food as he or she goes through the lunch line. Physically, he or she looks malnourished and appears skinnier than others. You know the student's circumstance and know he or she receives very little food at home. How do you respond? What might you do?

3. You are in charge of obtaining more student input about the food service program. What might you do? What questions would you ask students about improving food service or what happens in the cafeteria?

4. Describe how you think you should interact with students as they come through the cafeteria lines? What type of body language should characterize the food service workers?

5. You notice Mr. Smith, a parent, is bringing in breakfast from McDonald's to his child several days in a row. You know this is against the law, and you must have a conversation with Mr. Smith telling him he cannot continue to bring outside food into the cafeteria. How do you begin the conversation?

Customer Service Interview Questions
Position: Custodian/Maintenance

Prior to the interview, stage the room with issues custodial/maintenance staff would be in charge of fixing. Issues may include things like: replacing ceiling tiles, cleaning windows, removing bugs from lights, removing paper from mopping, dry or wet floor mopping, or painting walls. Make a list of these issues and have the list on hand for the interview.

Question for custodial candidate:

1. Look around the room and list several improvements you could make to this room if you were the custodian.

2. You notice a parent walking down the hallway who appears to be lost. How might you provide excellent customer service?

3. The desks in a particular classroom always have graffiti all over them. What would you do about it?

4. You notice that a parent parked in the visitor parking lot has a dead car battery. What would you do?

5. When you encounter a student or an adult, you want to exhibit good body language. Other than smiling, what communication strategies would you use to be approachable or inviting?

6. How can you ensure that you will notice issues such as negative signage, weeds, graffiti, and trash before leaders, parents, community members and students see it?

7. During a three hour athletic event, how would you make sure the restrooms are clean and well stocked? How about restrooms during a normal school day?

8. What does the statement "seeing issues before others see issues" mean to you?

Customer Service Interview Questions
Position: Secretary/Administrative Assistant

1. Answering the telephone is one of the duties associated with this position. Give me your best customer service method for answering the phone at our school. *(This is a situation that could be role-played between the applicant and the interviewer.)*

2. The school office plays an important role in communicating messages to everyone who enters the building. What makes an inviting school office? What would be the special touch you would bring to the school office?

3. A student's uncle comes to school to pick him up because he is sick. You look up information about the student, and the uncle is not listed as a possible pickup for the child. The principal is out of town at a conference and cannot be reached.
   a. What do you do?
   b. Role-play how you would tell the uncle he is not allowed to pick up his nephew.

4. A grandparent arrives to eat lunch with her grandchild. This

grandparent has never been at your school and is confused by
your directions to the cafeteria. What do you do?

5. It is quite hectic in the office at the end of the day as students
are getting on the bus to go home. There is some confusion
between the office and the teacher about a bus assignment for
one of the students. In a few minutes, a parent arrives at the
office and is frantic because their child did not get off the bus.
    a. What do you do?
    b. After the child is found, a few minutes later, what are
       some things you need to do?

6. How can you give great customer service to your immediate
supervisor?

7. How can your immediate supervisor give great customer
service to you?

Customer Service Interview Questions
Position: Transportation/Bus Driver

1. During your normal morning route, you drive past a designated stop, but are unaware of it until you are dropping
students off at the school. You learn later that afternoon—as
you are loading the buses for home—that these students were
marked as tardy. What would you do?

2. What would you want to know about the students riding
your bus?

3. How would you get to know the students who ride your bus?
How long would it take?

4. You are driving the football team to an away game. A parent
asks you for directions.
    a. What would you do?
    b. What would you do if you are unsure of the directions?

5. How would the riders on your bus learn a little about you?

6. How might you reward students for good behavior?

7. You want to share an approximate time with the parents for
pickups and drop-offs for your route. How might you do this?

8. What could you learn from tour bus guides that might be effective on your school bus?

9. What are some positive behavior management techniques that you could utilize on your bus?

10. Discuss how you might converse with parents in order for them to get to know you.

11. You see that a student forgets to put his window up as he moves into the isle to leave the bus? How do you handle this situation?

Customer Service Interview Questions
Position: Coach

1. How would you communicate your philosophy and your goals to parents of athletes in your program?

2. You team can only accommodate a set number of student athletes. After tryouts, how would you let students know they did not make the team?

3. How would you handle conflicts with practice or game schedules with players who opt to participate in multiple school functions and activities?

4. How do you communicate with parents concerning scheduling of practices on snow days, holidays, and special occasions?

5. Discuss your philosophy concerning the role of social media as a communication tool.

6. You are the varsity coach at the high school and have found out that the middle school coach, who you helped select, cusses at and berates the players. There are rumors that some players are thinking about quitting. How would you handle this situation?

7. Do you believe the assistant coaches are a reflection of you and the entire program? What type of mentoring and/or training would you provide for them? How would you develop their leadership and customer service skills?

8. How would you make sure your players have the supplies and resources necessary to participate on your team?

9. How would you take ownership of your student athletes in their academic and extracurricular pursuits? What types of one-on-one discussions would you have with your athletes about goals, college, and career readiness?

10. Under what circumstances would you:

    a. want a parent to bring a concern to you?

    b. contact your immediate supervisor?

    c. apologize to a player or a parent?

11. You just made a huge mistake and yelled at the wrong player. The player is very upset. How would you handle this situation?

12. What are some of your best strategies for promoting your program and your players at school and in the community?

Customer Service Interview Questions
Position: School Administrator

1. What type of customer service would you provide for your frontline employees?

2. What types of customer service expectations would you have for your office secretaries, coaches, bus drivers, and custodians?

3. What types of customer service expectations would you have for your teachers?

4. What types of bad service would necessitate an employee being confronted for giving that service to a parent or student?

5. If an employee made a mistake, describe your expectations for "fixing" the mistake in terms of time frame and the employee's actions.

6. You call the school and do not like how the secretary answers

the telephone. You've heard that she is sometimes negative to staff and students. How would you handle this situation?

7. How do school facilities and/or signage contribute to the customer service experience?

8. How would you reward employees for exceptional customer service?

9. How would you monitor and evaluate employees for customer service?

10. How would you connect with all your staff to foster positive relationships?

11. How would you give exceptional customer service to your staff?

12. Would there ever be an exception to when you would follow school policy? Why or why not?

4

Interviewing: What to Look for in a Quality Candidate

Applicable Concepts: Hiring

☐ Good nonverbal communication:
1. Eye contact with each member of committee.
2. Smiling.
3. Tone of voice.
4. Listening.

☐ High energy and enthusiasm with a sense of humor.

☐ Is able to see "gray area." Does not come across as inflexible.

☐ Ability to go above and beyond what is expected. Does candidate mention customer service ideas such as:
1. walking guests to their destination?
2. visiting students and/or parents at home?
3. dressing and behaving as professionals?
4. desiring to get to know students?
5. having a willingness to fix mistakes and problems?

☐ Past evidence of working with students outside the normal school day. Willingness to coach a sport, tutor students after school, or run a club.

☐ An understanding about customer service and its importance.

☐ An understanding of the benefits of school culture.

☐ An understanding of the importance of student

relationships and can give good specific examples of being able to show they care about students.

☐ Willingness to pursue various avenues to help students be successful beyond the regular school day.

☐ An understanding about competition that exists for public school students (private schools, home schools, charter schools).

☐ Their responses to interview questions . . . :
   1. go beyond generalities and jargon.
   2. demonstrate good content knowledge & expertise.
   3. give application examples.

☐ Gives great examples of how they will communicate with parents.

☐ Is agreeable to doing home visits.

☐ Asks interview committee good, specific questions.

5

Interview Committee Checklist

Applicable Concepts: Hiring, Plan and Reflect

☐ Review board policies on hiring, school consultation policy, and union contract hiring policy.

☐ Put together interview committee. (Team leader department chair, council members, content or grade level representative, parent.)

☐ Develop a list of desired personal attributes for the prospective candidate.

☐ Develop a list of professional criteria for vacancy.

☐ Seek input from central office and superintendent on job applications, background checks, etc.

☐ Decide how many candidates will be interviewed.

☐ Decide on a timeline for notifying candidate about whether or not he or she got the job.

☐ Decide how candidates will be notified of decision? Will you call or send a letter? Who will call?

☐ Check and see which extra-curricular and co-curricular positions are vacant.

☐ Where will you interview? Which room? Did you reserve a location?

☐ Check room temperature. Make sure room is clean.

☐ Provide paper and pens for interviewers and interviewees.

☐ Will there be food and/or drinks? Who is going to pick it up and set it up for interview sessions? Trash cans?

☐ Decide whether there will be a tour of the building. If so, who will give it?

☐ Create signs directing interviewees where to sit and wait. Post signs if interviewing when school is not in session.

☐ Decide whether someone is going to be available to greet and wait with the candidates. Make sure to incorporate customer friendly practices, including smiling, welcoming the person to the school, offering the person something to drink, and making sure they know where the restroom is located.

☐ Select date(s) for interviews. Will you call or will someone else call the candidates?

☐ Select times for interviews. Determine how long each will last *(approximately)*.

☐ Confirm dates and times with candidates and committee if interview has been scheduled several days in advance.

☐ Prepare a school information packet to provide to candidate (school calendar, salary schedule, school brochure, and other pertinent information).

☐ Develop a list of interview questions related to the position, to the values and priorities of the school and based on obtaining information about the personal and professional qualities related to the position.

☐ Call the candidate. Give him or her the date, time, and approximate length of the interview (within a range).

☐ Provide directions, if needed. Give interviewee your cell phone number in case they get lost and school is not in session.

☐ Share with the candidate the approximate number of people on the interview committee.

☐ Share what information might be useful for the candidate to bring:
1.   Portfolio
2.   Resume
3.   Samples of work

☐ Thank the candidate for their interest in working at your school, and share that you look forward to meeting the candidate in person.

☐ With the interview committee, go over questions that are off-limits or questions that you are legally not allowed to ask the candidate. (You cannot put the bees back in the hive.)

☐ Decide who will be asking questions during the interview. Will everyone ask a question or will one person be responsible for asking all the questions.

☐ Determine who will look over portfolios. Will you even look at them? How will you handle electronic portfolios? What are the "look-fors" in the portfolio?

☐ Decide on a timeframe for answering questions.

☐ Discuss whether you will follow up if an interviewee does not give you the answer you want on a particular question.

☐ Discuss seating arrangements for candidate and committee members.

☐ Brainstorm with committee possible anticipated questions from candidate. Be prepared to answer questions such as types of teacher support systems, the initiatives within the school/district, etc. Be prepared to "sell" your school.

☐ Emphasize the importance of welcoming and making a comfortable environment while ensuring the need to maintain professionalism. (State that everyone is expected to turn off cell phones.)

☐ Escort candidate to interview location and introduce each person on the committee.

☐ Explain process to candidate (who is asking questions, timeframe, who to give portfolio to, and your gratitude for their time).

☐ Gain commitments during the interview by asking: "Will you do home visits?" "Would you tutor students after school if needed?" "Would you be willing to coach or sponsor a club?"

☐ Give the candidate the opportunity to ask any questions.

☐ Share with the candidate the process and an approximate timeline for notification.

☐ Express appreciation for the candidate's time and interest in the position. Stand up and shake hands with the candidate as you escort him or her to the door or out of the school.

☐ With the committee, discuss initial impressions of the candidate. Discuss strengths and weaknesses related to the characteristics for the position.

☐ Discuss any adjustments that need to be made in the process.

☐ Discuss each candidate after each interview. Rank candidates and discuss how well you think each one would fit in the school?

☐ If the committee is having a hard time deciding among the candidates, is a second round of interviews needed?

☐ Make sure everyone is on the same page before you leave the room and after you make the decision. It is okay to disagree behind doors but when we leave this room, we speak with one voice. Remember this quote:

"When we are debating an issue, loyalty means giving me your honest opinion, whether you think I'll like it or not. Disagreement, at this stage, stimulates me. But once a decision has been made, the debate ends. From that point on, loyalty means executing the decision as if it were your own."

—Colin Powell[242]

☐ As principal, make sure to reserve self-time to make the decision and to contact references prior to offering position. Make an effort to contact someone beyond the list of references provided. Do a Google search and a Facebook search to look at information about the candidate.

☐ Call the person who you decided was the best fit for the position first. Make sure that person accepts and you have it in writing before you call everyone else.

☐ For those whom you will not hire, will you ask them if they'd like to be put on your list for future job openings?

☐ Send a letter or email to the superintendent, letting him or her know who you are recommending for hire. Be sure this written notification occurs after the required 30-day notice. Your note will probably appear in the school board minutes.

☐ After the hire, follow up to see how you can help the new hire transition into your school and community.

☐ Provide a factsheet about water, cable, and electric. Give a list of moving companies, realtors, places to shop, and salon.

☐ Provide information on babysitters or daycare.

☐ Are there certain school-friendly people you want to send

them to for business, insurance, or services? (This is a great way to build relationships with the community and increase positive PR about your school.)

☐ Set aside a time when you can have a face-to-face discussion about your expectations. Have a professional colleague attend. Introduce him or her as someone they can also contact or ask questions about the school. Provide important dates related to training and events.

☐ Communicate with the new employee the need to contact the district office and be prepared to present documents required for their personnel file.

6

Example of Customer Service Training for All School Office Personnel

Applicable Concepts: Training

Training is a very important piece to the entire customer service puzzle. Who in your district has the ability to train staff members? How might you go about training various groups? What might be important parts of your training. The next few pages may help you get you started on developing your training program. Included are some topics I have utilized in customer service trainings along with possible schedules and reflections.

8:00—Breakfast provided.

8:30—Introduction and get-to-know-each-other activity.

9:00—Group activity—discuss good and bad customer service stories and relate stories to public school situations.

9:45—Break.

9:55—Teach a customer service concept using a clip such as the one from *Seinfeld* about renting a car at the airport to explain under-promise and over-deliver. Work with a partner and discuss how to use this concept in your job.

10:55—Discuss competition—List all the different forms of competition to public schools.

Show the rise in home-school numbers in the past 30 years. Show the increase in charter schools. Discuss the number of personnel that must be cut for every 30 students lost to the competition.

Discuss how retirement systems are starting to change and how we all could be impacted by competition.

11:45—Nice lunch, leaders and office personnel eating together. Again, an example of providing great customer service to the people.

12:45—Review a video clip from the movie *Five Easy Pieces*. Discuss good and bad customer service pieces in the clip. How is this clip similar to a public school?

1:45—How could your leader provide better customer service to you? Work in groups and develop a list. Now share what leaders said about what the best office professionals do.

2:30—Develop a list of customer service expectations for a specific department—school office personnel, for example. With help from the presenter, a brochure will be created, stating expectations for all employees in the department. The beauty of this activity is that the employees are setting their own standards. (See 7, "Customer Service Requirements for Anyone Who Works Within School Offices" below for a sample brochure.)

3:30—Teach how to flip a mad customer. Provide research on how to recover well when you make a mistake. Any examples from the first activity?

4:30— Reflect upon and review material from the book *Simply The Best* regarding students' opinions on qualities that make the best adults.

Second Day

8:30—Develop customer service monitoring and evaluating instruments:
1. Develop a questionnaire for students
2. Develop a questionnaire for parents
3. How can leadership reward exceptional customer service?

10:30—Evaluate a fun customer service video or discuss more examples of customer service.

11:15—Develop a guide about yourself for your students and parents. Create business cards and have the district pay for them.

12:00—Lunch together and hand out customer service training certificate—take pictures and recognize on website, district Facebook page, and at school board meetings.

7

15 Thoughts on a Customer Service Training Plan for Public Schools

Applicable Concepts: Training, Leadership

☐ The program must be endorsed and monitored by school and district leadership.

☐ Make trainings enjoyable and give great service to employees during each training. Feed the employees during the trainings and be sure to have great snacks.

☐ Leadership must attend the trainings.

☐ Trainings must occur each year and there needs to be a system to train both employees who are absent and new employees to the district.

☐ Think about methods to reward personnel for attending trainings. Extra 25 cents per hour for those who are "customer service certified"? Extra personal day?

☐ All employees can attend an initial customer service training with guest speaker. However, the more specific the employee group, the more the training can be customized to meet the customer service expectations of the employee or department.

☐ The larger the school or district, the more specific the work group. A large school or district may only be able to provide customer service training for one department at a time; for example, all the secretaries within a district. A small school or district may be able to provide one training for multiple departments: custodians, bus drivers, secretaries, and nurses, for example.

☐ Leaders and direct reports need to attend all customer service sessions in order to know what each employee has been trained on and thus expected to do. Leaders can now hold them to those expectations.

☐ Think about starting the training with the school board and superintendent.

☐ While some outside help may be needed, many trainings can be handled by district personnel.

☐ Customer service should be discussed at every meeting, and customer service should be a part of everyone's evaluation.

☐ Customer service awards should be given to staff who excel at service.

☐ Once employees are trained in customer service, they will be easier to confront when they give poor service.

☐ Leaders must plan to monitor and reward exceptional customer service.

☐ Book studies, guest speakers, local merchants, and visits to other schools can all be utilized in a school or district improvement plan.

8

Customer Service Requirements for Anyone Who Works Within School Offices

This brochure on the following page was created
by school office staff
Applicable Concepts: Training

1. Answer the phone with a smile on your face and a smile in your voice.

2. Answer the phone within three rings.

3. Identify yourself.
   ☑ "Good morning, Newport Independent Schools. This is ___. How may I help you? (Feel free to create your own greeting.)

4. Have "live" personnel answer the phone.
   ☑ Someone needs to be available from 7:45 A.M. to 4:30 P.M. every day with the exception of the major holidays (Christmas, Thanksgiving, New Years, Fourth of July).

5. Listen!
   ☑ Never take complaints personally.
   ☑ Hear what the "customer" is not saying, as well as what they say.

☑ Take notes. Let the caller know you are taking notes. Include phone numbers, date, and time, as well as the person's name. Once you have written the gist of the issue, use the person's name and read the information back to the customer for accuracy.

6. Speak enthusiastically.

7. Be conscious of your tone!
   ☑ 82% of ear-to-ear communication is tone of voice (only 18%- words you use).

8. Own the problem.
   ☑ Put yourself in the "shoes" of the customer.
   ☑ Do not hand off an issue without giving the caller a way to call you back if they are not satisfied.

9. Make an emotional connection. (Talk about things such as: Hair cuts, shirt, shoes, family, sports, music, interests.)

10. Know how to direct personnel through the chain of command.
    ☑ Have you spoken with teacher, principal, superintendent?
    ☑ Assure caller or visitor they will be able to talk with who they request.

11. Screen calls after discussion with immediate supervisor.
    ☑ Know what calls get through and when, as well as which calls never get through.

12. Be in the moment.
    ☑ Make eye contact

13. Walk or have a student/ volunteer walk "guest" to destination.

14. Find a way to **WOW** people.
    ☑ What can we do for students and parents that they do not expect?

15. Abide by the 24 hour rule. (Make sure everyone else abides by the same rule.)

16. Make sure office looks professional. Keep backstage items backstage (discipline, negative talk, nurse issues, etc.)

17. Make sure you dress and act as a professional.
    ☑ You are always on stage (24/7).

18. Know the importance of body language.
    ☑ 55% of face to face communication is body language
    ☑ 38% tone and only
    ☑ 7% what you actually say

19. Know how to recover well when mistakes are made.
    ☑ Must be immediate
    ☑ Show sincere empathy
    ☑ Must equal the offense

20. Demonstrate an understanding of the demands of the job.
    ☑ There are times when you may need to work beyond normal time.
    ☑ Show initiative.

21. Make leaders aware of problems before they happen.
    ☑ Help diffuse rumors.

22. Maintain confidentiality at all times.

23. Make your immediate supervisor look good.

24. Smile. Enjoy your job!

25. Have a positive attitude at all times. (Remember: It is not personal when you have an angry student or parent.)

26. Let parents and students know what you are doing for them. (Remember: Southwest Airlines is always reminding people that bags fly free!)

27. **Under-promise and over-deliver!**
    ☑ If you think it might take an hour for the principal to return a call, tell the caller it will be at least three hours. Always try to exceed expectations.

28. Create "positive gossip" about your school
    ☑ Facebook
    ☑ Twitter
    ☑ QR Codes
    ☑ Grandparent's Day

29. Always look for ways to improve. In customer service, we never arrive!

30. Be able to connect with the student!

9

Example Information Collected About School Cafeterias

Applicable Concepts: Walk in the Shoes of the Customers, Collect Reliable Information, Plan and Reflect

This is a list of information I found from my visit to the school cafeteria (story from Walk in the Shoes of the Customers concept) and in my focus groups with students (story from the Collect Reliable Information concept). In addition to the findings, I've listed the goals that came out of this visit.

1. We were able to count the number of students who brought or packed their breakfast and lunch from home before and after we implemented the changes.
2. We compared student discipline issues in the cafeteria before and after the changes.
3. We surveyed staff, students, and parents before and after the cafeteria changes.
4. We wanted to improve the presentation of food.
5. We wanted 3 to 5 choices for breakfast and at least 8 different choices each day for lunch.
6. We wanted food samplings to occur in our cafeterias.
7. We wanted students' voice in the menus.
8. We wanted milk bottles instead of cartons.
9. We preferred spoons and forks instead of sporks.
10. We wanted the cafeterias to be clean, well lit, and the tables and chairs to be age appropriate.
11. We wanted staff to smile and be friendly to students.
12. We continued meeting with our student focus groups in each

school. In addition to getting student feedback, this was a way for us to make sure the students knew we were making changes based on their concerns and recommendations.

13. We asked teachers and administrators what they were hearing about the changes from students.

14. We asked school leaders to eat in the school cafeterias and give feedback at monthly meetings.

15. After implementing changes, I continued to meet with principals, the food service director, managers, cooks, and cafeteria monitors to gather feedback on changes and what else could be tweaked.

16. It is important to be realistic about changes: How much money are we making, or is it going to cost food service additional funds?

17. Would there be an increase in the number of staff who ate in the school cafeteria?

10

Collect Reliable Information Lessons Learned

Applicable Concepts: Collect Reliable Information, Plan and Reflect

Changing our cafeterias helps improve the entire culture of each school and the school district.

1. As in any other change initiatives, there were plenty of people who tried to stop it. Without the high levels of leadership being involved, these changes would have never occurred.
2. What gets monitored gets done.
3. Once students got involved in the cafeteria decision making, they complained less about school food. People will support what they help create, especially students.
4. Principals raved about how there were no longer discipline issues in the cafeteria.
5. The more students ate in the cafeteria, the more money food service made and thus could even expand their offerings.
6. After our first year, our director and managers came up with very creative ideas that surpassed anything we could have imagined.
7. Adults truly forget how important breakfast and lunch is to our students and sometimes need to be reminded that, if we do not have students eating in the cafeterias, we will not have food service jobs.
8. Evaluation of programs needs to occur as soon as possible after the program.

11

C'mon Man! Examples of Dumb Mistakes from Public Education

Applicable Concepts: Don't Do Dumb Things!

1. A teacher catching a kid with chewing tobacco and making him swallow it.
2. A student suspended for hugging a teacher.
3. A teacher paddling a student in front of an entire elementary class.
4. A student suspended for a weapons violation when he made a hat with a plastic army man holding a plastic gun on the hat for Hat Day. The hat was made to honor his father who was in the military.[243]
5. A student who brought baseball cards to a middle school and the principal refused to return them even at the end of the year.
6. Public discipline of students, like making students sit in isolated cubicles in the lunchroom or somehow making them stand out, so as to show they're being punished. Are we permitted to do this to teachers who make mistakes?
7. Taking student cell phones away and keeping them for weeks and months.
8. Marking students' hands to remind parents that they need to add money to their lunch account. Do we need to humiliate a kid in order to send a parent a message?
9. Group punishment, like keeping a whole class from going to recess because of the behavior of one or a few students.
10. Athletic coaches having inappropriate outbursts at their players. They are kids first and foremost, let's not forget that.

11. Suspending a first-grader and sending him to a 45-day program for problem children because he brought his own camping knife and fork set to lunch, violating the school's zero tolerance "weapons" policy. I couldn't make this stuff up![244]

12. In Utah 40 students had to dump their food trays in the trash when they got to the register to pay and did not have enough money. They were all over their allotted lunch charges. Students were then only allowed to consume the accompanying fruit and milk.[245]

13. Eighteen New Jersey students suspended three days for paying for their school lunch in pennies to protest the short lunch periods.[246]

14. Teachers ganging up on a parent in school meetings or special education meetings to give negative reports about their child. I call this "gang tackling" parents.

15. A teacher walking out of parent-teacher night with parents waiting to meet him because it was 5 minutes past the scheduled end time.

16. A teacher telling students there is nothing they can do about her not teaching them. She is tenured and this is her last year. They will just have to suffer.

12

Giving Great Service Up and Down the Organizational Chart

Applicable Concepts: Leadership, Give Great Service to Employees

"Small disconnects between [leaders] and their peers
actually look like major rifts to people deeper in the organization.
And when those people deeper in the organization try to resolve
the differences among themselves, they often become engaged in
bloody and time-consuming battles, with no possibility for resolution.
And all of this occurs because leaders higher in the organization
failed to work out minor issues, usually out of fear of conflict."
—Patrick Lencioni[6]

Public schools generally have dozens, if not hundreds, of job descriptions, with many tiers and layers of organizational structure. Look at the organizational chart of any public school and you will see the challenge of ensuring that customer service reverberates throughout the district and eventually makes its way to the primary customers: the students and parents. If we expect our employees to give great customer service to our students and parents, we must model and give great service throughout our organization. If we do not give great service to one another we cannot expect the same from our staff. On the following page, you'll find a graphic of giving customer service up and down the hierarchy of a public school system. Note that these arrows do not go one way—that great service should be seen as something we give and get from everyone we interact with in our schools.

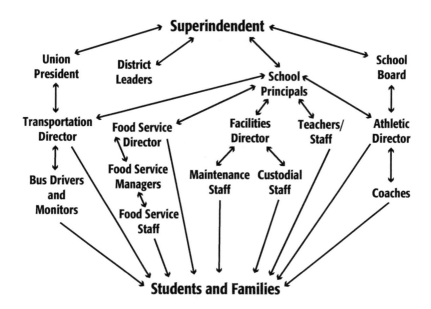

On the next few pages, I've included several job-specific forms with customer service expectations from one employee to another. People support what they help create so, again, I encourage you to only use these as a guide as you develop these standards with staff in your district.

Great Customer Service
from the Superintendent to the School Board

The Superintendent will:

1. never surprise school board members at school board meetings. We never want to look incompetent in front of the media. (Supports the Keeping Backstage Issues Backstage concept.)
2. include customer service in the district improvement plan.
3. help school board members plan conferences by scheduling hotel rooms, transportation, etc.
4. keep all board members informed of important dates so they can attend school functions.
5. not have "favorite" board members. While it may be necessary for the superintendent to communicate more often with the board chair, it may behoove the superintendent to spend equal amounts of time with each member.
6. make an attempt to get to know each board member.
7. investigate all matters brought to board members and give accurate information back to members within 24 to 48 hours.
8. give all school board members the superintendent's personal cell phone number to be called 24/7 in case of emergency.
9. always give credit to the school board and take responsibility when things go wrong.
10. always take phone calls from his or her school board members 24/7 and/or call members back within 24 hours.
11. assure that all school leaders will look into matters brought to board members.
12. try to have all school board member information to school board members four days prior to the school board meeting.
13. provide water to all school board members at each meeting.
14. help and train school board members with administrative tasks like how to fill out travel requests.

15. seek input from school board members on major school issues.

16. organize get-togethers, retreats, etc. for school board members to help build a sense of team with all members.

17. be evaluated on district customer service standards and give a report on the standards at one board meeting each year.

18. review customer service standards with district department every year.

19. provide a board member induction program for all new school board members.

_____   _____

Superintendent   Date

Great Customer Service
from the Superintendent to the Union President and
the Union President to the Superintendent

We will:

1. communicate once each month and will operate with a no-surprises mentality.
2. make decisions in the best interest of students and staff.
3. make every effort to abide by the bargaining contract and will discuss issues on a regular basis.
4. work together for everyone involved.
5. understand there are multiple sides to every story, and we will work together to find the best possible solutions when issues arise.

_____   _____
Superintendent   Date

_____   _____
Union President   Date

Great Customer Service
from the School Board Member to the Superintendent

The School Board will:

1. not surprise the superintendent at a board meeting. We never want to look incompetent in front of the media. (Goes with Keeping Backstage Issues Backstage concept.)
2. make an attempt to get to know the superintendent and other school board members.
3. give the superintendent a heads-up when they hear of district or school issues.
4. funnel all issues through the superintendent, who will handle through his or her leadership team.
5. work with the superintendent to make decisions in the best interest of all students.
6. be positive PR agents for the school system and thus the superintendent.
7. weave customer service into the superintendent's evaluation.
8. look for ways to be an asset to the superintendent whenever needed.
9. work together to be a high-performing team.
10. try to help everyone come together and be a positive team when one board member is not behaving appropriately or seems to have a set agenda.
11. realize that there are two sides to every story, and will send complaints back through the proper chain of command.
12. help address rumors, making sure that accurate information is presented to the public.

_____   _____
Name   Date

_____   _____
Name   Date

_____

Name   Date

Great Customer Service from
the Superintendent to District Leaders and
School Principals

The Superintendent will:

1. give all direct reports (including all district leaders and principals) his/her emergency cell phone number to be called 24/7 in case of emergency.
2. always realize that there are two sides to every story. When someone calls or writes regarding a school issue, the superintendent will remain neutral until all facts are received.
3. be mindful of everyone else's time. The district will do long-range calendar planning.
4. evaluate each employee and each department in the area of customer service.
5. make regular visits to each school and to school functions.
6. give positive feedback to all leaders and will always give constructive criticism in private.
7. always give credit to the school leaders and staff.
8. take phone calls from his or her leadership team 24/7.
9. work as a team with his or her key leaders and will listen to their feedback.
10. work with principals and direct reports to find needed resources.
11. assign district liaisons to each school. Liaisons are to be a support to the school principal and an advocate for the school at district meetings.
12. include the building leadership in all decisions that directly affect their schools.
13. give the building level leadership team the ability to make commonsense customer service decisions without fear of retribution for mistakes.

14. always speak positively about the schools, leadership, and staff in public.
15. not hold any leader back from other career opportunities.
16. strive to be equitable and ethical in all decisions.
17. provide all leaders and staff with growth opportunities.
18. hold effective meetings and recognize the value of others' time.
19. organize get-togethers with direct reports, including end-of-year and/or before-school get-togethers.
20. expect school leaders to be candid on school improvement and with district office. Different opinions will be valued and will not be held against anyone.

_____   _____

Superintendent   Date

Great Customer Service
from School Principal to District Leadership
(Superintendent and District Leaders)

The Principal will:

1. always communicate major issues to the school superintendent or liaison.
2. hold everyone in the school accountable to the customer service standards.
3. make customer service a top priority and consider every school touch point and customer service expectation.
4. always speak positively about the district, district leadership, and the school board in public.
5. keep up with current educational trends.
6. The principal will hold his or her administrative team accountable to the same customer service standards
7. hold everyone accountable to give great customer service to their staff.
8. be available 24/7 to answer phone calls from the superintendent or liaison in case of emergency.
9. not blame the district leadership team or criticize anyone in public.
10. not use the superintendent and district leadership team to get initiatives accomplished. Example: "We have to do this because the superintendent said so." "The superintendent walked through this building and said we must keep the building cleaner."
11. work closely with the special education director on placement of students and teachers. Include Individual Learning Plans (ILPs), special education suspensions, etc.
12. work closely with the food service director on meals, meal times, field trips, etc.
13. work closely with the transportation director in handling student discipline in a timely matter.
14. work closely with the district facilities director on hiring

and training all custodians and maintenance employees in customer service.

15. plan every event with a customer service focus.

_____   _____

Name   Date

Great Customer Service
from School Principals to Teachers and Staff

The School Principals will:

1. give all staff members his or her personal cell phone number to be called 24/7 in case of emergency.
2. get to know his or her entire staff and be approachable to all staff each day.
3. provide customer service training to each staff member, along with other needed and required training.
4. check on staff when they are sick.
5. return emails and phone calls from staff in 24 hours.
6. help new hires become acclimated to the school and community.
7. provide induction programs for every new employee.
8. celebrate good times with staff and be there for staff in the tough times. Examples: Attend weddings and funerals.
9. make every attempt to speak to and check on every employee each day. Check on every substitute teacher at least twice daily.
10. plan for events in advance and give a weekly calendar of events via email to each staff member every week.

_____   _____

School Principals   Date

Great Customer Service from the Transportation Director to Bus Drivers, Principals, Students, and Parents

The Transportation Director will:

1. train all direct reports each year in customer service and review customer service expectations with all direct reports.
2. make sure that drivers give great service to students.
3. train and provide training refreshers for all drivers and monitors.
4. provide survey information to students and staff, including coaches, concerning customer service of their drivers.
5. be on call to the superintendent/liaison school leadership team 24/7.
6. return emails and phone calls from staff members within 24 hours and give all direct reports an emergency cell number.
7. make sure that the transportation website is updated on a regular basis with bus route information and other information.
8. build teamwork with the mechanic, drivers, and monitors at the bus garage.
9. celebrate the successes of all transportation direct reports.
10. utilize various techniques to promote the department. For example employ Facebook, Twitter, etc.
11. attend district functions, setting up booths to answer questions from parents and guardians.
12. organize get-togethers with direct reports. Examples: end of year, Transportation Week.
13. plan and coordinate bus schedules with school principals each year. After the first day, hold a meeting with school principals to work out transportation issues.
14. create an equitable and fair system for drivers to execute after-school trips.
15. notify all parents by use of a one-call system on school closures and give reasons for closures.

16. have drivers provide information to parents and staff about the driver.

17. have a nice, clean, well-maintained bus garage to build camaraderie among staff. See "A Sample School First Impression Checklist" in Appendix.

_____   _____

Transportation Director   Date

Great Customer Service
from the Food Service Director to Food Service Managers, Principals, Students, and Parents

The Food Service Director will:

1. be on call to the superintendent or liaison 24/7.
2. make sure the food service managers and cooks are trained in customer service each year.
3. place menus with nutritional information on the school website.
4. offer a minimum of three breakfast choices and six lunch choices every day.
5. make sure that all cafeteria seating is age appropriate.
6. ensure that the highest degree of confidentiality is maintained with students and parents with regard to methods of payment.
7. ensure use of good judgment when dealing with students on alternative meals. For example, throwing away food because a student does not have the money to pay is unacceptable.
8. ensure that the tables are well-cleaned between lunch shifts.
9. work with principals and the facilities director to ensure that all floors are cleaned each night.
10. develop a food service survey for students and parents to receive feedback on the cafeteria experience.
11. evaluate the food service managers on the customer service offered to students.
12. keep a listing of special days during the school year and plan meals accordingly.
13. develop a method to interact with students by use of Facebook, Twitter, etc.
14. develop a webpage to help staff follow directions. For example: how to notify food service managers when taking students on field trips, catering, etc.

15. set up taste tests for students in order for students to have a voice in food service decisions.
16. be involved in school and district functions to answer questions from parents, staff, and students.
17. ensure that parents and guardians can pay for student meals online.
18. keep up with the latest technologies used in school food service.
19. organize get-togethers with direct reports. Examples: end of year, Food Service Week.

_____   _____

Food Service Director   Date

Great Customer Service
from the Facilities Director to Maintenance, Custodial Staff, Principals, Students, and Parents.

The Facilities Director will:

1. own every physical touch point of the school campus.
2. make sure that all custodians receive proper training on how to clean facilities and use the equipment.
3. make sure that all custodians and maintenance personnel have the proper equipment for doing their jobs well.
4. train all custodial and maintenance employees in customer service.
5. make sure all custodians have and wear uniforms that are clean.
6. create a monitoring survey for anyone who rents the district facilities to evaluate the customer service received.
7. work with the school principals to create fair and balanced scheduling for all custodians and maintenance personnel.
8. monitor, praise, and reward all custodial and maintenance employees on all shifts.
9. work with building principals to help provide excellent customer service to our customers at all major events.
10. consistently look for ways to make school facilities more customer service friendly.
11. look at all signage throughout the district and make sure that areas are well-marked and signs are customer service friendly.
12. make sure all snow and ice is removed from every possible walkway on the campus to keep our customers safe.
13. abide by "A Sample School First Impressions Checklist" (see Appendix).
14. be customer service friendly and make sure that all employees under his or her supervision do the same.

15. work with the school principal and do school and classroom checks a minimum of four times each year.

_____   _____

Facilities Director   Date

Great Customer Service
from Teachers to Parents and Students

Teachers will:

1. get to know his or her students and will call them by name.
2. call home to students who miss class two days in a row.
3. visit the home of students/parents/guardians each year.
4. keep themselves informed of important school and district events.
5. take all necessary precautions to keep every child safe at all times.
6. notify parents/guardians in case of emergency.
7. give parents/guardians good times to contact them, including phone numbers, email addresses, etc.
8. create a brochure that tells a little about themselves.
9. have a welcoming school classroom. Examples: Student work displayed, material about certain topics covered on the walls, desks free of graffiti, vents cleaned, good lighting, and appropriate room temperature.
10. give parents a personal cell number in case of an emergency.
11. keep a classroom website/Edmodo updated for parents.
12. do a weekly or monthly newsletter to keep parents informed.
13. attend nightly functions of the school/parent meetings and high school graduation.
14. be clear and as helpful as possible when communicating with customers and guests, including limited use of educational jargon.
15. respond within 24 to 48 hours to emails or phone calls. If it is an emergency, the teacher/staff member should respond immediately.

_____   _____

Teacher/Staff Member   Date

Great Customer Service
from Head Coaches to Parents and Students

Coaches will:

1. allow all students an opportunity to try out for his or her respected teams.
2. speak individually with those who are not able to make the team. Posting who made or did not make the team is not necessary.
3. go over student and parent expectations for the team.
4. provide schedules and amendments as quick as possible to parents.
5. provide directions to events.
6. be organized and plan well.
7. make sure that students have appropriate uniforms for competition.
8. give great customer service to transportation and food service departments as necessary.
9. never embarrass or humiliate students at events.
10. be responsible for assistant coaches and their actions.

_____   _____

Coach   Date

Great Customer Service
from Athletic Directors to Head Coaches and Principals

Athletic Directors will:

1. recruit and hire the best possible head coaches for student athletes.
2. train all coaches in customer service each year.
3. help head coaches recruit and hire good assistant coaches.
4. make sure student athletes have nice, appropriate uniforms for competitions.
5. make sure head coaches have proper equipment and practice facilities for student athletes.
6. make sure coaches are well trained and adhere to district customer service standards.
7. evaluate coaches on customer service standards.
8. make sure athletic facilities are immaculate.
9. make sure there is good signage, appropriate parking, and handicapped parking.
10. give great service to officials at home games.
11. attend events.
12. help schedule events and make sure events are posted on webpage.
13. notify school principal of any possible major athletic issues.
14. organize events as necessary for our students, such as college signing events, fundraising events, etc.

_____   _____

Athletic Director   Date

13

The Importance of Having
Customer Service Standards

Applicable Concepts: Leadership

To the Rescue: Customer Service Standards

In education we love standards and benchmarks! In an era where accountability is used to characterize almost everything associated with schools, it seems everyone has a solution for its improvement. Standards are at the forefront of many of those proposed solutions. Content organizations have standards; teacher evaluation models have standards; and there are technology standards. Analysis of public school standards reveals a focus primarily on rigor and relevance, on what to teach, and on what tools to use to teach more effectively. It also focuses on teacher training, evaluation, and professional growth. Remarkably, one aspect that is continually absent from professional conversations is an intentional focus on relationships in public schools. What makes this even more astounding is the plethora of research on the importance of school culture to school improvement efforts. Can one have a great culture without a focus on the relationships existing in schools? I would argue that an emphasis on relationships and customer service should be the gold standard in public schools.

The pursuit of excellence is a team effort and, as such, our goal of being the best begins with the development of relationships among our students, families, staff, and community. Exceptional customer service and satisfaction are expected and practiced and will be evident in the following standards. These standards may seem simplistic and common sense, but I believe implementing these standards is critical to a successful school's mission and vision.

*For the sake of definitions, when I use the term "staff member" on the following pages, I mean **any person on the school payroll.***

Standard: Welcoming Environment

1. All customers (students, parents/guardians, visitors, vendors and guests):
   - will be acknowledged and greeted by courteous staff members.
   - can expect to find welcoming, positive, and helpful signs that guide their visit.
   - can expect to find an area of the office or school for waiting that is customer-friendly.
   - can expect a clean and safe environment throughout the school and campus.
   - can expect to see current student work posted on the walls including a description of the curricular connection.
2. Each staff member will create an inviting, friendly environment.

Standard: Respect

1. All customers will be greeted promptly and in a courteous manner.
2. Each staff member will:
   - ensure confidentiality and respect for each customer's situation.
   - maintain a positive demeanor in his or her interactions.
   - use the name of the customer or visitor, if known, in his or her interactions.

Standard: Problem Solving & Responsiveness

1. Each staff member will do his/her best to honor the 24-hour

rule: responding to inquiries via phone or email within a 24-hour time period.

2. Each staff member will be an active listener as the customer shares concerns, needs, or ideas, directing the individual to the appropriate place to address any issue or answer any question.

3. Each staff member will "own the problem or concern" until the appropriate party is reached. For example, if a cafeteria server is asked by a visitor how she can find the History teacher, that server will be responsible for personally bringing that visitor to the teacher, or else ensure that she is passed on to an employee who will take her to that teacher.

4. Each staff member will be trained in the art of recovery.

Standard: Communication (External)

1. Each staff member will smile and use appropriate tone and body language when interacting with customers.

2. Each staff member will be clear and as helpful as possible when communicating with customers and guests, including limited use of educational jargon.

3. All phone calls will be answered within three rings by a trained person and not an automated system during business hours. The staff member will have a smile in his/her voice and will identify the location and who he/she is, appropriately assisting the customer.

4. Each staff member, when transferring a call, will provide the name and number of the person who can provide assistance. If this individual is unavailable, a message will be taken.

5. All customers will be provided with accurate information.

6. Each staff member will be "in the moment" with each customer, refraining from personal conversations with students or other staff members.

7. Each staff member will get to know the customer personally.

Standard: Communication (Internal)

1. Each staff member will interact with colleagues in a courteous and professional manner.
2. Each staff member will respect coworkers by not conversing negatively about colleagues or problems with, or in front of, customers.
3. Each staff member will work cooperatively and collaboratively with an emphasis on success for colleagues and ensuring quality experiences for customers.
4. Each staff member will be apprised of issues within the school district using One Clear Voice that clarifies the situation and provides accurate and timely information.
5. Each supervisor will model and provide good customer service to staff.

These customer service standards represent our commitment as a school district to not only pursuing excellence related to teaching, but excellence in our interactions with students, parents, and the community. If students and parents are going to be active partners in the educational process, and if student achievement is a priority for all students, schools must be intentional about developing relationships. Remember, inviting schools are ones where each person is valued.

14

Examples of Public School Customer Service Standards in ACME School District

Applicable Concepts: Leadership, Training, Confront

Below are some public school standards you can use as a guide for your school district. I start out by providing a list of general standards that can apply to any employee. You'll also find examples of job-specific customer service standards for immediate supervisors to develop within their departments. To reduce redundancy, if I included a standard in the general list, I did not include the standard in the job-specific list. I advise leaders to look through all lists provided in this section and develop their own standards unique to their school district and departments. You may want to start by customizing the general standards list for all employees at your school. None of these lists are all-inclusive and everyone is encouraged to look for other standards in other resources that may fit their own individual needs.

General Customer Service Standards
For All Staff Members

I will:

1. know and fulfill the district slogan "We're About Kids."
2. speak to everyone and acknowledge their presence when anyone comes within five feet of me. I will smile, say please and thank you, my pleasure, or other positive terms when communicating with our customers.
3. keep myself current and well-informed with facts and events going on within my school and the district.
4. address school rumors or criticism and share this information with my immediate supervisor in an effort to dispel the myth and disperse the truth.
5. when possible, address parents and students by name and escort parents/guardians and other visitors to their destinations instead of just giving directions.
6. answer the phone within three rings, using proper telephone etiquette and a smile in my voice as I identify myself to the caller.
7. always focus on what I "can do" for the student or parent versus what I "cannot do."
8. take pride in my personal appearance at all times because I am a professional for this school system.
9. take pride in the cleanliness and repair of the school and the equipment.
10. provide 100% effort respecting and working closely with my fellow staff members.
11. always be a positive PR agent for the school and district. I understand that making negative comments about other staff, our schools, or administration is not acceptable.
12. always alert my immediate supervisor to any issue that may adversely affect staff or students.
13. practice the art of recovering well when I make mistakes.

I will make it immediate, mean what I say, and make the apology equal the mistake.

14. always remain calm when dealing with difficult people and situations, understanding that seldom are their criticisms personal.

15. get back with everyone within 24-48 hours when I receive phone calls or emails.

I agree to follow the policies of the ACME School System, knowing my efforts will contribute to the overall success of our school district.

_____   _____

Name   Date

Customer Service Standards
for Secretaries and Office Staff

We will:

1. greet our customers with a smile and in a courteous and professional manner.
2. stay informed about events at our school and district-wide. We will communicate these events to our students, parents, and community.
3. answer telephones promptly (within three rings) whenever possible.
4. answer phone calls in a courteous manner (with a smile in our voices). Tone is 38 percent of how well the discussion over the phone is received.
5. answer the phone during school hours. We will only let calls go through to voicemail after hours and on weekends.
6. own customer issues and not hand off issues until someone else owns the issue.
7. seek ways to improve office procedures in order to help us offer better customer service.
8. dress and act in a professional manner.
9. keep the office well decorated, bright, and clean with a nice aroma.
10. always alert the school principal to issues that could adversely affect students and staff.
11. always discuss positive aspects about the schools and districts while working or after hours out in the community.
12. always look for ways to improve our customer service. We will take customer service ideas to our immediate supervisor.
13. be in the moment when talking with customers. If the phone rings while talking with a customer, we must place caller on hold and then finish with customer.
14. keep soft drinks and snacks out of the direct sight of customers. (Keep Backstage Issues Backstage).

15. personally call parents of absent students instead of using the automatic system.
16. check all documents for grammar and spelling mistakes. We will also monitor what is placed on our school walls, bulletin boards, etc.
17. make sure everyone returns calls or emails within 48 hours.
18. use names of our customers as much as possible when speaking on the phone or in person.
19. keep conversations with coworkers to a minimum while within earshot of customers. Confidential conversations will not occur around our customers.
20. practice the art of recovering well when we make mistakes. Make it immediate. Mean what you say. Make the apology more positive than the negative mistake.
21. be proficient with computers and check our school email at least once daily.

_____   _____

Name   Date

Customer Service Standards for School Bus Drivers

We will:

1. say hello and good-bye to every student boarding and departing the bus each day.
2. clean the interior of the bus each day. We will inspect each passenger seat every morning.
3. wash our buses at least once each week and sweep our buses out every day.
4. stay informed about major district events and remind our students each day.
5. strive to know the names of all students on our buses the very first week of school.
6. have a positive interaction with all parents of the students we transport.
7. have a professional brochure that tells the students and parents something about us (See "Customer Service Requirements for Anyone Who Works Within School Offices" in Appendix).
8. make ourselves available to parents and students who have questions or concerns at school open houses.
9. work cooperatively with school principals and staff to address transportation needs and concerns.
10. be well-groomed—dress and look professional each day.
11. have well-managed school buses, where students feel safe and are well-trained in procedures and routines.
12. do our best to pick up and drop off students at the appropriate time each day.
13. be on time to take students to after-school activities.
14. let students know where they are supposed to sit, and give bus expectations to each rider on the very first day of school.
15. practice routines and procedures the first two weeks of school.
16. make driving decisions based on the safety of all students.

17. look for ways to improve our customer service and make recommendations to our immediate supervisors.
18. report accidents immediately to our immediate supervisors.
19. survey students on our bus to give us feedback on our customer service.
20. help parents with directions to co-curricular and extra-curricular events.
21. be proficient with computers and check our school email at least once daily.

_____   _____
Name   Date

Customer Service Standards for Food Service Staff

We will:

1. greet students with a smile each day.
2. never embarrass students who do not have money to pay for meals.
3. never throw away student meals because a student is over their charge limit.
4. work with the school principal to train all students in cafeteria procedures and routines. Train students on how to use appropriate voice levels in the cafeteria.
5. provide students with multiple breakfast, lunch, and afternoon snack options. For example: a minimum of three breakfast choices and six lunch choices each day.
6. survey students on their favorite breakfast, lunch, and afternoon snack choices. Share results of study and try to accommodate student requests.
7. ensure cafeteria tables are cleaned using sanitary methods between each lunch period.
8. make sure cafeteria tables and chairs are at age-appropriate heights and everything in cafeteria is age appropriate.
9. keep cafeteria clean and bright with appropriate materials on walls.
10. allow students to sample new food items.
11. work with administration to make sure students are provided meals regardless of ability to pay.
12. train or make sure new teachers each year know how to plan for field trips requiring sack lunches.
13. when asked, explain why we cannot provide certain foods and soft drinks.
14. continue to find ways to model going green for students, especially on Environmental Friendly Day or Arbor Day.
15. stay involved with school events and use meals to enhance these experiences.

16. celebrate culture diversity with meal choices.

17. list meal options in English and Spanish.

18. celebrate special holidays with appropriate food choices.

19. regularly meet with students on how to improve their food service experience.

20. create a food service Facebook page and Twitter account so students can keep up with food offerings and other food service department news.

21. keep our menus on our website with appropriate allergy labels.

22. do our very best to make sure all lunch shifts are treated equally.

23. be proficient with computers and check our school email at least once daily.

24. always look for ways to have fun! Dress up for special occasions like Halloween. Serve King Cake for Mardi Gras and wear beads. Serve burgoo soup for the Kentucky Derby.

25. let students know a little about ourselves. Example: One cafeteria keeps the pictures of all workers with names up on the walls. Routinely, under the pictures, they will have something about them. Who was their favorite cafeteria worker when they were a student? Who will win the Super Bowl? What are their picks for the Kentucky Derby?

26. equip our cafeterias with the latest technology. Examples: Parents and staff have the ability to pay via the internet. Menus and nutrition information are placed on district website, etc.

27. keep the cafeteria open throughout the day to feed hungry students.

28. wet-mop cafeteria floors every day after school.

29. train students to ask the manager or someone within the cafeteria questions if they have a problem or issue.

30. provide students with a survey to measure students' perceptions of their school cafeteria.

31. attend school events to answer food service questions for

parents, students, and staff, especially at "Back to School" fairs and PTA/PTO events.

32. create a way for students to see meal choices listed as they enter the cafeteria or while they are in line, well before stepping up to the counter to make a selection.

33. make sure proper eating utensils are provided for students. For example, sometimes sporks may not be appropriate for meat entrees.

34. be mindful that extra food may be necessary after long weekends or school breaks. Make sure all students have opportunities to eat on school weather delays.

_____   _____

Name   Date

Customer Service Standards
for Maintenance/Custodial Staff

We will:

1. look for items to fix, weeds to pull, and graffiti to paint over before leadership sees these items.

2. wear our uniforms each day and be well-groomed and professional at all times.

3. look for opportunities to help our teachers and other staff give great service to our customers.

4. be ready to assist anyone on our campus. Example: A parent with a flat tire in our parking lot needs help.

5. always be able to be reached by our immediate supervisor and his or her designee in case of emergency.

6. adhere to response times and follow up with staff after completing tasks.

7. keep facilities clean and well maintained. We will quickly remove or fix anything that detracts from our facilities.

8. walk the grounds every day and any sign of graffiti will be removed or painted over immediately.

9. routinely check trash cans and make suggestions for additional placements of trash cans.

10. check student desks daily for any signs of graffiti or damages.

11. be well-trained on maintaining clean floors, waxing, windows, etc.

12. have a set schedule for checking restrooms daily. Restrooms will be monitored every hour and will be clean and well maintained. All graffiti must be removed, sinks cleaned, lights working, etc.

13. replace mulch as needed and keep weeds from landscaping. We will constantly monitor and remove dead plants, trees, etc.

14. notice lights that need replacing and replace them immediately.

15. have a set schedule for checking and cleaning all windows as needed. Particular attention will be paid to the main office and high traffic areas.
16. report and/or fix all signage, including but not limited to exit signs and direction signs.
17. smile and speak to all our customers when asked to do other duties, such as parking cars at events.
18. look at outside lighting and make sure our campus is well lit and well maintained.
19. help leadership notice when mulch is needed or grass needs to be cut, as well as all other necessary items that need constant attention.
20. keep our immediate supervisor updated about ongoing issues.
21. be on time to work each day.
22. remove all ice and snow from all walking paths on our property for staff and student safety.
23. routinely check faculty and staff restrooms—stock restrooms, install hooks for coats and purses, and include scent sprays for staff restrooms.
24. not have food and beverages in sight of our customers. We will keep backstage issues backstage.
25. keep an inventory of our supplies and maintenance items and take great care of all our equipment.
26. remove and clean all handprints from all surfaces, including windows and glass, especially in high traffic areas.
27. check water fountains daily for proper maintenance and cleaning.
28. only display positive signage. For example: "Please do not walk on our newly waxed floors. We want them to be as clean as possible for students, visitors, and staff."
29. learn all facets of building maintenance as needed, including checking the temperature on cafeteria freezers and refrigerators and on boilers.

30. make sure we give great customer service to health and fire inspectors.

31. check dates on all fire extinguishers and other items as necessary.

32. check and clean all carpets. Carpeting must be securely attached to the floor. Rugs and carpets must be free of wrinkles or bulges.

33. practice the art of recovering well when we make mistakes. Make it immediate. Mean what you say. Make the apology more positive than the negative mistake.

34. be proficient with computers and check our school email at least once daily.

35. be on call 24/7 in case of a school emergency.

_____   _____

Name   Date

Customer Service Standards for Technicians/Aides

We will:

1. handle all technology issues as quickly as possible. We strive to have a three-day turnaround from the time an issue is reported.
2. keep written evidence of the time of the reporting issue until completion.
3. provide efficient methods for staff members to get their equipment and to turn in their equipment at the end of the year.
4. try to offer replacements when we need to repair staff computers, iPads, or other devices.
5. offer computer training as needed to all staff members.

_____   _____

Name   Date

Customer Service Standards
for Payroll/Accounts Receivable Staff

We will:

1. handle all individual staff accounts with confidentiality.
2. provide payroll dates to all staff members yearly.
3. personally explain the situation to the staff member should there be a payroll issue.
4. keep the office open after hours, when necessary, to meet with staff members concerning payroll.
5. communicate with all school vendors about pay dates.
6. have a finance link to our main website that can help answer all payroll questions.
7. be trained in health insurance matters, allowing us to assist other staff members with inquiries and decisions.
8. be available to staff members when they have issues with our finance providers.
9. direct deposit all payroll checks and use the E-Stub system, allowing past deposits and W-2 information to be accessed at any time.
10. explain all payroll deductions on our website.
11. have as many forms as possible on our website in order to streamline our processes and make it an easy process for our employees.

_____   _____

Name   Date

15

Home Visit and Transition Day Checklists

Applicable Concepts: Forge Relationships, Plan and Reflect

These are sample Home Visit and Transition Day checklists for the entire processes in my district. The person responsible will depend on what makes sense for your school or district. Also, you'll want to tailor the date of completion to your own school timeline. These are here for guidance.

Home Visit Checklist

Check-Off	Activity	Person(s) Responsible	Date
	Contact building principals to determine the school's home visit coordinator that will be on the district team	District Administrator	April 1
	Schedule a Home Visit Meeting with building and central office personnel	District Administrator	April 15
	Meet with Building Home Visit Coordinators, ELL teachers, and others to discuss: • Scheduling the Home Visit date 1. Establish the central location for the districtwide luncheon 2. Tent locations 3. Lunch menu 4. News coverage 5. Teacher materials for home visits: business cards, T-shirts, candy, door hangers, bags, pencils, etc. 6. Banners to announce the Home Visit date and times on school property 7. Review the Home Visit expectations and reimbursement	District Administrator	May 1

Check-Off	Activity	Person(s) Responsible	Date
	• Conduct a Home Visit Information Meeting with teachers • Information for business cards and T-shirt sizes to place order	Building Home Visit Coordinator	May 15
	Spanish translation on door hangers and bags	ELL Teachers	May 15
	Send home information flyers with students (Save the Date)	Building Home Visit Coordinator	Last week of school
	Information on new hires, transfers, or resignations, who will be conducting Home Visits, who will be sent to the District Administrator to add to the business cards and T-shirt list for home visits.	HR Officer Building Principals	Ongoing (last date to send info is 15 days prior to Home Visit Day)
	• Review information on business cards, door hangers, and bags and send information to printer • Determine T-shirt logo style (We're About Kids) from a selection designed by the company	District Administrator	June 15

	• Inform city officials about the Home Visit date and time
	• Contact news personnel to inform them about the Home Visit date and time
	• Place orders for the following:
	  o Lunch
	  o Candy for bags
		District Administrator	July 5

	• Complete PO for business cards, door hangers, and bags • Complete PO for T-shirts	District Administrator	July 5
	Order additional business cards and T-shirts for new hires or transfers	District Administrator	15 days prior to Home Visit Day
	Display Home Visit banners on school property	Facilities Director	15 days prior to Home Visit Day

Check-Off	Activity	Person(s) Responsible	Date
	• Assign tent locations and time slots for district office personnel to work during the Home Visit time frame • Send the information to district personnel and make any necessary changes, due to scheduling conflicts	District Administrator	15 days prior to Home Visit Day
	Set-up: • Tents • Cafeteria (tables, chairs, trash cans, etc.)	Facilities Director	Day before home visit
	Teacher materials will be taken to the designated areas: • Business cards • T-shirts • Pencils • Candy • Door hangers • Bags • Maps • Sign-in sheets • Home Visit log sheet • Rosters with student addresses and phone numbers	District Administrator Building Home Visit Coordinators	Day before Home Visit
	• Check the cafeteria to see if additional items are needed and clean up the cafeteria after the luncheon • Coolers with water are at the designated tent areas for staff	Facilities Director	Home Visit Day

	• Distribute the Home Visit materials to teachers:
	  o Business cards
	  o T-shirts
	  o Pencils
	  o Candy
	  o Door hangers
	  o Bags
	  o Maps
	  o Rosters
	• Review the Home Visit Expectations and Home Visit Log
	• Make sure all staff have signed the sign-in sheet (give the final copy to District Administrator)
		Building Home Visit Coordinators	Home Visit Day

Check-Off	Activity	Person(s) Responsible	Date
	Assist the building Home Visit coordinators with ensuring that all staff have all materials to conduct home visits	Curriculum Department	Home Visit Day
	Oversee the luncheon table	HR Agent	Home Visit Day
	• Collect individual teacher Home Visit logs • Send the Home Visit logs to the finance department to issue payment for the stipend	Building Home Visit Coordinators/ Building Principals	End of September
	Pay teachers Home Visit Stipend of $250 each	Finance Department	October 15th

Transition Day Checklist

Check-Off	Activity	Person(s) Responsible	Date
	Contact building principals to determine the school's Transition Day Coordinator who will be on the district team	District Administrator	March 1st
	Schedule a Transition Day Meeting with building and central office personnel	District Administrator	March 15th
	Meet with Building Transition Day Coordinators, HR Agent, Facilities Director, District Administrators, ELL teachers, and others to discuss: 1. Purpose of Transition Day 2. Schedule the Transition Day Date 3. Busing Plan (loading and unloading) 4. Attendance, lunch, and medicine 5. Building plans for movement of students in the building and Transition Day Expectations 6. T-shirt order 7. Move-Up Day letter 8. Building checklist for Move-Up Day	District Administrator	April 1st

Check-Off	Activity	Person(s) Responsible	Date
	• Conduct a Transition Day meeting with teachers: o Review the district level plans o Review the school's plan and expectations • Send T-shirt sizes to District Administrator	Building Transition Day Coordinator	April 15th
	Spanish translation for Move-Up Day letter	ELL Teachers	April 15th
	Order Move-Up Day T-shirts	District Administrator	April 25th
	• Teachers will submit their Transition Day lesson plan to the building principal • Building principals will review the plans and provide feedback	Building Principals	May 1st
	Distribute T-shirts to buildings	District Administrator	Week prior to Transition Day
	Assign district personnel to building locations for Move-Up Day	HR Agent, District Administrator	Week prior to Transition Day
	Send home the Move-Up Day letter home to families	Building Home Visit Coordinator	Week prior to Transition Day
	Publicity: • Buildings will announce the Move-Up Day during announcements • Marquees will display Move-Up Day information • Move-Up Day banners will be posted on school property	Building Principals	Week prior to Transition Day

Check-Off	Activity	Person(s) Responsible	Date
	Building nurses will send a medication list for 2nd and 6th grade students to central office (the list will include the student name, name of medication(s), and contact information)	Building Nurse Building Principal	Week Prior to Transition Day
	Buses will report to the designated schools at time indicated on the bus list to transfer students in grades (2nd and 6th) to middle and high schools	Facilities Director	Transition Day
	District staff will report to assigned school		Transition Day
	Nurses will check and make sure that all student medication has been received for 2nd and 6th grade students	Building Principals	Transition Day
	Reflection meeting with district and school Transition Day coordinators	District Administrator	1 week after Transition Day

16

Events Checklists

Applicable Concepts: Plan and Reflect

Gym Pre-Season Customer Service Checklist

Job Task	Completed	Initials
1. Clean bleachers a. Clean all garbage from under the bleachers, sweep and mop under the bleachers b. Clean all garbage in the bleachers c. Wipe bleachers down d. Vacuum carpet on bottom row of bleachers		
2. Clean and wipe down chairs, vacuum rug under the chairs		
3. Deep clean ALL locker rooms and bathrooms a. vacuum/mop, clean out lockers, wipe walls and lockers, clean showers and restrooms		
4. Deep clean offices/officials' locker rooms a. Vacuum/mop, dust, wipe walls, and clean carpets b. Organize if also used as office		
5. Paint and touch up gym walls and locker rooms		
6. Put up signs/banners (Wildcats sign, sponsor banners)		
7. Put up pennants/flags (Wildcats pennants, American flag)		
8. Check scoreboard (light bulbs, controls)		
9. Check sound system—music, microphones		
10. Check lights—replace bulbs if needed		

Job Task	Completed	Initials
11. Refinish the floor (certain years) Yearly: a. Wax floor b. Mop and clean court/floor		
12. Set up and clean scorers table a. Check table lighting b. Check possession arrows for basketball		
13. Evaluate additional needs/improvements in locker rooms, restrooms, etc.		

Gym PreGame
Customer Service Checklist

Job Task	Completed	Initials

1. Clean Bleachers
a. Clean out all garbage in the bleachers
b. Vacuum carpet on bottom row of
  bleachers
c. Make sure bleachers are pulled so there
  are no gaps
d. Cover gaps on walkway with rubber mats		

2. Clean and wipe down chairs, vacuum rug under chairs		
3. Clean all locker rooms and bathrooms. Vacuum/mop, clean showers and restrooms. Empty trash		
4. Clean offices/officials' locker rooms a. Vacuum/mop, empty trash b. Organize if also used as office		
5. Empty all trash		
6. Check scoreboard (light bulbs, controls)		
7. Check sound system—music, microphones		
8. Check lights		
9. Dust mop and clean court/floor		
10. Set up scorers' table		
11. Windex backboards if needed		
12. Volleyball—players set up and tear down nets		

Stadium Cleanup and Game Procedure
Customer Service Checklist

Job Task	Completed	Initials
1. Walk the field, grass, track, and area inside and outside the fence to clean up any garbage as well as weeds, branches, and anything else that is not supposed to be there		
2. Use Billy Goat or blower to clean debris off of track if needed		
3. Walk the driveway in front of the maintenance garage and to the coaches' parking lot to pick up garbage and/or debris		
4. Clean and sweep/blow the area in front of the youth concessions and outside the varsity locker rooms		
5. Clean out garbage in front of the stands and sweep/blow in front of the stands		
6. Clean and sweep/blow the area in front of the varsity concessions		
7. Clean and sweep the bathrooms and bathroom hallway		
8. Clean and sweep the tunnel		
9. Clean and sweep the home/visitor locker rooms		
10. Clean and sweep the track/officials' locker room		
11. Clean and sweep the press box		

Job Task	Completed	Initials
12. Setup for games: a. Football—All yard markers, pylons, goalposts and pads must be set. Chains should be on location, ready to use. Check scoreboard and lights. Turn on pressbox air conditioner. Set up ticket tables at each entrance gate. Set signs for team personnel and officials only on the field. b. Soccer—Goals and nets should be set. Corner flags set in place. Check scoreboard and lights. Turn on pressbox air conditioner. Set up ticket table at Gate 1 by the concessions. Set signs for team personnel and officials only on the field.		
13. During Game: a. Monitor garbage cans and empty as needed during the games b. Periodically check the restrooms for cleanliness and trash c. Keep locker rooms locked. Only open for teams at halftime and after game d. Help when needed or as directed by athletic director or game manager		
14. After Game: a. Remove trash from the stands and empty cans b. Lock all gates and doors c. Begin at step #1 again		

17

Possible Customer Service Objectives for School Improvement Plans

Applicable Concepts: Leadership, Plan and Reflect

The following list contains possible objectives that may appear in a school's Improvement Plan if they are focused on improving customer service:

* School leaders will collaborate to increase positive relationships with staff, students, and parents by providing customer service training by [DATE] as measured by survey data throughout the year.

* School leaders will collaborate with teachers to decrease the amount of discipline referrals by 50 percent by [DATE] through implementation of customer service training and measured by discipline data collected throughout the year.

* School leaders will collaborate to support positive relationships with staff, students and parents through implementation of home visits for all students, by [DATE] as measured by home visit logs and surveys throughout the year.

* The transportation director will collaborate with school leaders and bus drivers to decrease the amount of bus discipline referrals by 25 percent by [DATE] through implementation of customer service training and measured by discipline data collected throughout the year.

* The food service director will collaborate with school leaders to provide customer service training for cafeteria staff to build more positive relationships with students and staff by [DATE] as measured by survey data throughout the year.

References

(Endnotes)

1   "John F. Kennedy." *The American Presidency Project.* Web. Accessed August 25, 2017. https://goo.gl/RZn8dc

2   "Confidence in Institutions." *Gallup.* 2017. Web. Accessed August 16, 2017. https://goo.gl/AghjhS

3   "History of education in the United States." *Wikipedia.* Web. Accessed August 25, 2017. https://goo.gl/fJ9KvV

4   "Homeschooled Students." *The Condition of Education.* https://goo.gl/zVyvg1

5   "A Growing Movement: America's Largest Charter School Communities." *National Alliance for Public Charter Schools.* November, 2015. Web. Accessed July 27, 2017. https://goo.gl/M2ysF9

6   PDK International. "The 49th Annual PDK Poll of the Public's Attitude Toward the Public Schools." *Pdkpoll.org.* Web. Accessed December 23, 2017. https://goo.gl/sLvDBz

7   Dr. Seuss. *The Sneetches and Other Stories.* New York, New York: Random House, 1953. Print.

8   PDK International. "The 49th Annual PDK Poll of the Public's Attitude Toward the Public Schools." *Pdkpoll.org.* Web. Accessed December 23, 2017. https://goo.gl/MjJ31u

9   Kimmett, Colleen. "10 Years After Katrina, New Orleans' All-Charter School System Has Proven a Failure." *In These Times.* August 28, 2015. Web. Accessed August 25, 2017. https://goo.gl/PcDV9z

10   *The Wizard of Oz.* Victor Fleming. Metro-Goldwyn-Mayer. 1939. Film.

11   Tschohl, John. *Achieving Excellence Through Customer Service.* Minneapolis, Minnesota: Best Sellers Publishing, 2007. Print.

12   Denove, Chris, and James Power. J. D. Power and Associates. *Satisfaction: How Every Great Company Listens to the Voice of the Customer.* New York, New York: Penguin Group, 2006. Print.

13   Hyken, Shep. "Customer Service Is Much More Than Rules And Policies—It's A Philosophy." *Forbes.* June 18, 2016. Web. Accessed August 15, 2017. https://goo.gl/kQ4tFc

14   Tarkenton, Fran. *The Power of Failure: Succeeding in the Age of Innovation.* Washington, D.C.: Regnery Publishing, 2015. Print.

15   Jones, Bruce. "Learning from the Front Lines of Customer Service." *Harvard Business Review.* March 8, 2016. Web. Accessed August 25, 2017. https://goo.gl/tG34VA

16   DiJulius III, John R. *Providing World Class Customer Service.* Hoboken, New Jersey: John Wiley & Sons, Inc., 2008. Print.

17   Frohlich, Thomas C., Evan Comen, and Samuel Stebbins. "Customer Service Hall of Shame." *24/7 Wall St.* August 23, 2016. Web. Accessed August 25, 2017. https://goo.gl/79ZC4h

18   "Pebbles' Birthday Party." *The Flintstones.* ABC. October 8, 1964. Television.

19   Maxwell, John. *The 21 Indispensable Qualities of a Leader: Becoming the Person Others Will Want to Follow.* Nashville, Tennessee: Thomas Nelson, Inc., 1999. Print.

20   Markel, Howard. "How the Tylenol murders of 1982 changed the way we consume medication." *PBS Newshour.* September 29, 2015. Web. Accessed August 25, 2017. https://goo.gl/SfAcuZ

21   Rehak, Judith, and International Herald Tribune. "Tylenol made a hero of Johnson & Johnson : The recall that started them all." *The New York Times.* March 23, 2002. Web. Accessed August 25, 2017. https://goo.gl/tXY8nJ

22   "Credo." *Johnson & Johnson.* Web. Accessed August 25, 2017. https://goo.gl/83DH5H

23   Birger, Jon. "30-Year super stocks." *Money Magazine.* October 9, 2002. Web. Accessed August 25, 2017. https://goo.gl/tZhhzm

24   Solomon, Jesse. "Southwest Airlines: Top Stock of 2014. *CNN*

Money. November 18, 2014. Web. Accessed August 25, 2017. https://goo.gl/ve8iaB

25   Associated Press. "American joins long list of airline bankrupt-cies." *Boston.com.* November 29, 2011. Web. Accessed August 25, 2017. https://goo.gl/2mVioe

26   Southwest Airlines mission statement. "Mission Statement." *Southwest.* Web. Accessed August 25, 2017. https://goo.gl/MqJkf9

27   Maxon, Terry. "Tales from the Beat: Herbert D. Kelleher." *Dallas News.* September 2015. Web. Accessed August 25, 2017. https://goo.gl/RXW6R8

28   — — —.

29   Purkey, William W., and Paula H. Stanley. *The Inviting School Treasury.* New York, New York: Scholastic Inc., 1994. Print.

30   Mahoney, Tom. *The Great Merchants: The Stories of Twenty Famous Retail Operations and the People Who Made Them Great.* New York, New York: Harper, 1955. Print.

31   "Chapter Twenty-Four." *Boston Public.* Fox. November 5, 2001. Television.

32   Maxwell, John. *The 21 Irrefutable Laws of Leadership: Follow Them and People Will Follow You.* Nashville, Tennessee: Thomas Nelson, Inc., 1998. Print.

33   "Chapter Eleven." *Boston Public.* Fox. January 22, 2001. Television.

34   Zemeckis, Robert. *Forrest Gump.* Paramount Pictures. 1994. Film.

35   "Alexander the Great Quotes." *Brainyquote.com.* Web. Accessed August 25, 2017. https://goo.gl/kM2neK

36   "The Scandinavian Airline Story" *YouTube.com.* June 4, 2014. Web. Accessed August 25, 2017. https://goo.gl/WTV25n

37   Carlzon, Jan. *Moments of Truth: New Strategies for Today's Customer-Driven Economy.* New York, New York: HarperCollins Publishers, 1989. Print.

38   "Branch Rickey Quotes: Luck is the residue of design." *Brainyquote.com.* Web. Accessed August 25, 2017. https://goo.gl/KcBTK9

39   Kober, Jeff. "At Disney Everyone Picks Up Trash." *Mouse Planet.* August 30, 2007. Web. Accessed August 25, 2017. https://goo.gl/6mJHhT

40   Team, Trefis. "Disney Sees Solid Growth Across Segments; Frozen Helps Post 23% Earnings Growth." *Forbes.* February 5, 2015. Web. Accessed August 25, 2017. https://goo.gl/hmwHmt

41   Byland, Anders. "How Walt Disney Co. Has Changed in the Last 10 Years." *Forbes.* March 15, 2017. Web. Accessed August 25, 2017. https://goo.gl/5p1k8W

42   Tarson, Mike, and Abigail Brooks. "5 Stunning Stats About Disney." *CNN Money.* Web. Accessed August 25, 2017. https://goo.gl/DNNSm6

43   Benchmark Education Company. "Read About Best Practices in Planning for the First Day of School." *Benchmark Education.* Web. Accessed June 29, 2017. https://goo.gl/i6FzbA

44   Andersen, Erika. "21 Quotes from Henry Ford on Business, Leadership and Life." *Forbes.* May 31, 2013. Web. Accessed June 29, 2017. https://goo.gl/MgE1CB

45   Taylor, Bill. "Hire for Attitude, Train for Skill." *Harvard Business Review.* February 1, 2011. Web. Accessed August 25, 2017. https://goo.gl/DnsEVA

46   Meiert, Jens Oliver. "An Ex-Google Employee Explains What It Means To Be 'Googley'." *Business Insider.* August 13, 2013. Web. Accessed August 25, 2017. https://goo.gl/dYtBPG

47   Feloni, Richard. "Zappos' sneaky strategy for hiring the best people involves a van ride from the airport to the interview." *Business Insider.* December 3, 2015. Web. Accessed June 29, 2017. https://goo.gl/VnnhY9

48   Moore, Karl. "Millennials Work For Purpose, Not Paycheck." *Forbes.* October 2, 2014. Web. Accessed August 25, 2017. https://goo.gl/wvGjn5

49   Miller, Adam. "3 things millennials want in a career (hint: it's not more money)." *Fortune.* March 25, 2015. Web. Accessed August 25, 2017. https://goo.gl/5Gr2KN

50   Malcolm, Hadley. "Millennials will take a happier workplace over better pay." *USA Today.* April 14, 2016. Web. Accessed August 25, 2017. https://goo.gl/4CkFqe

51   Jordan, Heather R., Robert L. Mendro, and Dash Weerasinghe.

"Teacher Effects on Longitudinal Student Achievement." *Review of Educational Research.* July, 1997. Print.

52 "Social Media Raises the Stakes for Customer Service." *American Express News.* May 2, 2012. Web. Accessed August 25, 2017. https://amex.co/2rzRa0s

53 "In Here You Call Me The Governor." *The New Celebrity Apprentice.* NBC. January 2, 2017. Television.

54 Konoske, Graf, Annette, Partelow, and Meg Benner. "To Attract Great Teachers, School Districts Must Improve Their Human Capital Systems." *Center for American Progress.* December 22, 2016. Web. Accessed July 27, 2017. Source: https://ampr.gs/2qREX6S.

55 Hayes Publishing Company. "Getting the Best That Is in Your Clerks, and Make Them Help You by Helping Themselves." *The Retail Druggist.* 1921: 58. Print. https://goo.gl/U34akL

56 LeBoeuf, Michael. *How to Win Customers and Keep Them for Life.* New York, New York. Berkley Books, 1987. Print.

57 Portnoy, Gary. "The Cheers Story." Accessed July 27,2017. https://goo.gl/zkDULN

58 Zappos (@FormerlyZappos). "Dunn nun . . . Dunn nun . . . Duunn nun Duunn nun . . . Dun nun Dun nun Dun nun Dun nun . . . " June 23, 2016, 1:30 p.m. Tweet. https://goo.gl/FwNK9K

59 — — —. "LIVE on #Periscope: Vans x Nintendo! Check out this amazing new line from @vans_66 #vans #nintendo #lasvegas." June 3, 2016, 4:16 p.m. Tweet. https://goo.gl/pgGRTp

60 — — —. "#Boston, you were great—on to the next one! Want @ DJKhaled to deliver your Zappos order? http://zps.to/DJKhaled." June 6, 2016, 2:48 p.m. Tweet. https://goo.gl/t8tC4Z

61 Jensen, Eric. *Teaching with Poverty in Mind: What Being Poor Does to Kids' Brains and What Schools Can Do About It.* Alexandria, Virginia: ASCD, 2009. Print.

62 Comer, James, and Ruby Payne. "Nine Powerful Practices." *Educational Leadership: Poverty and Learning.* April 2008: 48-52. Print. https://goo.gl/hiNVU5

63   Geisel, Theodor Seuss. *The Lorax*. New York, New York: Random House, 1971. Print.

64   Jensen, Eric. *Teaching with Poverty in Mind: What Being Poor Does to Kids' Brains and What Schools Can Do About It*. Alexandria, Virginia: ASCD, 2009. Print.

65   Smith, John M. *Dangerous Minds*. Buena Vista Pictures. 1995. Film.

66   Jensen, Eric. *Teaching with Poverty in Mind: What Being Poor Does to Kids' Brains and What Schools Can Do About It*. Alexandria, Virginia: ASCD, 2009. Print.

67   Middleton, Kelly E., and Petitt, Elizabeth A. *Simply the Best: 29 Things Students Say the Best Teachers Do Around Relationships*. Bloomington, Indiana: AuthorHouse, 2010. Print.

68   Jensen, Eric. *Teaching with Poverty in Mind: What Being Poor Does to Kids' Brains and What Schools Can Do About It*. Alexandria, Virginia: ASCD, 2009. Print.

69   Bell, Chip R., and Ron Zemke. *Managing Knock Your Socks Off Service*. New York, New York: AMACOM, 2007. Print.

70   Brickman, Paul. *Risky Business*. Warner Bros. 1982. Film.

71   Ford, Lisa, David McNair, and William Perry. *Exceptional Customer Service: Going Beyond Your Good Service to Exceed the Customer's Expectation*. Avon, Massachusetts: Adams Business, 2001. Print.

72   Edmiston, Jake. "Service Insights Blog." *Customer Expressions*. March 18, 2014. Web. Accessed June 29, 2017. http://www.customerexpressions.com/blog/customer-service/secrets-of-zappos-call-center/

73   Taylor, Bill. "Why Zappos Pays New Employees to Quit—And You Should Too." *Harvard Business Review*. May 19, 2008. Web. Accessed June 29, 2017. https://goo.gl/1r7B7h

74   Feloni, Richard. "Zappos' sneaky strategy for hiring the best people involves a van ride from the airport to the interview." *Business Insider*. December 3, 2015. Web. Accessed June 29, 2017. https://goo.gl/39Ty1U

75   Borek, Steve. "Zappos Goes Beyond the Mission Statement." *Endgame Business*. February 9, 2014. Web. Accessed June 29, 2017. https://goo.gl/g7rrHw

76   Andersen, Erika. "21 Quotes from Henry Ford on Business, Leadership and Life." *Forbes.* May 31, 2013. Web. Accessed June 29, 2017. https://goo.gl/9QoDQS

77   Maxwell, John C. *Winning with People: Discover the People Principles that Work for You Every Time.* Nashville, Tennessee: Thomas Nelson, Inc., 2004. Print.

78   "Undercover Boss." CBS.

79   Stevens, Drew. "How to Address the Customer Service Gap." *Ezine Articles.* July 8, 2008. Web. Accessed July 27, 2017. https://goo.gl/hsY3Pm

80   Burnstein, David C. "How Lay's Is Tapping Its Audience For Its Next Big Chip Idea." *Fast Company.* August 1, 2012. Web. Accessed July 3, 2017. https://goo.gl/gq5kQW

81   Eckert, Robert, A. "The Two Most Important Words." *Harvard Business Review.* April, 2013. Web. Accessed July 3, 2017. https://goo.gl/EY9wXQ

82   "Potty Training Books." *Amazon.com.* Web. Accessed July 3, 2017. https://goo.gl/qbExUD

83   John Maxwell Team (@JohnMaxwellTeam). "How do we know if people need encouragement? If they have a pulse, they need encouragement! ~John Maxwell #JMTeam." October 23, 2016, 9:12 p.m. Tweet. https://goo.gl/hVFnbr

84   Blanchard, Ken. *Whale Done!: The Power of Positive Relationships.* New York, New York: Blanchard Family Partnership, 2002. Print.

85   — — —.

86   Evans, James R., and William M. Lindsay. *Managing for Quality and Performance Excellence.* Mason, Ohio: Cengage Learning, Inc., 2009. Print.

87   Blanchard, Ken. *Customer Mania: It's Never Too Late to Build a Customer-Focused Company.* New York, New York: Free Press, 2004. Print.

88   Bryant, Adam. "At Yum Brands, Rewards for Good Work." *Business Day.* July 11, 2009. Web. Accessed July 3, 2017. https://goo.gl/8oGVuo

89   — — —.

90   — — —.

91   Blanchard, Ken. *Whale Done!: The Power of Positive Relationships*.
       New York, New York: Blanchard Family Partnership, 2002. Print.

92   Gruenert, Steve and Todd Whitaker. *School Culture Rewired: How to
       Define, Assess, and Transform It*. Alexandria, Virginia: ASCD, 2015.
       Print.

93   Judge, Mike. *Office Space*. Twentieth Century Fox. 1999. Film.

94   "Pest." Lifelock TV Commercial. *Ispot.tv*. Web. Accessed July 3,
       2017. https://goo.gl/dSqLhc

95   Adams, Bob. "Delivering a Great Guest Experience is a Balance
       of Art and Science." *27gen*. March 27, 2014. Web. Accessed July 3,
       2017. https://goo.gl/3KhzVL

96   Bradberry, Travis. "10 Mistakes Intelligent People Never Make
       Twice." *Entrepreneur*. October 26, 2015. Web. Accessed August 15,
       2017. https://goo.gl/Bsz1mv

97   "Jay Samit Quotes." *Brainyquote.com*. Web. Accessed July 3, 2017.
       https://goo.gl/ZYCYUH

98   Pitts, Anna. "You Only Have 7 Seconds to Make a Strong First
       Impression." *Business Insider*. April 8, 2013. Web. Accessed July 3,
       2017. https://goo.gl/6XBccf

99   Goman, Carol Kinsey. "Seven Seconds to Make a First Impres-
       sion." *Forbes*. February 13, 2011. Web. Accessed July 3, 2017.
       https://goo.gl/bqTv5D

100   Kober, Jeff. "At Disney Everyone Picks Up Trash." *Mouse Planet*.
       August 30, 2007. Web. Accessed August 25, 2017.
       https://goo.gl/3VGZBz

101   Black, John A., and English, Fenwick W. *What They Don't Tell You
       in Schools of Education about School Administration*. Lancaster, Penn-
       sylvania: The Scarecrow Press, Inc., 2001. Print.

102   Numeroff, Laura. *If You Give a Mouse a Cookie*. New York, New
       York: HarperCollins Publishers, 1985. Print.

103   "Abraham Lincoln Quotes." *Brainyquote.com*. Web. Accessed July
       4, 2017. https://goo.gl/qApbpU

104 robatsea2009. "classic Heinz Ketchup Anticipation TV ad 1979." *Youtube.com.* July 8, 2010. Web. Accessed August 28, 2017. https://goo.gl/6rVB2U

105 Park, Sadie. "The Evolution of Heinz Ketchup Bottles." *Timetoast.* Web. Accessed August 28, 2017. https://goo.gl/hzws9x

106 Collins, Jim. *Good to Great: Why Some Companies Make the Leap and Others Don't.* New York, New York: HarperBusiness, 2001. Print.

107 Shan, Khushbu. "Arby's New Hook For Millennials: 'We Have The Meats.'" *Eater.* July 30, 2014. Web. Accessed July 4, 2017. https://goo.gl/SYrZUp

108 Nefer, Barb. "Facts About Disney World in Florida." *USA Today.* Web. Accessed July 4, 2017. https://goo.gl/1d3dbc

109 D'Onfro, Jillian. "Source: Amazon Is Planning Its Own Private Fleet of Delivery Trucks." *Business Insider.* March, 13, 2014. Web. Accessed July 4, 2017. https://goo.gl/eRsaET

110 Blodget, Henry. "Here's a Picture of Amazon Locker, the New Delivery Box Amazon Is Using to Take Over the World." *Business Insider.* August 24, 2012. Web. Accessed July 4, 2017. https://goo.gl/L2BUjE

111 Rubin, Ben Fox. "Amazon Prime Air drone completes its first US public delivery." *Cnet.com.* March 24, 2017. Web. Accessed July 4, 2017. https://goo.gl/NbXnCi

112 Oches, Sam. "Inside Chick-fil-A's Drive-Thru Strategy." *QSR Magazine.* October, 2016. Web. Accessed July 4, 2017. https://goo.gl/hk8Zq8

113 Eastwood, Clint. *Heartbreak Ridge.* Warner Bros. 1986. Film.

114 "For the Love of All." *The Huffington Post.* February 23, 2015. Web. Accessed August 22, 2017. https://goo.gl/1Ndqp6

115 Luce, Ron. *The Power of One: Stand Up, Be Counted, Make a Difference.* United States. Maxwell Motivation, Inc., 2004. Print.

116 bdot02. "Terry Tate, Office Linebacker." *YouTube.com.* May 3, 2012. Web. Accessed July 4, 2017. https://goo.gl/ZH3U2E

117 "Maslow's Hierarchy of Needs." Wikipedia. Web. Accessed July 4, 2017. https://goo.gl/s9zBpR

118 Rath, Tom, and Jim Harter. *Wellbeing: The Five Essential Elements.* New York, New York: Gallup Press, 2010. Print.

119 — — —.

120 — — —.

121 "By the Numbers: A Psychologically Healthy Workplace Fact Sheet." *American Psychological Association Center for Organizational Excellence.* November 20, 2013. Web. Accessed July 4, 2017. https://goo.gl/giAMHM

122 Achor, Shawn. *The Happiness Advantage: The Seven Principles of Positive Psychology that Fuel Success and Performance at Work.* New York, New York: Crown Business, 2010. Print.

123 Rinke, Wolf J. *Winning Management: 6 Fail-Safe Strategies for Building High-Performance Organizations.* Clarksville, Maryland: Achievement Publishers, 1997. Print.

124 Gordon, Seth. *Horrible Bosses.* New Line Cinema. 2011. Film.

125 Keith, Kent M. "The Paradoxical Commandments." *Paradoxical-Commmandments.com.* 1968. Web. Accessed July 4, 2017. https://goo.gl/nnttJQ

126 Booher, Dianna. *Communicate Like a Leader: Connecting Strategically to Coach, Inspire, and Get Things Done.* Oakland, California: Berrett-Kohler Publishers, Inc., 2017. Print.

127 O'Connor, Claire. "America's Best Employers 2015." *Forbes.* March 25, 2015. Web. Accessed July 4, 2017. https://goo.gl/TBcbEx

128 Dill, Kathryn. "America's Best Employers 2016." *Forbes.* March 23, 2016. Web. Accessed July 4, 2017. https://goo.gl/9E3xMM

129 Kauflin, Jeff. "America's Best Employers 2017." *Forbes.* May 9, 2017. Web. Accessed July 4, 2017. https://goo.gl/1ZXntR

130 Bert, Julie. "Tour Google's Luxurious 'Googleplex' Campus in California." *Business Insider.* October 6, 2013. Web. Accessed July 12, 2017. https://goo.gl/bJhPCz

131 "Should a Summer Internship Secure a Permanent Position?" *thisiswhatgoodlookslike.com.* June 9, 2013. Web. Accessed July 12, 2017. https://goo.gl/cwmtZ5

132 Greer, Mark. "A Happier, Healthier Workplace." *American Psy-

chological Association. December, 2004. Web. Accessed July 4, 2017. https://goo.gl/wr3asx

133   Gruenert, Steve, and Todd Whitaker. *School Culture Rewired: How to Define, Assess, and Transform It.* Alexandria, Virginia: ASCD, 2015. Print.

134   Bauman, Margaret. "Good Times Means Good Business at Pike Place." *Alaska Journal.* November 26, 2006. Web. Accessed July 12, 2017. https://goo.gl/AVC8jt

135   Sealy, Geraldine. "In Search of Work-Life Balance, Companies Get Creative." *ABC News.* May 4. Web. Accessed July 12, 2017. https://goo.gl/x7psur

136   Lelyveld, Nita. "Fish Market Markets Success." *The Washington Post.* August 20, 2000. Web. Accessed July 12, 2017. https://goo.gl/4ZSL7t

137   Lattman, Peter. "The Origins of Justice Stewart's 'I Know It When I See It.' *The Wall Street Journal.* September 27, 2007. Web. Accessed July 12, 2017. https://goo.gl/xMhgmH

138   "Is Your School's Culture Toxic or Positive?" *Education World.* Web. Accessed July 12, 2017. https://goo.gl/9LUhCb

139   Gruenert, Steve, and Todd Whitaker. *School Culture Rewired: How to Define, Assess, and Transform It.* Alexandria, Virginia: ASCD, 2015. Print.

140   Achor, Shawn. *The Happiness Advantage: The Seven Principles of Positive Psychology That Fuel Success and Performance at Work."* New York, New York: Crown Business, 2010. Print.

141   Achor, Shawn. *The Happiness Advantage: The Seven Principles of Positive Psychology That Fuel Success and Performance at Work.* New York, New York: Crown Business, 2010. Print.

142   PDK International. "The 49th Annual PDK Poll of the Public's Attitude Toward the Public Schools." *Pdkpoll.org.* Web. Accessed December 23, 2017. https://goo.gl/A1e5gg

143   Konen, Jon. "9 Reasons Culture Trumps Strategy." *Teacher.org.* October 7, 2016. Web. Accessed November 3, 2017. https://goo.gl/j1yYS8

144 "Lagniappe." *Dictionary.com.* Web. Accessed December 19, 2017. https://goo.gl/N8DqtY

145 "MLK Quote of the Week: "All labor that uplifts humanity has dignity and importance and should be undertaken with painstaking excellence." *The King Center.* April 9, 2013. Web. Accessed July 12, 2017. https://goo.gl/vDME7Q

146 Denove, Chris, and James D. Power IV. *Satisfaction: How Every Great Company Listens to the Voice of the Customer.* New York, New York: Penguin Group, 2006. Print.

147 Sanborn, Mark. *The Fred Factor: How Passion in Your Work and Life Can Turn the Ordinary Into the Extraordinary.* New York, New York: Currency Doubleday, 2004. Print.

148 — — —.

149 Blanchard, Ken, and Barbara Glanz. *The Simple Truths of Service: Inspired by Johnny the Bagger.* Naperville, Illinois: Simple Truths, 2017. Print.

150 Blanchard, Ken. "San Diego Padres." Web. Accessed July 12, 2017. https://goo.gl/y2LVCg

151 "Napoleon Bonaparte Quotes." *Brainyquote.com.* Web. Accessed October 25, 2017. https://goo.gl/UrfMWk

152 "The Alternate Side." *Seinfeld.* NBC. December 4, 1991. Television.

153 Wagstaff, Keith. "Happiness Equation Solved: Lower Your Expectations." *NBC News.* August 4, 2014. Web. Accessed July 12, 2017. https://goo.gl/aArLp3

154 "Relics." *Star Trek: The Next Generation.* CBS. October 12, 1992. Television.

155 Kaufman, Ron. *Lift Me UP! Service With a Smile: World-Class Quips and Action Tips to Brighten Up Your Services!.* Singapore: Ron Kaufman Pte Ltd., 2005. Print.

156 Matthews, Mark. "Quotable Quote." *Goodreads.* Web. Accessed July 12, 2017. https://goo.gl/95bRX2

157 "Benjamin Franklin Quotes." *Goodreads.com.* Web. Accessed July 12, 2017. https://goo.gl/NEA5Rn

158 Wish a Friend. "I Am Sorry Quotes." *Wishafriend.com.* Web. Accessed July 12, 2017. https://goo.gl/wtcEN4

159 Blanchard, Ken, and Margaret McBride. *The One Minute Apology: A Powerful Way to Make Things Better."* New York, New York: HarperCollins, 2003. Print.

160 Araton, Harvey. "Apologizing, Woods Sets No Date for Return to Golf." *The New York Times.* February 19, 2010. Web. Accessed July 12, 2017. https://goo.gl/YH2euA

161 Hoynes, Paul. "Umpire's missed call spoils Armando Galarraga's bid for a perfect game as Tigers post 3-0 victory." *Cleveland.com.* June 2, 2010. Web. Accessed July 12, 2017. https://goo.gl/xgjC8B

162 "Ump Joyce on Controversial Call." *MLB.com.* Web. Accessed July 12, 2017. https://goo.gl/qby1j4

163 Associated Press. "Starbucks' New Pledge: We'll Be Perfect." *NBC News.* February 27, 2008. Web. Accessed July 12, 2017. https://goo.gl/SsuJ1r

164 Zappos. "Shipping and Returns." *Zappos.com.* Web. Accessed July 12, 2017. https://goo.gl/1vKZUX

165 sonsofmaxwell. "United Breaks Guitars." *YouTube.* July 6, 2009. Web. Accessed July 12, 2017. https://goo.gl/JBJ82s

166 Wilson, Richard. "A Public Relations Disaster: How saving $1,200 cost United Airlines 10,772,839 negative views on YouTube." *Sentium.* 2011. Web. Accessed July 12, 2017. https://goo.gl/ZPZcku

167 Gibbons, Kevin. "United Airlines Lose Millions following YouTube Complaint Song!" *White.com.* July 23, 2009. Web. Accessed July 12, 2017. https://goo.gl/yy8ag6

168 *Consumer Attorneys of California.* Web. Accessed July 12, 2017. https://goo.gl/WrdR4B

169 Bryan, Luke. "Crash My Party." By Clawson, Rodney, and Gorley, Ashley. *Crash My Party.* Capitol Nashville, 2013. Digital Music Download.

170 Bane, Joshua. "Your Dirty Laundry Belongs in the Basket, Not on Facebook." *Bane Tech.* February 13, 2014. Web. Accessed July 13, 2017. https://goo.gl/oTxhQp/

171 DiJulius, John R. *What's the Secret?: To Providing a World-Class Customer Experience.* Hoboken, New Jersey: John Wiley & Sons Inc., 2008. Print.

172   Voltaire, Dictionnaire Philosophique, (1764).

173   James, Geoffrey. "World's Dumbest Branding Move." *CBS Money Watch*. March 28, 2007. Web. Accessed July 13, 2017. https://goo.gl/YZcBdt

174   Associated Press. "Burger King takes no shoes rule to the next level asking mom with shoeless 6 month old baby to leave." *NY Daily News*. August 7, 2009. Web. Accessed July 13, 2017. https://goo.gl/quLqKi

175   Aryeh, Dima. "LG Launches Balloons with G2 Vouchers, 20 People Hurt by BB Guns." *Android and Me*. August 12, 2013. Web. Accessed July 13, 2017. https://goo.gl/3tMqKi

176   *The Huffington Post*. "James Tate Banned From Shelton High School Prom For Romantic Gesture (Video)." May 11, 2011. Web. Accessed July 13, 2017. https://goo.gl/Ni8r7K

177   Ossad, Jordan. "Connecticut Teen Garnering Support After Prom Ban." *CNN*. May 13, 2011. Web. Accessed July 13, 2017. https://goo.gl/QvVnYu

178   *The Today Show*. "The Prom Must Go On." June 5, 2011. Web. Accessed July 13, 2017. https://goo.gl/vmCqtj

179   Ossad, Jordan. "Connecticut Teen Garnering Support After Prom Ban." *CNN*. May 13, 2011. Web. Accessed July 13, 2017. https://goo.gl/qXEy7u

180   Liptak, Adam. "Strip-Search of Girl Tests Limit of School Policy." *The New York Times*. March 23, 2009. Web. Accessed July 13, 2017. https://goo.gl/hVENo3

181   Barnes, Robert. "Supreme Court Rules Strip Search Violated 13-Year-Old Girl's Rights." *The Washington Post*. June 26, 2009. Web. Accessed July 13, 2017. https://goo.gl/bkRJYW

182   Meek, James Gordon. "Supreme Court rules school's strip search of teen Savana Redding unconstitutional." *New York Daily News*. June 25, 2009. Web. Accessed July 13, 2017. https://goo.gl/1j139p

183   Associated Press. "NJ School Bus Takes Wrong Students on Field Trip." *NBC 24 News*. May 21, 2010. Web. Accessed July 13, 2017. https://goo.gl/kC9ges

184 "Turkeys Away." *WKRP in Cincinnati.* CBS. October 30, 1978. Television.

185 Merchant, Nilofer. "Situational Leadership." *Business Insider.* May 4, 2011. Web. Accessed July 13, 2017. https://goo.gl/P8bSkb

186 "Bags Fly Free." *SouthwestAirlines.com.* Accessed July 13, 2017. https://goo.gl/cF6y7Q

187 Snyder, Brett. "How Southwest Made Hay With 'Bags Fly Free.'" *CBS Money Watch.* July 29, 2010. Web. Accessed July 13, 2017. https://goo.gl/nekWzg

188 Martin, Hugo. "Southwest Airlines Will Keep Its 'Bags Fly Free' Policy." *LA Times.* July 28, 2015. Web. Accessed July 13, 2017. https://goo.gl/GFqyyz

189 Griffin, Elle. "Brand Ambassadors vs. Employee Advocates (& Why You Need Them)." *Everyonesocial.* October 18, 2016. Web. Accessed July 13, 2017. https://goo.gl/HTqcTz

190 ———.

191 "Trust in Employee Engagement: Data Reveals Employee Trust Divide." *Edelman.* 2016. Web. Accessed July 13, 2017. https://goo.gl/3E1cjP

192 Griffin, Elle. "Brand Ambassadors vs. Employee Advocates (& Why You Need Them)." *Everyonesocial.* October 18, 2016. Web. Accessed July 13, 2017. https://goo.gl/WxRxSW

193 Cervellon, Marie-Cecile, and Lirio, Pamela. "When Employees Don't 'Like' Their Employers on Social Media." *MIT Sloan Management Review.* November 22, 2016. Web. Accessed July 19, 2017. https://goo.gl/Rso5wA

194 Fisher, Anne. "How Patagonia Keeps Employee Turnover 'Freakishly Low'." *Forbes.* June 9, 2016. Web. Accessed July 19, 2017. https://goo.gl/RxGuAe

195 Chhabra, Esha. "Why This Company is Giving Away All of Its Profits from Black Friday." *Forbes.* November 23, 2016. Web. Accessed July 13, 2017. https://goo.gl/Lbdwer

196 Addady, Michael. "Patagonia's Donating All $10 Million of Its Black Friday Sales to Charity." *Fortune.* November 29, 2016. Web. Accessed July 13, 2017. https://goo.gl/DoKpiM

197   Lauletta, Tyler. "Patagonia is donating 100% of its Black Friday
      sales to charity this year." *Business Insider.* November 23, 2016.
      Web. Accessed July 13, 2017. https://goo.gl/jdV1ch

198   Kavilanz, Parija. "Patagonia's Black Friday sales hit $10 million—
      and will donate it all." *CNN.* November 29, 2016. Web. Accessed
      July 13, 2017. https://goo.gl/9KmFqk

199   Broderick, Ryan. "US Airways Just Tweeted Out One Of The Most
      Graphic Things You've Ever Seen A Brand Tweet." *BuzzFeed News.*
      April 14, 2014. Web. Accessed July 14, 2017. https://goo.gl/nSGbue

200   Glenza, Jessica. "Bud Light sorry for 'removing no from your
      vocabulary for the night' label." *The Guardian.* April 29, 2015. Web.
      Accessed July 14, 2017. https://goo.gl/DwHHur

201   Lawrence, Laurent. "Biggest PR Disasters of 2014." *PR Say.*
      January 9, 2015. Web. Accessed July 14, 2017.
      https://goo.gl/dG79mB

202   New, Catherine. "Lululemon Yoga Pants Yanked from Shelves
      Because Fabric Too Sheer." *Huffingon Post.* March 19, 2013. Web.
      Accessed July 14, 2017. https://goo.gl/2qn3hy

203   Phasin, Kim. "Shunning Plus-Size Shoppers Is Key To Lulu-
      lemon's Strategy, Insiders Say." *Huffington Post.* August 9, 2013.
      Accessed July 14, 2017. https://goo.gl/dPD8XK

204   Ohlheiser, Abby. "Urban Outfitters apologizes for its blood-red-
      stained Kent State sweatshirt." *The Washington Post.* September 15,
      2014. Web. Accessed July 14, 2017. https://goo.gl/NCkoY1

205   Lawrence, Laurent. "Biggest PR Disasters of 2014." *PR Say.*
      January 9, 2015. Web. Accessed July 14, 2017.
      https://goo.gl/P8WDTN

206   — — —.

207   Colorado School Public Relations Association. Web. Accessed July
      14, 2017. https://goo.gl/6oSWey

208   Associated Press. "Superintendent suspended for pulling down
      board VP's pants." *Fox News.* October 3, 2017. Web. Accessed
      November 8, 2017. https://goo.gl/DNmt7R

209   Morris, Tricia. "17 Sensational Customer Service Quotes to Inspire

You this Summer." *Customer Think.* June 25, 2012. Web. Accessed November 21, 2012. https://goo.gl/zdXVf8

210 Head & Shoulders. "First Impression: Vintage Head & Shoulders Commercial." *YouTube.com.* October 17, 2015. Web. Accessed July 14, 2017. https://goo.gl/sThWXx

211 Wahba, Phil. "Walmart Brings Back Greeters to Improve Service and Fight Theft." *Fortune.* May 4, 2016. Web. Accessed July 14, 2017. https://goo.gl/LSmLAq

212 Middleton, Kelly E., and Elizabeth A. Petitt. *Simply the Best: 29 Things Students Say the Best Teachers Do Around Relationships.* Bloomington, Indiana: AuthorHouse, 2010. Print.

213 Sanborn, Josh. "How Every Generation of the Last Century Got Its Nickname." *Time.* December 1, 2015. Web. Accessed July 14, 2017. https://goo.gl/hQiiaz

214 Silletto, Cara. *The Millennial Mindset: Why Today's Workforce Thinks Differently.* Crescendo Strategies, 2016. Print.

215 Kaufman, Leslie, and Claudia H Deutsch. "Montgomery Ward to Close Its Doors." *The New York Times.* December 29, 2000. Web. Accessed July 14, 2017. https://goo.gl/q94VTB

216 Walmart. "Our Story." *Walmart.com.* Web. Accessed July 14, 2017. https://goo.gl/N5LTwT

217 Sauter, Michael B,. and Samuel Stebbins. "America's Most Hated Companies." *24/7 Wall St.* January 10, 2017. Web. Accessed July 14, 2017. https://goo.gl/u2HEje

218 Anderson, Mae, and Michael Liedtke. "Hubris—and Late Fees—Doomed Blockbuster." *NBC News.* September 23, 2010. Web. Accessed July 14, 2017. https://goo.gl/KM23x2

219 Walker, Nell. "The Rise of Netflix." *USA Business Review.* August 25, 2016. Web. Accessed July 14, 2017. https://goo.gl/dzkHXZ

220 Masters, Kim. "The Netflix Backlash: Why Hollywood Fears a Content Monopoly." *The Hollywood Reporter.* September 14, 2016. Web. Accessed July 19, 2017. https://goo.gl/iK6XQx

221 LaMonica, Paul R. "Netflix is No House of Cards: It's Now Worth $70 Billion." *CNN Money.* May 30, 2017. Web. Accessed July 14, 2017. https://goo.gl/diLXgq

222 Alba, Davey. "Uber Just Launched Its Food-Delivery UberEats App in First US Cities." *Wired*. March 15, 2016. Web. Accessed July 14, 2017. https://goo.gl/NV96Tv

223 — — —. "Only Amazon Could Make a Checkout-Free Grocery Store a Reality." *Wired*. December 6, 2016. Web. Accessed July 14, 2017. https://goo.gl/FmGxxZ

224 Bray, Hiawatha. "Amazon wants to get inside your home. Just for a moment or two." *The Boston Globe*. October 25, 2017. Web. Accessed November 15, 2017. https://goo.gl/7CvxXH

225 KIRO 7 News. "Controversial Amazon Key launches in Seattle area, but will people use it?" *KIRO7 News*. November 8, 2017. Web. Accessed November 15, 2017. https://goo.gl/qJ7BWs

226 Willis, Damien. "N.M. Schools Roll Out High-Tech Sleep Pods for Students." *USA Today*. March 1, 2017. Web. Accessed July 14, 2017. https://goo.gl/Dgjqns

227 Neighmond, Patti. "Stressed-Out High Schoolers Advised to Try a Nap Pod." *NPR*. May 15, 2017. Web. Accessed July 14, 2017. https://goo.gl/Nzcn3x

228 — — —.

229 *Open Yale Courses*. http://oyc.yale.edu/courses

230 Middleton, Kelly, and Elizabeth A. Petitt. *Who Cares: Improving Public Schools Through Relationships and Customer Service*. Tucson, Arizona: Wheatmark Publishing, 2007. Print.

231 Geisel, Theodor. "Dr. Seuss Quotable Quote." *Goodreads.com*. https://goo.gl/7CmgwK

232 Leadership Geeks. "Ray Kroc Leadership Profile." *Leadership-Geeks.com*. August 10, 2016. Web. Accessed October 25, 2017. https://goo.gl/5swQNE

233 "Dwight D. Eisenhower Quotes." *Brainyquote.com*. Web. Accessed October 25, 2017. http://bit.ly/2I6IEAA

234 "John C. Maxwell Quotes." *Brainyquote.com*. Web. Accessed October 25, 2017. https://goo.gl/zeyMuq

235 Maxwell, John. *The 21 Indispensable Qualities of a Leader: Becoming*

the Person Others Will Want to Follow. Nashville, Tennessee: Thomas Nelson, Inc., 1999. Print.

236 Leadership Geeks. "Andrew Carnegie Leadership Profile." *LeadershipGeeks.com.* August 10, 2016. Web. Accessed October 25, 2017. https://goo.gl/LjQ14G

237 "Henry Kissinger Quotes." *Brainyquote.com.* Web. Accessed October 25, 2017. https://goo.gl/1r2KgB

238 "Arnold H. Glasow Quotes." *Brainyquote.com.* Web. Accessed October 25, 2017. https://goo.gl/dV3jxY

239 Nayar, Vineet. "Leadership Redefined." *Harvard Business Review.* September 23, 2008. Web. Accessed October 25, 2017. https://goo.gl/VwDxhP

240 Romney, Mitt. "Mitt Romney's Florida Victory Speech." *Real Clear Politics.* January 31, 2012. Web. Accessed October 25, 2017. https://goo.gl/1WR7NQ

241 Maxwell, John. "7 Factors that Influence Influence." *The John Maxwell Company.* July 8, 2013. Web. Accessed October 25, 2017. https://goo.gl/MhHoq8

242 Bouck, Cory. *The Lens of Leadership: Being the Leader Others Want to Follow.* New York, New York: Aviva Publishing, 2013. Print.

243 Associated Press. "School Bans Hat Over Toy Soldiers' Guns." *CBS News.* June 18, 2010. Web. Accessed October 25, 2017. https://goo.gl/5AEsXF

244 Urbina, Ian. "It's a Fork, It's a Spoon, It's a . . . Weapon?" *The New York Times.* October 11, 2009. Web. Accessed October 25, 2017. https://goo.gl/aGmigX

245 Foster, Matthew. "School Tossed Kids' Lunches in Trash Over Money Owed." *ABC News.* January 30, 2014. Web. Accessed October 25, 2017. https://goo.gl/efuE9s

246 Lencioni, Patrick. *The Four Obsessions of an Extraordinary Executive.* San Francisco: Jossey-Bass, 2000. Print.

247 Vossekuil, Brian, Fein, Robert A., Reddy, Marisa, Borum, Randy, and William Modzeleski. "The Final Report on the Safe School Initiative: Implications for the Prevention of School Attacks in the United States." United States Secret Service and United States

Department of Education. July, 2004. Web. Accessed April 4, 2018.
http://bit.ly/2G4Krjr

248   Mulvey, E. P., and Elizábeth Cauffman. "The inherent limits of
      predicting school violence." American Psychologist. October,
      2001. Print.

About the Author

Kelly E. Middleton has thirty years of experience in public education and is currently Superintendent of Newport Independent Schools in Northern Kentucky. Kelly has a diverse background as an educator, serving in the roles of teacher, coach, administrator, and university professor. Kelly has served as a principal at every school level. When Kelly transferred from school principal to district administrator, one of his job responsibilities was public relations. This title and its job responsibilities would completely alter his entire career. Kelly has coauthored two books: *Who Cares? Improving Public Schools Through Relationships and Customer Service* and *Simply The Best: 29 Things Students Say the Best Teachers Do Around Relationships*. His newly released third book is titled *Competing for Kids: 21 Customer Service Concepts from Top Companies that Public Schools Can Use to Attract and Retain Students*. This new book provides public schools strategies to compete for students. In the next decade, schools that fail to treat students and parents as valuable customers will become extinct.

Kelly has also authored numerous articles focusing on customer service and on building relationships in public schools.

Kelly has presented many times at the National School Boards Conference and the National School Public Relations Conference, and he conducts customer service staff development for all job descriptions in schools throughout the United States.
You can contact Kelly via email or connect with him on social media.

Email: kellye3m@gmail.com
Twitter: @kellsinfotweets
Facebook: Kelly Middleton
Instagram: kmiddleton33

What Others are Saying . . .

"As the person who gave Kelly his first job in education, it gave me great pride a few years ago to be able invite him back to conduct a professional development session for our leadership team on the importance of providing great customer service. We had completed a book study of *Who Cares*, and his presentation hit home, showing us how important it is to not become complacent in how we view our students and parents, who are indeed our customers. In today's "war on public education" these concepts are even more imperative. We must make every effort to let our students, our parents, and our community be assured that we hold their most valuable possession in high esteem and are here to make sure that we give them our BEST. Kelly's book is a practical, common sense guide to remind us we must do just that!"

—Marvin Moore, Superintendent,
Rowan County Schools

"Kelly Middleton has written a practical, yet powerful book on the value and importance of customer service concepts in schools and districts. It is chock-full of business examples relevant to schools with personal anecdotes, insight, and a ready-to-use training guides schools can begin implementing immediately. School culture depends on excellent customer service and this book is a prodigious resource for school leaders everywhere!"

—Lisa McCane, Superintendent,
Augusta Independent School District

"As a secondary school educator and school board member with almost forty years of experience, I continually seek best practices for improving student achievement. I have witnessed firsthand how the customer service concepts articulated by Kelly Middleton can transform a school district, impacting every aspect of schooling. While serving in the capacity of school board chair, our district won the prestigious MAGNA Award from the National School Board Association in 2010 due to the implementation of Kelly's concepts such as relationship building and home visits. He has been instrumental in assisting other schools and districts throughout the country in implementing these customer service concepts.

Competing for Kids is not only timely in the current climate of policy makers advocating school choice options for students, it also prompts one to pause for reflection about ways schools can successfully compete in today's educational marketplace."

—Ann Porter, Retired Teacher and School Board Chair,
Mason County Schools
Maysville, KY

"This book is an insight to Kelly's servant heart. How he translates this to illustrating how we are to fully serve students and to servant leadership is compelling. As a former teacher and coach I'm proud to see that Kelly still holds the strong values that made him an excellent student, athlete, and superintendent."

—Steve Butcher, Superintendent,
Pulaski County Schools

"Much like his previous book *Who Cares?*, this book is loaded with helpful, commonsense information that we all too often take for granted. As public school educators, serving children should always be our first and most important priority and, if done with a caring, sincere heart, our sphere of influence will extend well beyond this generation of children."

—Chuck Adams, Superintendent,
Spencer County Schools,
2012 Administrator of the Year

"Kelly Middleton presented several times in my school district while I was Superintendent. Each and every time he came to our district, my faculty and staff huddled around his customer service ideas and couldn't wait to implement them! This is a must-read for all stakeholders in schools and communities, understanding the need for customer service in every aspect of education."

—Nancy L. Hutchinson, Chief Executive Officer,
Kentucky Educational Development Corporation

"Over the past twenty years in public education, we find it increasingly difficult to create a safe and caring environment for students to learn and grow. Kelly helps his readers to see how using customer service concepts can turn a school or district around."

—Dr. Anthony Strong, Superintendent,
Pendleton County Kentucky Schools,
Coauthor of *A Guide to Kentucky's Next Generation*
Leadership Series for Onboarding New Superintendents
Finalist for Kentucky Association of School Administrator,
Superintendent of the Year in 2017 and 2018

"The commonsense approach used in *Competing for Kids* reminds us that being servant leaders to our customers (students and families) must be our first priority. This book enlightens educators to the reality that customer service can make or break a business or school. I love his previous book, *Simply the Best*, but this one really hit me as a school leader. *Competing for Kids* is a must-read for all educators!"

—Mike Jones, Principal,
Crawford Middle School, Fayette County Public Schools

"Concerns about the demise of public education have been voiced repeatedly in recent years. *Competing For Kids* shows concrete ways educators can produce exceptional results by focusing on providing outstanding service for our customers—students and their families. Mr. Middleton's unique, comprehensive approach to addressing each area of school function will surely refresh your commitment to developing amazing schools, faculties and students."

—Dr. Randy Poe, Superintendent,
Boone County Schools,
2015 F.L. Dupree Outstanding Superintendent Award,
Kentucky Association of School Administrators 2013
Kentucky Superintendent of the Year

"In this age of technology, everyone is fixed on a device that removes the human element. "Soft skills" are necessary to be successful in all walks of life. Kelly Middleton has curated great customer service concepts used all over the world. We must revisit the need to train and exercise all people in the art of "Soft Skills." A must read!!!"

—Dr. Jack Herlihy, Retired Superintendent
and University Professor of Leadership

"The 21 concepts promoted within this book are absolutely necessary in order to be competitive when recruiting and retaining staff and students. Kelly does an outstanding job of blending concepts and actions along with some excellent real-life examples from his life and educational experiences."

—Kerry L. Hill, Transportation Director
Retired Assistant Superintendent
Campbell County Schools, Alexandria, KY

"Kelly takes the core principles of customer service and outlines how schools can apply them in ways that work to best support students. Using examples from his own experience and from schools across the country, he paints a picture of how schools can create a model based on what best serves students."

—Grace Todd McKenzie, Associate Director
Family Partnership, Partners for Education, Berea College

"Each concept in this book speaks to one basic principle that we are taught at young age: Treat people the way you want to be treated. The concept on Recovering Well enlightens us and encourages us to embrace the value of putting ourselves in the place of others so that we may understand their story and make the right decision when we have messed up. We in public education say, Thank you Kelly Middleton. Never stop fighting the good fight."

—Ramona Malone, Chairperson
Newport Board of Education